# Deck Officer Study Guide

## FIFTH EDITION

*Preparation for the United States Coast Guard
Merchant Marine License Examinations*

# VOLUME 7
*LIFEBOATMAN*

*Edited by:*

CAPTAIN JOSEPH S. MURPHY, II
Professor, Department of Marine Transportation
Massachusetts Maritime Academy

## Academy Publishing Company
6 Munroe Parkway
Wareham, Massachusetts 02571

*ISBN 1-881349-06-3 (Volume 7)*
*ISBN 1-881349-02-0 (6 Volume Set)*
*Printed in the United States*

# TABLE OF CONTENTS

## VOLUME 7 -LIFEBOATMAN

### PART 1 - LIFESAVING

#### Safety of Life at Sea

#### Survival at Sea

#### Lifeboats - Lifeboat Davit Systems

# PART 1 - LIFESAVING

# PART 2 - MARITIME LAW

# PART 3 - Distress & Emergency Signals

# PART 4 - Offshore Supply Vessels (OSV) - Survival Craft

WITHOUT FEAR, COURAGE CANNOT EXIST. COURAGE IS NOT THE ABSENCE OF FEAR BUT RATHER THE WILL TO GO ON IN THE FACE OF EXTREME ADVERSITY.

I WILL SURVIVE BECAUSE I WILL NEVER GIVE-UP!

# PREFACE

## GOAL

The *Deck Officer Study Guide, Lifeboatman, Volume 7* was compiled to assist prospective deck license candidates enrolled in a structured curriculum or studying independently with their preparation for the following U.S. Coast Guard Merchant Marine license examinations and open-book renewal exercises:

### Certification Examinations:
- Able Seaman/Lifeboatman, All Grades of Certification
- Lifeboatman, Original Issue, Any Waters
- Lifeboatman, Mobile Offshore Drilling Units, Original Issue, Any Waters
- Lifeboatman (Limited), Survival Craft, Original Issue, Any Waters

### Review & Renewal Exercises:
- Comprehensive Renewal Exercise, All Grades of Certification

## PURPOSE

The U.S. Coast Guard posts the Merchant Marine examination question bank on the Internet which constitutes publication of the questions in the public domain. This information is made available to afford the public an opportunity to review and comment upon the questions' clarity and accuracy. The data base file contains the U.S. Coast Guard questions for all grades of license. The Merchant Marine examination bank is not an examination study guide. It is merely a question and answer file which divides the deck license questions up into five generic topic areas. The questions are not organized into specific categories and appear in random fashion.

The *Deck Officer Study Guide, Lifeboatman, Volume 7* eliminates the need for computer know-how and expensive computer equipment. *Volume 7, Lifeboatman of the Deck Officer Study Guide* substantially reorganizes the sequence of the examination questions into clear-cut sections for each of the five deck disciplines. The objective of this effort is to provide you with quick access to definitive areas of required expertise in order to accelerate systematic study and stimulate cognitive learning. Each section of the *Deck Officer Study Guide* isolates the key concepts affording you an opportunity for a comprehensive self-testing program. This methodology defines your individual starting point for additional research and remedial skill development.

## COMPREHENSIVENESS

The primary reference source consulted during the compilation of the *Deck Officer Study Guide* was the U.S. Coast Guard Merchant Marine question bank. The multiple choice questions in this publication are the actual questions which will appear on the current series of Merchant Marine license examination modules and renewal exercises. During the collation of this publication, more than 15,000 U.S. Coast Guard multiple choice questions, answers and associated references were analyzed and regrouped into specific examination subjects. **See: Merchant Mariner Info Center; Deck Exam Info; Deck Exam Questions (http://www.uscg.mil/stcw/index.htm)**

## TEXT ARRANGEMENT

The *Deck Officer Study Guide* is designed to be *"User Friendly"*. It provides quick access to definitive subject areas and/or key concepts. The body of the text is organized into the following seven distinct volumes:

- VOLUME 1      Deck General
- VOLUME 2      Navigation General
- VOLUME 3      Deck Safety
- VOLUME 4      Rules of the Road
- VOLUME 5      Navigation Problems Parts "A" & "B"
- VOLUME 6      Deck Examination Illustration Book COMDTPUB P16721.6A
- VOLUME 7      Lifeboatman (Lifeboatman Examination Only)

The seven volumes address the subject matter embodied in all sections of the current Merchant Marine license examination modules for all grades of deck license. The arrangement and content of each section was determined by utilizing the U.S. Coast Guard's examination specifications, as detailed in Table 46 CFR 10.910-2, *"License Codes"*.

The arrangement format for *Volume 7, Lifeboatman* presents each question with a sequential number which indicates both the volume number and a number unique to each question, next the U.S. Coast Guard database question number, followed by an appropriate Rule reference, the applicable system of Rules, a stem, which supplies needed information and poses the question, and four possible answers. The U.S. Coast Guard's keyed answer to each question in the *Volume 7, Lifeboatman* is indicated by the anchor symbol "⚓".

      **080064/DS03984**          **MIL, WSM, *46 CFR 160.51**
As shown in the illustration, item #8 would be a(n) _____? See Diagram D014SA
- A. recognition light
- ⚓ B. rain water catchment tube assembly
- C. pressure relief valve
- D. floating sheath knife

## ILLUSTRATIONS

Some of the questions in this publication require the use of an illustration or diagram to answer the question correctly. All of the illustrations and diagrams were contained in COMDTPUB P16721.6A, *Merchant Marine Deck Examination Illustration Book, and January 1992 edition*. Volume 6, *Deck Examination Illustration Book* of the *Deck Officer Study Guide* is a reproduction of COMDTPUB P16721.6A. The National Maritime Center (NMC) no longer publishes a paper copy of the Deck Examination Illustrations. They are available on line at the NMC's website. If a question requires the use of an illustration or diagram, it will be specifically stated in the lead-in sentence or stem of the question.

      **080064/DS03984**          **MIL, WSM, *46 CFR 160.51**
As shown in the illustration, item #8 would be a (n) _____? See Diagram D014SA
- A. recognition light
- ⚓ B. rain water catchment tube assembly
- C. pressure relief valve
- D. floating sheath knife

## REFERENCES

*Deck Examination Reference Texts* have been cited whenever possible. Refer to and review the list of *Deck Examination Reference Texts* contained in *Volume 1, Deck Safety* of the *Deck Officer Study Guide*. **Preference has been given to the Examination Room Reference texts which are always preceded by an asterisk (\*).** Use the <u>examination room</u> reference books as desk companions while studying and during self-testing exercises. Listed references may appear as an abbreviation or code. A table following the Preface in *Volume 1, Deck General of the Deck Officer Study Guide* lists the abbreviations and codes in alphabetical order and identifies the title of the reference. Some of the references listed are no longer available. As new questions are developed, they are drawn from current references. Over time, older references go out of print or are revised. If new reference material is published the U.S. Coast Guard reviews the questions in current use to ensure that they are still valid. The entire contents of any authorized Deck Examination Reference text may be used during all parts of the license examination with the exception of Rules of the Road during which NO reference material of any kind may be used.

## MERCHANT MARINE EXAMINATION QUESTION STRUCTURE

All of the deck license examination modules are randomly generated. The examination questions do not follow in the same question sequence as those found in the *Deck Officer Study Guide*. Therefore, you must <u>NEVER</u> memorize lists of answers. This technique will not produce the desired results. The U.S. Coast Guard computer system is not programmed with an answer randomization capability but many of the questions in the test bank use identical question stems and/or similar answers with the answers rearranged in a different sequence; therefore, you must <u>NEVER</u> memorize answers by letter identity alone. New questions and updated examination modules will be generated by the U.S. Coast Guard in order to reflect changes in national and international regulations, shipboard procedures, or evolutionary changes in the marine industry. You must always be prepared to demonstrate your proficiency and knowledge of the subject matter rather than your mastery of the rote memorization of the questions themselves.

## DECK LICENSE EXAMINATION GUIDANCE

The *Guide for Administration of Merchant Marine Deck Examinations (Deck Guide)*, (February 2002) and a table of *Deck Examination Subjects* outline the examination administration procedures, module rotation, and basic module structure for various grades of deck license. The U.S. Coast Guard Regional Examination Centers (RECs) are allowed some degree of latitude with regard to the administration of examinations. **You should personally confirm the module sequence, starting times and dates at the Regional Exam Center (REC) well in advance of your test day. See: Merchant Mariner Info Center; Deck Exam Info; Deck Exam Guide (http://www.uscg.mil/STCW/deck.pdf).**

The *Guide for Administration of Merchant Marine Deck Examinations (Deck Guide), (February 2002)* should be consulted on line at the address above. The assessment guidelines will help you to be better prepared. We fear things in direct proportion to our ignorance of them. The more you know about your exam and your rights the better off you will be.

The *Deck Examination Subjects Table* is designed to provide prospective license applicants with a detailed explanation of what subject areas may potentially appear in specific examination module. Be advised that, identical subject areas appear in different examination sections for various grades of license. Not every topic listed for a module will appear on every test, and different forms of a module can have different areas of emphasis. U.S. Coast Guard's examination specifications, as detailed in Table 46 CFR 10.910-2, "*License Codes*" contain the end caption:

"Any other subject considered necessary to establish the applicant's proficiency."

This catch-all statement has been rather liberally interpreted by the U.S. Coast Guard Merchant Marine Examination Branch to mean: "*No holds barred - Anything goes!*"

## ACKNOWLEDGMENTS

A practical study guide of this scope and depth must acknowledge many debts - to other study guides of this and former generations, to maritime educators, marine scholars and authorities who have worked so diligently to improve the educational standards and professional skills of American Licensed Deck Officers.

The names of the scholars which follow have contributed primarily because of their commitment to the diffusion of knowledge. A preface is superfluous in respect of a work with such obvious purpose as this; but some acknowledgments are truly in order.

A collective acknowledgment of indebtedness is gratefully made to my colleagues, one and all, from the Department of Marine Transportation at the Massachusetts Maritime Academy for their support, expertise and helpful suggestions made in informal conversations.

I am particularly grateful to:

Department of Marine Transportation, Massachusetts Maritime Academy
- CAPT. Craig Dalton, Professor
- CAPT. Earl Mayhofer, Jr.
- CAPT. Ed Bruce, Lab Assistant
- CAPT. Edward Vacha, Lab Assistant
- CAPT. John Carlisle, Instructor
- CAPT. Karen Arnold, Assistant Professor
- CAPT. Kerry Chicoine, Instructor
- CAPT. Kurt DeCicco, Lab Assistant

LAPWARE, LLC
- Mr. Richard Plant

for their continuing scholarship, valued counsel and years of dedication to Marine Science; and most of all, To my students at the Massachusetts Maritime Academy who have contributed ideas through their work and classroom discussions.

The opinions and guidance, herein, are my own, none of the mentioned contributors bears any responsibility for any of the material contained in this book.

JOSEPH S. MURPHY, II
Professor, Department of Marine Transportation
Massachusetts Maritime Academy

| EXAM STRUCTURE SHEET NO. 5-10 | License Type: **Lifeboatman** License Group: **Any Appropriate Tonnage** License Action: **Original Issue** License Condition: **Any Waters** | | **EXAM CODE** 48AA |
|---|---|---|---|
| **Number of Modules:** One (1) | | **Number of Questions** | **Minimum Passing Score** |
| 481XX - Deck Safety + Rules of the Road | | 70 | 70% |

Notes:
1) Applicants for certification as Lifeboatman desiring an endorsement for proficiency in survival craft must meet the provisions of the STCW Regulation VI/2, paragraph 1, and the appropriate provisions of Section A-VI/1 paragraph 2.1.1 and regulations in accordance with 46 CFR 12.10-5.
2) Applicants must also complete the Lifeboatman Practical demonstration in ESS 5 – 16 in addition to the written examination indicated above.

| EXAM STRUCTURE SHEET NO. 5-11 | License Type: **Lifeboatman** License Group: **Any Appropriate Tonnage** License Action: **Renewal** License Condition: **Any Waters** | | **EXAM CODE** 48RE |
|---|---|---|---|
| **Number of Modules:** One (1) | | **Number of Questions** | **Minimum Passing Score** |
| 489XX - Renewal Exercise[1] | | 20 | 90% |

Notes:
1) The Renewal Exercise is open book.
2) If an applicant does not receive a passing score on the first attempt then they should be allowed the opportunity to correct the questions they have missed and be re-graded for the second attempt. If they still fail on the second attempt, they should then be given a different module for the third and final try before undergoing a two-month waiting period.
3) Applicants who successfully complete an approved refresher training course are not required to complete the Renewal Exercise module.

The Lifeboatman written examination will consist of seventy (70) multiple choice questions. The passing grade on the Lifeboatman written examination is 70%. You must, therefore, get not more than twenty-one (21) questions wrong. The U.S. Coast Guard usually allows up to 3-1/2 hours to complete the Lifeboatman written examination.

REFERENCE:   Guide for Administration of Merchant Marine Deck Examinations (Deck Guide) November 2007.
See: http://www.uscg.mil/nmc/mmic_deckexquest.asp

# LIFEBOATMAN MODULE DESCRIPTIONS

| EXAM STRUCTURE SHEET NO. 5-12 | License Type: **Lifeboatman** <br> License Group: **Mobile Offshore Drilling Unit** <br> License Action: **Original Issue** <br> License Condition: **Any Waters** | | **EXAM CODE 49AA** |
|---|---|---|---|
| **Number of Modules:** One (1) | | **Number of Questions** | **Minimum Passing Score** |
| 491XX - Deck Safety + Rules of the Road | | 50 | 70% |

Notes:
1) This endorsement is only to be used for testing industrial workers employed on offshore drilling platforms and does not apply in qualifying for ratings forming part of a navigational watch.
2) Applicants must also complete the Lifeboatman Practical demonstration in ESS 5 – 16 in addition to the written examination indicated above.

| EXAM STRUCTURE SHEET NO. 5-13 | License Type: **Lifeboatman** <br> License Group: **Mobile Offshore Drilling Unit** <br> License Action: **Renewal** <br> License Condition: **Any Waters** | | **EXAM CODE 49RE** |
|---|---|---|---|
| **Number of Modules:** One (1) | | **Number of Questions** | **Minimum Passing Score** |
| 489XX - Renewal Exercise[1] | | 20 | 90% |

Notes:
1) The Renewal Exercise is open book.
2) If an applicant does not receive a passing score on the first attempt then they should be allowed the opportunity to correct the questions they have missed and be re-graded for the second attempt. If they still fail on the second attempt, they should then be given a different module for the third and final try before undergoing a two-month waiting period.
3) Applicants who successfully complete an approved refresher training course are not required to complete the Renewal Exercise module.

The Lifeboatman written examination will consist of seventy (70) multiple choice questions. The passing grade on the Lifeboatman written examination is 70%. You must, therefore, get not more than twenty-one (21) questions wrong. The U.S. Coast Guard usually allows up to 3-1/2 hours to complete the Lifeboatman written examination.

| EXAM STRUCTURE SHEET NO. 5-14 | License Type: **Lifeboatman (Limited)**<br>License Group: **Survival Craft**<br>License Action: **Original Issue**<br>License Condition: **Any Waters** | | EXAM CODE **44BA** |
|---|---|---|---|
| **Number of Modules:** One (1) | | Number of Questions | Minimum Passing Score |
| 441XX – Survival Craft | | 50 | 70% |

Note: Applicants must complete in addition to module 441XX either an approved course on Proficiency in Survival Craft , or the practical demonstrations sited in ESS 5 – 9 and in ESS 5 – 16 part III – Liferaft Launch Procedures and are limited to service on vessels not equipped with lifeboats.

| EXAM STRUCTURE SHEET NO. 5-15 | License Type: **Lifeboatman (Limited)**<br>License Group: **Survival Craft**<br>License Action: **Renewal**<br>License Condition: **Any Waters** | | EXAM CODE **44RE** |
|---|---|---|---|
| **Number of Modules:** One (1) | | Number of Questions | Minimum Passing Score |
| 449XX - Renewal Exercise[1] | | 20 | 90% |

Notes:
1) The Renewal Exercise is open book.
2) If an applicant does not receive a passing score on the first attempt then they should be allowed the opportunity to correct the questions they have missed and be re-graded for the second attempt. If they still fail on the second attempt, they should then be given a different module for the third and final try before undergoing a two-month waiting period.
3) Applicants who successfully complete an approved refresher training course are not required to complete the Renewal Exercise module.

The Lifeboatman written examination will consist of seventy (70) multiple choice questions. The passing grade on the Lifeboatman written examination is 70%. You must, therefore, get not more than twenty-one (21) questions wrong. The U.S. Coast Guard usually allows up to 3-1/2 hours to complete the Lifeboatman written examination.

# LIFEBOATMAN PRACTICAL EXAMINATION

| EXAM STRUCTURE SHEET NO. 5-16 | LIFEBOATMAN PRACTICAL DEMONSTRATION | |
|---|---|---|

**46 CFR 12.10-5(a) requires applicants for certificates or endorsement as lifeboatman to demonstrate their ability to effectively carry out all the duties that may be required of a lifeboatman. They must demonstrate that the training they have received has been effective in all operations connected with the launching of lifeboats, liferafts, and other survival craft; that they can understand and carry out the usual orders given, in English, incident to launching and recovery of survival craft; that can demonstrate the practical skills in the handling of lifeboats and the use of oars; and that they are capable of taking command of the crew of a lifeboat or other survival craft.**

1. **REC responsibilities.** Applicants for lifeboatman and not having completed an approved course are to be administered the appropriate written examination. For applicants needing to perform and be assessed in skill demonstrations, personnel in the REC should not be required to conduct these assessments unless the full scale equipment and assistance of a knowledgeable active duty or reserve BM or QM is available to observe the demonstration. As an alternative you may accept a Letter of Proficiency similar to the one shown on page 5-23. Applicants may only use one-quarter scale models to describe or identify components of a lifeboat provided in PART I, page 152. Only actual equipment may be used to demonstrate the proficiencies listed in Parts II and III in the use of survival craft. The services of a boat and crew are required in Part II to demonstrate ability to handle a lifeboat and command a crew underway which are typically not available at all RECs.

2. **Procedures to be followed:**

(a) **PART I – COMPONENT IDENTIFICATION.** Applicants must identify the equipment used in lifeboats and other survival craft. Ideally this will be done using the actual equipment. They should describe under what circumstances and in which craft the equipment would be found, the method in which it is used, and any special precautions regarding its construction or use. For the purpose of standardization award 1 point for identification and 1 point for description as per the checklist provided. Time allowed 30 minutes. Applicant must accumulate a minimum of 70 points to demonstrate proficiency.

(b) **PART II - PROCEDURES.** The applicant must be assessed as to their proficient performance of the skills involved in the launching, handling and recovering of a lifeboat (PARTS II-1, II-2 and II-3). The processes shown in Column A are to be compared to the standards provided in the checklist on pages 5 – 17 through 5 – 20. Time allowed is 60 minutes.

(c) **PART III – PROCEDURES.** An applicant for Lifeboatman or Lifeboatman Limited must demonstrate the procedural steps involved in the launching, righting and boarding of liferafts. An applicant for lifeboatman limited to vessels not equipped with lifeboats must have successfully completed module ESS 5 –14 and have demonstrated the ability to launch and board a liferaft. Time allowed is 30 minutes.

*Reference: Guide for Administration of Merchant Marine Deck Examinations (Deck Guide) NOV 2007.* This publication provides guidance for examination room proctors and other personnel who actively monitor applicants in the exam room (COMDTPUB P16721.35B). See: http://www.uscg.mil/nmc/mmic_deckexquest.asp

# LIFEBOATMAN PRACTICAL EXAMINATION

| LIFEBOATMAN PRACTICAL EXAMINATION | PART I COMPONENT IDENTIFICATION |
|---|---|

**REFERENCE: 46 CFR 199.175**

| COMPONENT | POINTS | COMPONENT | POINTS |
|---|---|---|---|
| Bailer | | Provisions | |
| Bilge pump | | Pump | |
| Boathook | | Radar reflector | |
| Bucket | | Rainwater collection device | |
| Can Opener | | Repair kit | |
| Compass | | Sea anchor | |
| Dipper | | Searchlight | |
| Drinking Cup | | Seasickness kit | |
| Fire extinguisher | | Signal, smoke | |
| First aid kit | | Signal, hand flare | |
| Flashlight | | Signal, parachute flare | |
| Hatchet | | Skates and fenders | |
| Heaving Line | | Sponge | |
| Instruction card | | Survival instructions | |
| Jackknife | | Table of lifesaving signals | |
| Knife (non-folding) | | Thermal protective aids | |
| Ladder | | Tool kit | |
| Mirror, signaling | | Towline | |
| Oars/Paddles | | Water | |
| Painters | | Whistle | |

| LIFEBOATMAN PRACTICAL EXAMINATION | PART II-1  PROCEDURES |
|---|---|

Applicants shall demonstrate their ability to prepare and safely launch survival craft and clear the ship's side quickly; give the correct commands for launching and boarding survival craft, clear the ship and handling and disembarking persons from survival craft. These checklists represent one set of assessment criteria for determining the success of these performance demonstrations. Others may be used such as those enclosed with NMC Policy Letter 08-01.

### PART II-1  LIFEBOAT LAUNCH PROCEDURES

| Applicant performs or describes in detail the steps involved in the lowering and launching of a lifeboat from gravity type davits.<br>Applicant must identify at least forty (40) of the steps listed in this column in order to be asked the questions in column B for the steps omitted in column A.<br>If an applicant fails to initially describe forty (40) steps in column A, it is a failure. | A | Questions for the Examiner to ask an applicant for a step he has failed to include in column A. If an applicant correctly answers a question for a step he omitted give him credit in column B. The total of the credits in column A and B of Parts II-1 and II-3 combined is the final score. Seventy (70) points is the passing grade. (For further information see NMC Policy Letter 08-01.) | B |
|---|---|---|---|
| Muster the crew. | | How do you know everyone assigned is present? | |
| Ensure that each crewmember knows their duties. | | How do you know the crew is trained? | |
| Where are the duties of the crew listed? | | | |
| Ensure crew and passengers are protectively dressed. | | How should persons who are preparing to abandon ship be dressed? | |
| Ensure crew and passengers have properly donned lifejackets and immersion suits. | | Where are immersion suits not required? (32N to 32S) | |
| Ensure lifejackets and immersion suits have proper equipment in good working order. | | What should be attached to a lifejackets and immersion suits to attract attention? | |
| Ensure boat properly suspended from falls. | | How should boats be suspended to perform maintenance on them, the winch or falls? | |
| Ensure gripes in place and secure. | | What secures the boat in its cradle? | |
| Remove lifeboat stowage cover and strongback. | | Stow clear of launch and debarkation area. What protects the interior of a stowed lifeboat? | |
| Ensure tricing pendants properly rigged and secure. | | How should the trip lines on the McCluney hooks be led? | |

## PART II-1  LIFEBOAT LAUNCH PROCEDURES (continued)

| | | | |
|---|---|---|---|
| Ensure Rottmer release gear handle pinned in closed position and has clear path to open. | | What prevents accidental release of the lifeboat from the falls? | |
| Ensure boat drain cap in place and secure. | | How is water prevented from entering the boat through its drain? | |
| Ensure that davit tracks are clear. | | What should be checked prior to lowering to prevent the davit arm wheels from jamming? | |
| Release manropes (lifelines) and ensure they will run free as boat lowers. | | What is provided to protect the occupants in case the boat was to fall unexpectedly? | |
| Ship rudder and/or tiller. | | What is a sweep oar? | |
| Have sea painter led out, made fast forward as close to water as possible, with all slack removed. | | How do you ensure the waterborne boat will lay alongside at the embarkation station? | |
| Ensure painter properly led inboard of forward falls, outboard of everything else. | | What could cause the sea painter to foul during the launch process? | |
| Ensure sea painter is properly made fast to forward inboard thwart. | | Where is the sea painter made fast in the boat? | |
| Ensure toggle pin has a clear release path and releases into boat. | | How do you ensure a "clean" release of the sea painter when so ordered? | |
| Ensure everyone is out of boat. | | How do you prevent injury to occupants while lowering the boat to the embarkation deck? | |
| Have gripes released, removed, and stowed clear of launch and embarkation areas. | | What happens to the gripes after they are released? | |
| Ensure locking bar swung clear of track. | | What fitting or part locks the boat in the stowed position? | |
| Have embarkation ladder made ready for use. Remove cover. Ensure made fast to deck. | | How will the winch operator get off the ship? | |
| Ensure no personnel or other obstruction in lowering path. | | What should be checked prior to lowering to prevent damage to the boat or injury to people on deck? | |
| Have lifeboat lowered at a steady speed to the embarkation deck. | | What speed should be used when lowering the lifeboat? | |
| Ensure strain on tricing pendants just enough to hold boat securely alongside at embark deck. | | What happens if you continue to try to lower the boat past the embarkation deck? | |
| Have frapping lines passed. | | What helps to prevent occupants from being thrown from the boat when the tricing pendants are released? | |

## PART II-1  LIFEBOAT LAUNCH PROCEDURES (continued)

| | | | |
|---|---|---|---|
| Order crew and passengers into the boat. | | How should load be distributed in boat? | |
| Order everyone to be seated, using manropes. | | What should occupants do while the boat is being lowered? | |
| Have tricing pendants released. | | What happens if you continue to lower the boat below the embarkation deck? | |
| Have frapping lines eased out slightly. | | What keeps the boat from swinging while being lowered? | |
| Order boat lowered. | | What speed should be used in lowering the boat? | |
| When safely waterborne order boat released. | | Ideally, when should boat be released? (crest of wave or swell) | |
| Order engine started or oars deployed. | | What should be checked immediately after starting engine? (cooling water flow) What is Fleming gear? | |
| Shove off. | | How do you get the boat heading away from the ship is side? (use boathook not hands) | |
| Swing clear of ship. | | If vessel has way on what helps boat sheer away from ship? | |
| Release sea painter. | | What should you do once the boat has swung clear of the ship is side? | |
| Look for, and assist, survivors. | | What should you look for once safely clear of ship? | |
| Join other boats. | | What helps aircraft sight vessel survivors? | |

# LIFEBOATMAN PRACTICAL EXAMINATION

| LIFEBOATMAN PRACTICAL EXAMINATION | PART II-2 OAR COMMANDS |
|---|---|

Reference:    American Merchant Seaman's Manual

| COMMAND | MEANING | DEMONSTRATED CORRECTLY |
|---|---|---|
| STAND BY THE OARS | Each crewmember clears oar, ships rowlock, places blade flat, on gunwale forward, inboard of person in front of them. | |
| SHOVE OFF | Inboard bowman pushes off using boathook. When ordered bowman releases sea painter. | |
| OUT OARS | Place oars in rowlocks directly from the boated position or from "Stand-By The Oars" position. Oars horizontal, at right angles to keel, blades flat. | |
| GIVE WAY TOGETHER | Blades of oars are swung forward and dipped into the water. At the command, "Together", the stroke is started. At the end of the stroke, blades are feathered, swung forward, and another stroke is started. | |
| HOLD WATER | Complete the stroke, stop rowing, drop blade into water vertically, and gradually swing to a position at right angles to the keel, taking care not to overstress rowlock. | |
| PORT (STARBOARD) HOLD WATER | Used to turn boat more quickly. Ordered side completes stroke and holds water, other side continues to row. With boat stopped can be used with "Give Way" command to opposite side to turn boat while gathering minimal headway. | |
| STERN ALL | When rowing ahead, complete the stroke, and then commence to backwater, gradually increasing the depth of the blades. | |
| BACK WATER | Row in the astern direction | |
| OARS | Complete the stroke, stop rowing, and bring the oars horizontal, at right angles to the keel, with the blades held flat. | |
| TRAIL OARS | Complete stroke and carefully allow oar to trail alongside, fore and aft. | |
| BANK OARS | Given from the "Oars" position. Allows oarsmen to rest when laying to. Oars drawn through the rowlock and rested on opposite gunwale. | |
| IN BOWS | The bowmen complete the stroke, swing their oars forward, and boat them. They then stand by with boat hooks to fend off or receive a line. | |
| WAY ENOUGH | Given when approaching a landing. Complete stroke, toss oars to about 45 degrees and boat the oars, forward oars first, unship the rowlocks | |
| BOAT THE OARS | From "Oars" or "Toss Oars", place the oars in the boat on side thwart, blades forward. | |
| TRAIL OARS | The trim blades of the oars are brought alongside the boat and left trailing in the water in single banked boats fitted with swivel rowlocks. | |
| TOSS OARS | Complete the stroke, come to "Oars" position, raise the oars smartly to the vertical, rest handles on the footing and trim blades fore-and-aft. | |

## PART II-3  LIFEBOAT RECOVERY PROCEDURES

| Applicant performs or describes in detail the steps involved in the recovery of a lifeboat with gravity type davits. Grade with Part II-1 | A | Questions to assist the Examiner in assessing the applicant's competence when they have failed to include an item in Column "A". | B |
|---|---|---|---|
| Request and receive permission to come alongside. | | How do you communicate with the ship from a lifeboat? What is signal to recover boat? | |
| Inspect Rottmer release gear for free rotation. | | When do you close and lock Rottmer gear? | |
| Come alongside slightly forward of falls. | | To what position should you aim during your approach to the ship? | |
| Retrieve and secure sea painter to thwart. | | How is the boat secured to the ship? | |
| Maneuver into position under the davit heads. | | Where does the sea painter position the boat? | |
| Have the frapping lines eased out. | | What keeps the falls clear as boat maneuvers into position alongside? | |
| Have hooks engaged. | | How are hooks lowered? | |
| Have releasing gear secured. | | What prevents accidental release of hooks? | |
| Have boat raised to just short of davit head. | | How high is boat raised? Why? | |
| Have tricing pendants rigged. | | What prevents a Pelican hook from opening accidentally? | |
| Have boat lowered to embarkation deck. | | How is boat brought alongside at embarkation deck? | |
| Order occupants to disembark. | | How could occupants disembark from boat prior to raising? | |
| Have cap removed from drain. Have automatic drain ball checked for free flow of water. | | How do you remove standing water from boat? | |
| Stow frapping lines. | | What do you do with the frapping lines? | |
| Have tracks and travel path checked for obstructions. | | What should be done prior to raising boat to prevent jamming while raising? | |
| Have boat raised. | | At what speed should the boat be raised? | |
| Have limit switch operation checked. | | What automatic device prevents the boat from being raised too far? | |
| Have boat raised until about 12 inches short of the mechanical stops or stowed position. | | Where are the inboard ends of gripes secured? | |
| Secure power to the winch. | | When should power to the winch be secured? | |
| Hand crank winch to mechanical stops. | | What safety feature prevents injury if power down activated while hand raising the boat? | |
| Connect and tighten gripes and locking bar. | | What prevents a secured boat from lowering? | |
| Lower boat until it rests on keel. | | Does a fully raised boat rest on its keel? | |
| Have all gear properly stowed in boat. | | What should be done with the boat's gear? | |

## PART III  LIFERAFT LAUNCHING PROCEDURES

| Applicant performs or describes in detail the steps involved in launching and boarding an inflatable liferaft.<br><br>Applicant must describe at least ten (10) steps correctly in order to be asked the questions from part B for the omitted steps. | A | Questions for the examiner to ask an applicant for a step he has failed to include in column A. If an applicant correctly answers a question for a step he omitted give him credit in column B. Each credit in columns A and B is worth five percentage points. Seventy percent is passing. | B |
|---|---|---|---|
| Muster crew and passengers at raft. | | How do you know everyone assigned to the craft is present? | |
| Ensure everyone knows duties. | | Where are survival craft assignments and duties listed? | |
| Ensure every one dressed properly. | | Describe what people should and should not be wearing or carrying. | |
| Secure painter directly to vessel. | | Why is a cleat installed in the vicinity of the liferaft station? | |
| Have strap released that secures raft to cradle. | | Describe the different methods of releasing a liferaft from its cradle. | |
| Have raft container carried to launch point. | | How many crewmembers does it take to safely carry and launch a liferaft? | |
| Check for obstructions below. | | What do you check immediately prior to launching the liferaft? | |
| Have raft thrown into water. | | What equipment is used to launch the liferaft? | |
| Have painter pulled out to end. | | How do you inflate a liferaft? | |
| Have painter pulled sharply to inflate raft. | | How long does it take for the liferaft to inflate? | |
| Have crew and passengers board raft. | | Describe the different methods of boarding a raft. | |
| Have crewmember right inverted raft. | | What do you do if the raft inflates in the inverted position? How do you hold on to the raft while trying to right it? | |
| Have painter cut to releases. | | How do you cast off the painter? | |
| Have raft paddled clear of vessel. | | How do you propel the raft clear of the vessel? | |
| Look for, and assist, survivors. | | What should you do once safely clear of the vessel's side? | |
| Have sea anchor deployed. | | What keeps the raft from drifting downwind? | |
| Ensure liferaft interior has adequate ventilation. | | Should you seal up all openings to preserve warmth? | |
| Have double bottom inflated. | | How do you prevent heat from escaping to the seawater? How do you inflate double bottom? | |
| Have all rafts lashed together. | | What helps searchers spot waterborne survivors from the air? | |
| Assign watchstanding and other duties. | | What duties should be assigned to occupants? | |

The following reference texts and materials will be provided by the Coast Guard at the Regional Examination Center (REC) for use by license candidates for all grades of license.

1.      1981 Nautical Almanac
2.      Reprints from the 1983 Tide & Tidal Current Tables (COMDTPUB P16721.46)
            Part 1: 1983 Tide Tables (Atlantic Coast of N. America)
            Part 2: 1983 Tidal Current Tables (Atlantic Coast of N. America)
3.      Sight Reduction Tables for Marine Navigation, H.O. Pub. No. 229, Vol. 2, Latitudes 15°-30°, Inclusive
4.      American Practical Navigator, Pub No. 9, Volume II, 1981 edition
5.      International Code of Signals, H.O. Pub. No. 102, 1969 edition, revised 1993
6.      Reprints from the Light List Lists and Coast Pilots (COMDTPUB P16721.38)
            Part 1: Block Island and Eastern Long Island Sound
                  Section A: Light List - Volume I (blue pages)
                  Section B: Coast Pilot - 2 (white pages)
            Part 2: Chesapeake Bay Entrance and Approaches
                  Section A: Light List - Volume II (yellow pages)
                  Section B: Coast Pilot - 3 (green pages)
7.      U.S. Coast Pilot, Volume 5 (1988 ed. - Rivers & Western Rivers modules only)
8.      U.S. Coast Pilot, Volume 6 (1998 ed. Great Lakes modules only)
9.      U.S. Coast Pilot, Volume 7 (1989 ed. Rivers & Rivers other than Western Rivers modules only)
10.     * Radio Navigational Aids Pub. No. 117, 1997 edition
11.     Chemical Data Guide for Bulk Shipment by Water CIM 16616.6A, 1990 edition
12.     * Code of Federal Regulations §
A.      * 33 CFR Parts 1 to 124, Navigation Rules, Anchorages, Bridges
B.      * 33 CFR Parts 125 to 199, Oil Pollution, and Navigation Safety Regulations
C.      * 46 CFR Parts 1 to 40, Tanker Regulations, Manning Requirements
D.      * 46 CFR Parts 41 to 69, Marine Engineering and Load Line Regulations
E.      * 46 CFR Parts 70 to 89, Passenger Vessel Regulations
F.      * 46 CFR Parts 90 to 139, Cargo and Miscellaneous Vessels Regulations
G.      * 46 CFR Parts 140 to 155, Dangerous Cargo Regulations
H.      * 46 CFR Parts 156 to 165, Manning & Equipment Specifications (Subpart Q)
I.      * 46 CFR Parts 166 to 199, Small Passenger Vessel Regulations
J.      * 46 CFR 200-499, Maritime Administration, Great Lakes
K.      * 49 CFR Parts 100 to 177, Transportation of Hazardous Material
13.     Stability Data Reference Book
14.     Operating Manual COASTAL DRILLER (MODU examinations)
15.     Operating Manual DEEP DRILLER (MODU examinations)
16.     * Ship's Code Card

*All parts of the above license examination reference materials may be used on every section of the deck license examination with the exception of Rules of the Road during which no reference material of any kind may be used.*

*\* The effective date is the latest date available.*

## QUALIFICATION AS A LIFEBOATMAN AND CERTIFICATION AS PROFICIENT IN SURVIVAL CRAFT AND RESCUE BOATS

### _Assessments of Practical Demonstrations to Qualify as Proficient in Survival Craft and Lifeboatman_

1. **Skill demonstrations**

    a. Each applicant for STCW certification as Proficient in Survival Craft must meet the standards of competence set out in STCW Code, Table A-VI/2-1. Similar skills must be demonstrated by an applicant for an endorsement as lifeboatman in accordance with 46 CFR Subpart 12.10. A mariner who completes a U.S. Coast Guard approved or accepted course will meet these standards because the demonstrations are required to be included as part of the course's approval.

    b. Using actual equipment, each student must correctly demonstrate all the skills listed on the assessment standards on the following pages. Assessment standards establish the conditions under which the assessments will occur, the performance or behavior the student is to accomplish, and the measurements against which the performance is judged.

    c. Some of the assessments are supplemented by and referenced to checklists to ensure thorough coverage of skills that require the performance of numerous individual tasks. Where referenced in the assessment standards, the examiner must use the appropriate checklist in conducting assessments of practical demonstrations of skill to ensure that critical tasks are not overlooked when evaluating a student's performance. The checklists are located immediately following the assessment standards. Applicants must meet the criteria in both the assessment standards and the checklists to be considered proficient in the applicable area.

    d. Checklists for less complex skills have not been developed; however, individual assessors should consider the development of appropriate checklists for those areas to ensure that all areas are fully assessed.

    e. Applicants seeking a lifeboatman's endorsement valid for service on lifeboat equipped vessels must complete all of the assessments listed in this enclosure. Applicants for a lifeboatman's endorsement valid for service only on vessels not equipped with lifeboats are required to complete only the assessments for handling and launching of a rescue craft beginning on page 10 of this enclosure. All applicants must also complete the personal survival element of basic safety training.

    f. Applicants must also provide proof of training during lifeboat drills and sea service

2. **Knowledge requirements**

Knowledge based competencies must be assessed through a written multiple-choice examination administered at a U.S. Coast Guard Regional Examination Center.

### Assessments of Practical Demonstrations
### to Qualify as Proficient in Survival Craft and Lifeboatman

| Competence | Knowledge, understanding and proficiency | Performance Condition | Performance Behavior | Performance Standard |
|---|---|---|---|---|
| Take charge of a lifeboat during and after launch | Command launching the lifeboat Another type of survival craft that permits the applicant to demonstrate the required skills may be substituted for a lifeboat | Given a lifeboat properly stowed on a gravity davit system, when hearing the abandon ship signal or the order to lower the lifeboat, the student will give the correct commands to launch the boat. | When hearing an abandon ship signal or the order in English to lower the lifeboat, the student will command launching the boat. | 1. Commands are issued in proper sequence. 2. All tasks to launch the boat are verified. 3. The boat is launched in ten minutes. *Use check-list #1* |
| | Prepare and safely launch a lifeboat | Given a lifeboat properly stowed on a gravity davit system, when given orders to perform tasks necessary to prepare and launch a lifeboat, the student will correctly perform the tasks. | The student will perform the following tasks: 1. Ready the boat to launch; 2. Pass the sea painter; 3. Secure sea painter; 4. Attend the frapping lines; 5. Release tricing pendants; and, 6. Operate winch and brake. | 1. Remove boat cover and strong backs; plug drain; ready man ropes; ship tiller; check painter is secure to thwart; and remove gripes. 2. Lead painter inside falls; and outboard of all obstructions. 3. Remove slack; and secure well forward by a round turn and figure eights on the bitts. 4. Pass frapping lines around falls after the tricing pendants pull boat into side of the ship; slack as ordered during the boat's decent. 5. On command, let go tricing pendants. 6. On command, lift brake release and lower boat. *Use check-list #2* |

## QUALIFICATION AS A LIFEBOATMAN AND CERTIFICATION AS PROFICIENT IN SURVIVAL CRAFT AND RESCUE BOATS

| Competence | Knowledge, understanding and proficiency | Performance Condition | Performance Behavior | Performance Standard |
|---|---|---|---|---|
| | Safely recover a lifeboat | In a lifeboat in the water, | the student will command: 1. bringing the lifeboat under the falls; 2. hooking the boat to the falls; 3. raising the boat to the embarkation deck; 4. raising the boat to its stowed position; and, 5. securing the boat. | 1. Commands are issued in proper sequence. 2. All tasks needed to recover the boat are verified. 3. The boat is recovered and secured within 15 minutes. *Use check-list #3* |
| | Steer (command) a lifeboat under oars | In a lifeboat in the water, | the student will: 1. get the boat underway; 2. steer a course by LB compass; 3. turn to port in the shortest possible distance; 4. turn to starboard turn to starboard in the shortest possible distance; 5. stop; and 6. go astern while steering as straight a course as possible using both a rudder and oars. | 1. Commands are issued in proper sequence. 2. Courses are within ± 6°of direction given by examiner. 3. Oarsmen carry out commands together. *Use check-list #5* |
| Operate a lifeboat engine | Method of starting and operating a lifeboat engine and its accessories | In a lifeboat equipped with an inboard engine, | the student will start and operate the lifeboat engine. | 1. Student checks that oil and cooling water levels are in accordance with manufacturer's recommendation 2. Actions taken to start the engine are in accordance with operator's manual for the engine's starting system (hand crank, electric, or hydraulic). 3. The engine is operated in forward, neutral and reverse |

## QUALIFICATION AS A LIFEBOATMAN AND CERTIFICATION AS PROFICIENT IN SURVIVAL CRAFT AND RESCUE BOATS

| Competence | Knowledge, understanding and proficiency | Performance Condition | Performance Behavior | Performance Standard |
|---|---|---|---|---|
| Manage a lifeboat after abandoning ship | Row a lifeboat | In a lifeboat in the water, | the student will respond correctly to the following commands: 1. Stand by the oars; 2. Out oars; 3. Stand by to give way; 4. Give way 5. Oars; 6. Hold water; 7. Back water; 8. Way enough; and, 9. Boat the oars. | 1. Actions in response to the commands are correct. 2. The oarsmen carry out together the actions in response to commands. *Use check-list #6* |
| | Use lifeboat equipment | Using a SOLAS approved lifeboat, | the student will demonstrate the correct use of the following equipment: 1. Bilge pump; 2. Rainwater collection device; 3. Sea Anchor; and, 4. Thermal Protective Aids. | 1. The bilge pump is readied for pumping and operated. 2. The device is correctly deployed. 3. Simulates correct deployment of the sea anchor. 4. A TPA is correctly donned. |
| Use locating devices | Rig devices to aid location | Given a lifeboat radar reflector and a SART, | the student will correctly rig the following devices to aid location: 1. The boat's radar reflector; and, 2. The lifeboat SART. | 1. The radar reflector is rigged to maximize its radar return. 2. The SART is positioned to maximize its signal output. |

## QUALIFICATION AS A LIFEBOATMAN AND CERTIFICATION AS PROFICIENT IN SURVIVAL CRAFT AND RESCUE BOATS

| Checklist 1.<br>**While serving as the person-in-charge, give correct commands for launching a lifeboat or take appropriate steps to complete the listed actions** | PASS | FAIL |
|---|---|---|
| **Muster crew and verify boat assignment** | | |
| 1. Verify that individuals know their tasks as identified in the station bill | Y | Y |
| 2. Reassign tasks as necessary for missing or injured individuals | Y | Y |
| **Visually inspect crew and passengers** | | |
| 1. PFD's are properly worn | Y | Y |
| 2. Crew brings their survival suits, if required | Y | Y |
| 3. Hard hats are worn by launching crew; remainder have appropriate head covering | Y | Y |
| **Verify crewmembers bring equipment identified in their station bill as assigned** | | |
| 1. Radio Officer/Deck Officer – Radio, L/B VHF, SART | Y | Y |
| 2. GSU – Blankets | Y | Y |
| 3. Boat Engineer – Tools | Y | Y |
| **Prior to launch, visually inspect the following:** | | |
| 1. Hull | Y | Y |
| 2. Davits | Y | Y |
| 3. Sea painter | Y | Y |
| 4. Tricing pendants | Y | Y |
| 5. Releasing gear lever in closed position | Y | Y |
| 6. Vessel list to determine if lifeboat can be launched | Y | Y |
| 7. Davit tracks for damage or obstructions | Y | Y |
| 8. Obstructions below in way of boat | Y | Y |
| 9. Drain plug is in place | Y | Y |
| 10. Oars and Compass | Y | Y |
| **Prepare the lifeboat for launch** | | |
| 1. Remove cover and strongback from lifeboat (if fitted) | Y | Y |
| 2. Install boat plug | Y | Y |
| 3. Check releasing lever in the non-release position | Y | Y |
| 4. Lower man ropes | Y | Y |
| 5. Lead sea painter forward and makes fast | Y | Y |
| 6. Ship rudder | Y | Y |
| 8. Release gripes | Y | Y |
| **Lower boat to the embarkation deck** | | |
| 1. Raise winch brake handle to lower away to embarkation deck | Y | Y |
| 2. Reduce rate of descent and apply brake before tricing pendants take boat's weight | Y | Y |
| 3. Pass the frapping lines and make them taut | Y | Y |
| 4 Order crewmembers into boat and to be seated | Y | Y |
| 5. Order launch crew to release tricing pendants | Y | Y |
| **Lower boat to the water** | | |
| 1. Release brake and allow lifeboat to lower to the water | Y | Y |
| 2. Order crewmember to release boat from falls by changing the release lever position. | Y | Y |
| 3. Order crewmembers to manually release the falls in the correct sequence according to sternway or headway if lifeboat does not have automatic releasing gear | Y | Y |
| 4. Complete task in 10 minutes | Y | Y |

## QUALIFICATION AS A LIFEBOATMAN AND CERTIFICATION AS PROFICIENT IN SURVIVAL CRAFT AND RESCUE BOATS

| **Checklist 2.**<br>**While serving a member of a boat crew, prepare and safely launch a lifeboat** | PASS | FAIL |
|---|:---:|:---:|
| **Ready the boat for launch**<br>**On command, the student will:** | | |
| 1. Remove the boat cover and strong backs (if fitted) | Y | Y |
| 2. Insert the drain plug | Y | Y |
| 3. Ready the manropes | Y | Y |
| 4. Ship the tiller | Y | Y |
| 5. Check that the painter is secure to the thwart | Y | Y |
| 6. Remove gripes | Y | Y |
| **Pass and secure the sea painter**<br>**On command, the student will:** | | |
| 1. Lead painter inside falls and outboard of all obstructions | Y | Y |
| 2. Remove slack | Y | Y |
| 3. Secure to a bitt on the main deck well forward by a round turn and figure eights | Y | Y |
| **Attend frapping lines and tricing pendants**<br>**On command, the student will:** | | |
| 1. Pass frapping lines around falls after the tricing pendants pull boat into side of the ship | Y | Y |
| 2. Secure with figure eights to cleat on davit arm | Y | Y |
| 3. Slack as ordered during the boat's descent | Y | Y |
| 4. When ordered, release tricing pendants | Y | Y |
| **Operate winch and brake during lowering the boat**<br>**On command, the student will:** | | |
| 1. Lift brake release and lower boat as directed by person-in-charge | Y | Y |

## QUALIFICATION AS A LIFEBOATMAN AND CERTIFICATION AS PROFICIENT IN SURVIVAL CRAFT AND RESCUE BOATS

| Checklist 3. Safely recover a lifeboat | PASS | FAIL |
|---|---|---|
| 1. Recover the sea painter and secure to forward thwart | | |
| 2. Check that falls are not twisted and hooks are facing each other | Y | Y |
| 3. Ease frapping lines out | Y | Y |
| 4. Order crewmember to connect forward fall if vessel is making headway or to connect aft fall if vessel is making sternway | Y | Y |
| 5. Order crewmember to connect remaining fall | Y | Y |
| 6. Secure releasing gear | Y | Y |
| 7. Order boat raised by electrical hoist to just above the embarkation deck so that tricing pendants can be made fast | Y | Y |
| 8. Lower boat to embarkation deck to disembark passengers and crew | Y | Y |
| 9. Remove drain plug | Y | Y |
| 10. Order boat raised by winch | Y | Y |
| 11. Check limit switches | Y | Y |
| 12. Resume raising boat by winch until stopped by limit switches; turn off power to the winch | Y | Y |
| 13. Order the boat raised to the boat cradle using hand cranks for the last 12 inches (Don't allow winch brake to be used when hand cranks are in place or being used) | Y | Y |
| 14. Secure locking bars | Y | Y |
| 15. Pass the gripes and tighten the gripe turnbuckles until boat is pulled in against keel stops | Y | Y |
| 16. Lower boat until it rests on keel stops | Y | Y |
| 17. Release sea painter from forward deck and stow in boat | | |
| 18. Replace strongback and boat cover, if fitted | Y | Y |
| 19. Complete task in 15 minutes | Y | Y |

## QUALIFICATION AS A LIFEBOATMAN AND CERTIFICATION AS PROFICIENT IN SURVIVAL CRAFT AND RESCUE BOATS

| Checklist 5.<br>Steer (command) a lifeboat under oars | PASS | FAIL |
|---|---|---|
| **Give the command to fend off the bow**<br>**Give the command "Stand by the oars"** | | |
| 1. Crew picks up the oars at the loom so that the blade rests flat on the forward gunwales, pushes oars forward until the handles are over the respective thwarts | Y | Y |
| **Give the command "Out oars"** | | |
| 1. Crew lifts the oars and places them in the oar locks | Y | Y |
| **Give the command "Stand by to give way"** | | |
| 1. Crew holds oars horizontally, blades perpendicular, with the wrists straight and arms extended full length; leans forward until knuckles almost touch the backs of the persons in front | Y | Y |
| **Give the command "Give way"** | Y | Y |
| 1. Crew dips three-quarters of the blade into the water, braces feet against the stretcher, leans back, and draws the handle up to the chest | Y | Y |
| 2. At the end of the first stroke, crew feathers the oars by rotating the wrist downward | Y | Y |
| 3. Leans forward and repeats steps 1 and 2 | Y | Y |
| **Steer the lifeboat in a straight line by compass**<br>**Turn the lifeboat to port in the shortest distance.** | | |
| 1. Turn rudder to port (put tiller to starboard) | Y | Y |
| 2. Hold water port | Y | Y |
| 3. Give way starboard | Y | Y |
| 4. Backwater port | Y | Y |
| **Turn the lifeboat to starboard** | | |
| 1. Turn rudder to starboard (put tiller to port) | Y | Y |
| 2. Hold water starboard | Y | Y |
| 3. Give way port | Y | Y |
| 4. Backwater starboard | Y | Y |
| **Stop the lifeboat** | | |
| 1. Hold water all | Y | Y |
| **Steer astern** | | |
| 1. Backwater all | Y | Y |
| 2. Adjust steering as necessary to achieve a course within ± 6° of the desired heading | Y | Y |

## QUALIFICATION AS A LIFEBOATMAN AND CERTIFICATION AS PROFICIENT IN SURVIVAL CRAFT AND RESCUE BOATS

| Checklist 6.<br>Row a lifeboat | PASS | FAIL |
|---|---|---|
| **On the command "Stand by the oars"** | | |
| 1. Pick up the oar at the loom so that the blade rests flat on the forward gunwales, push oars forward until the handle is over the respective thwart | Y | Y |
| **On the command "Out oars"** | | |
| 1. Lift the oar and place it in the oar locks | Y | Y |
| **On the command "Stand by to give way"** | | |
| 1. Hold oar horizontally, blade perpendicular with the wrists straight and arms extended full length; lean forward until knuckles almost touch the back of the person in front | Y | Y |
| **On the command "Give way"** | | |
| 1. Dip three-quarters of the blade into the water, brace feet against the stretcher, lean back, and draw the handle up to the chest | Y | Y |
| 2. At the end of the first stroke, feather the oar by rotating the wrist downward | Y | Y |
| 3. Lean forward and repeats steps 1 and 2 | Y | Y |
| **On the command "OARS"** | | |
| 1. Complete the stroke, stop rowing, and bring the oar horizontal at right angles to the keel with the blades held flat | Y | Y |
| **On the command "HOLD WATER "** | | |
| 1. Complete the stroke, stop rowing, dip the oar about half way into water and hold water to stop the way on the boat | Y | Y |
| **On the command "BACK WATER"** | | |
| 1. Row in astern motion | Y | Y |
| **On the Command "WAY ENOUGH"** | | |
| 1. When rowing ahead, complete the stroke, raise oars with crook of elbow to about 30 degrees swing blade forward, and place oars in the boat | Y | Y |
| **On the command "BOAT THE OARS"** | | |
| 1. From "Oars", place the oars in the boat with blades forward | Y | Y |

## QUALIFICATION AS A LIFEBOATMAN AND CERTIFICATION AS PROFICIENT IN SURVIVAL CRAFT AND RESCUE BOATS

### Assessments for Launching and Recovery of Rescue Boats

| Competence | Knowledge, understanding and proficiency | Performance Condition | Performance Behavior | Performance Standard |
|---|---|---|---|---|
| Take charge of rescue boat during and after launch | Command launching the rescue boat. | Using a rescue boat properly stowed on single arm davit, mounted on a pier or a ship, when hearing an order in English to lower the rescue boat, | the candidate will command the launching of a rescue boat. | The candidate issued the following orders in proper sequence and verified they were properly carried out: 1. removed boat cover and securing lines; put in drain plugs if fitted, check fuel and lube oil levels, tested engine, and made sure all rescue gear is aboard; 2. checked that the sea painter is properly attached; 3. secured control lines (if fitted) at rescue boat bow and stern; 4. checked that the out drive had been lowered; 5. swung rescue boat to the embarkation position*; and, 6. lowered rescue boat to water.<br><br>* If it is unsafe for the rescue boat crew to ride the rescue craft from the embarkation position to the water, this task should be simulated. |
|  | Launch the rescue boat. | Using a rescue boat properly stowed on single arm davit, mounted on a pier or a ship, when hearing the orders in English to prepare and lower the rescue boat, | the candidates, acting as members of the launch crew, will prepare and launch a rescue boat.*<br><br>*Candidates must rotate through all assigned tasks to determine if they have achieved competence. | When ordered, the candidate correctly performed the following tasks: 1. readied the rescue boat for launch; 2. properly passed and secured the sea painter and control lines (if fitted); 3. lowered the outdrive; 4. positioned the rescue boat at the embarkation site; and, 5. lowered the boat on command. |

## QUALIFICATION AS A LIFEBOATMAN AND CERTIFICATION AS PROFICIENT IN SURVIVAL CRAFT AND RESCUE BOATS

| Competence | Knowledge, understanding and proficiency | Performance Condition | Performance Behavior | Performance Standard |
|---|---|---|---|---|
| Take charge of rescue boat during and after launch | Operate the rescue boat during launch. | Using a rescue boat, when hearing the order in English to man the rescue boat, | the candidate will act as coxswain and operate the rescue boat during launch. | The candidate:<br>1. boarded the rescue boat;<br>2. when afloat, started the engine;<br>3. ordered the release of the releasing hook, after control line (if fitted), forward control line (if fitted), and painter; and,<br>4. departed the ship's side at a shallow angle. |
|  | Operate the rescue boat during launch. | Using a properly stowed rescue boat, when hearing the order in English to man the rescue boat, | the candidate acting as the rescue boat crew will carry out all commands during launch. | The candidate:<br>1. boarded the rescue boat;<br>2. released the releasing hook, after control line (if fitted), forward control line (if fitted), and painter; and,<br>3. fended off as ordered. |
|  | Recover the rescue boat. | Given a rescue boat on the water connected to the fall of a single arm davit, mounted on a pier or a ship, when hearing the orders in English to recover and stow a rescue boat, | the candidates acting a members of the recovery crew will recover and stow the rescue boat.*<br><br>*Candidates will be rotated through all assigned tasks to determine if they have achieved competence. | When ordered, the candidate correctly performed the following tasks:<br>1. lowered the painter and control lines to the appropriate height above the water;<br>2. tended the forward and after control lines (if fitted);<br>3. lowered the hook when the boat operator signaled to do so;<br>4. when the boat operator signaled to begin hoisting, hoisted the rescue boat to the disembarkation position while tending the control lines ( if fitted)*;<br>5. disembarked the rescue boat crew;<br>6. swung the rescue boat to its stowed position; and ,<br>7. properly secured the rescue boat.<br><br>* If it is unsafe for the rescue boat crew to ride the rescue boat from the water to the disembarkation position, this task should be simulated. |

## QUALIFICATION AS A LIFEBOATMAN AND CERTIFICATION AS PROFICIENT IN SURVIVAL CRAFT AND RESCUE BOATS

| Competence | Knowledge, understanding and proficiency | Performance Condition | Performance Behavior | Performance Standard |
|---|---|---|---|---|
| Take charge of rescue boat during and after launch | Operate the rescue boat during recovery. | Using a rescue boat on the water and a single arm davit, mounted on a pier or a ship, when hearing the order in English to return to the ship, | the candidate will operate the rescue boat during recovery. | The candidate: 1. positioned the rescue boat under the sea painter's eye; 2. directed the crew to grab the sea painter; 3. rode the painter until the boat was in the appropriate position; 4. directed the crew to secure the sea painter on his/her command; 5. directed the crew to secure the forward control line (if fitted), and the after control line (if fitted); 6. directed the crew to secure the releasing hook to the rescue boat bridle; and, 7. secured the engine properly as safety requires. |
| | Command the recovery and stowage of the rescue boat. | Given a rescue boat on the water connected to the fall of a single arm davit, when hearing the order in English to recover the rescue boat, | the candidate will command the recovery and stowage of the rescue boat. | The candidate issued orders in proper sequence that resulted in the following actions and verified they were properly carried out: 1. painter and control lines were lowered to the appropriate height above the water; 2. forward and after control lines (if fitted) were tended; 3. the hook was lowered upon signal; 4. when the boat operator signaled to begin hoisting, ordered the recovery crew to hoist the rescue boat to the disembarkation position while tending the control lines ( if fitted)*; 5. the rescue boat crew disembarked; 6. the rescue boat was swung to its stowed position; and, 7. the rescue boat was properly secured. If it is unsafe for the rescue boat crew to ride the rescue boat from the water to the disembarkation position, this task should be simulated. |

# RECORD OF QUALIFYING SEA SERVICE

This record of the sea service acquired by _____, MMD no._____, will be used to qualify for a lifeboatman's endorsement or certification as proficient in survival craft. It should be signed by the mariner's department head indicating the dates of service, and the number of abandon ship drills in which the mariner participated.

| VESSEL | ROUTE[1] | SIGNED ON | DISCHARGED | DATES OF ABANDON SHIP DRILLS[2] | DATES BOAT LOWERED TO WATER AND CREW EXERCISED[3] | SIGNATURE (Include MMD no.) |
|---|---|---|---|---|---|---|
|  |  |  |  |  |  |  |
|  |  |  |  |  |  |  |
|  |  |  |  |  |  |  |
|  |  |  |  |  |  |  |
|  |  |  |  |  |  |  |
|  |  |  |  |  |  |  |
|  |  |  |  |  |  |  |
|  |  |  |  |  |  |  |
|  |  |  |  |  |  |  |

Notes:
1. Insert O for ocean routes; NC for near coastal routes; GL for Great Lakes routes; LBS for other lakes and bays or sounds.
2. Only include dates where the crew was instructed in abandon ship procedures and the launching and handling of survival craft
3. Only include a date in this column if the mariner served as member of the boat crew that was exercised at oars, otherwise insert

# RECORD OF COMPLETION OF PRACTICAL ASSESSMENTS
# TO QUALIFY AS A LIFEBOATMAN AND AS PROFICIENT IN SURVIVAL CRAFT

This checklist conveniently groups the STCW's competencies and the supporting knowledge, understandings, and proficiencies that apply to certification as proficient in survival craft and to issuance of a lifeboatman certification. Assessors who witness the successful demonstration of a mariner's competency, performed in accordance with the assessment standards, should sign the appropriate line in this checklist, print their name, and include their license number.

MARINER'S NAME _____ MMD NO.

_____

| STCW COMPETENCY | DATE | VESSEL TRAINING FACILITY | SIGNETURE/LIC. NO. |
|---|---|---|---|
| **I. LAUNCHING AND RECOVERY OF LIFEBOATS** | | | |
| 1. Command launching the lifeboat | | | |
| 2. Prepare and safely launch a lifeboat | | | |
| 3. Safely recover a lifeboat | | | |
| 4. Start and operate a lifeboat's engine | | | |
| 5. Steer (command) a lifeboat under oars | | | |
| 6. Row a lifeboat | | | |
| 7. Use lifeboat equipment | | | |
| 8. Rig devices to aid detection | | | |
| **II. LAUNCHING AND RECOVERY OF RESCUE BOATS** | | | |
| 1. Command launching the rescue boat | | | |
| 2. Launch the rescue boat | | | |
| 3. Operate the rescue boat during launch – Act as coxswain | | | |
| 4. Operate the rescue boat during launch – Act as boat crew | | | |
| 5. Operate the rescue boat during recovery | | | |
| 6. Command the rescue boat during recovery | | | |

* By signing, I acknowledge that I have had at least one year of sea service in a licensed capacity within the past five years and that I am serving as a licensed officer on the vessel upon which these assessments are being performed.

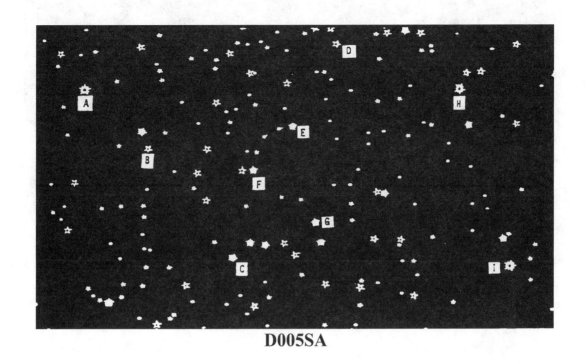

**D005SA**

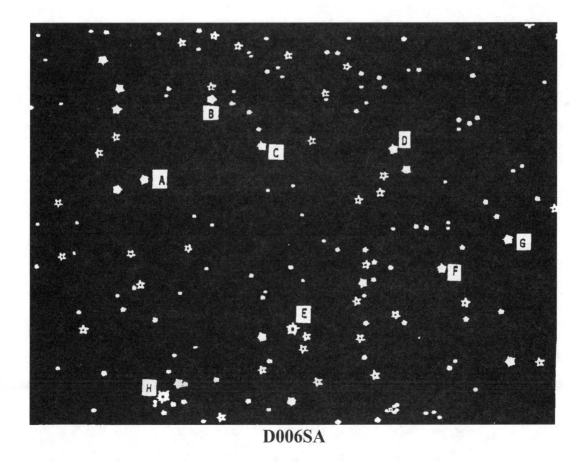

**D006SA**

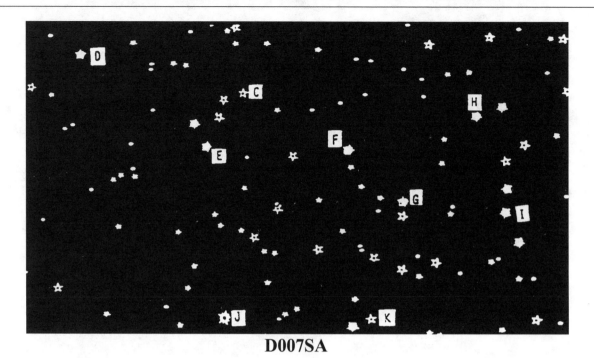

**D007SA**

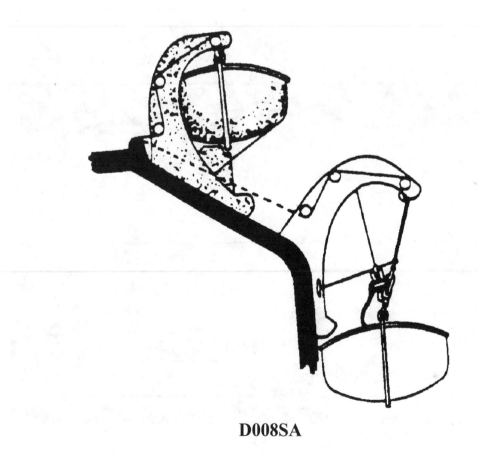

**D008SA**

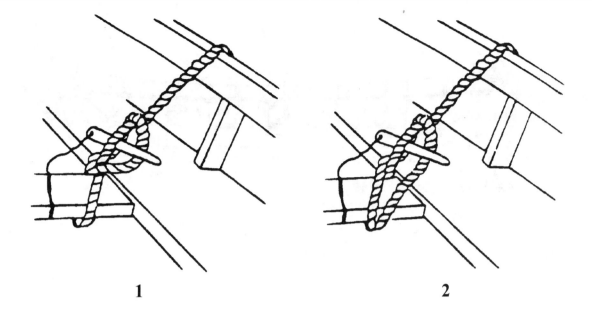

**1**          **2**

**D009SA**

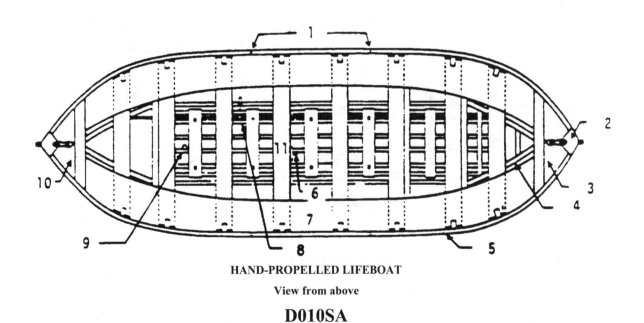

**HAND-PROPELLED LIFEBOAT**

View from above

**D010SA**

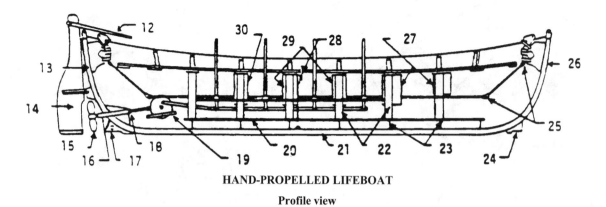

**HAND-PROPELLED LIFEBOAT**

Profile view

## D010SA

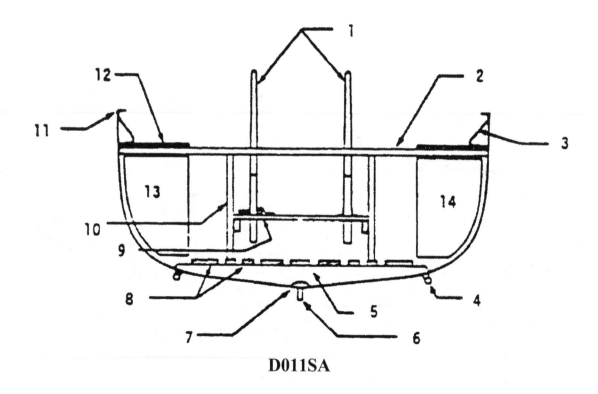

## D011SA

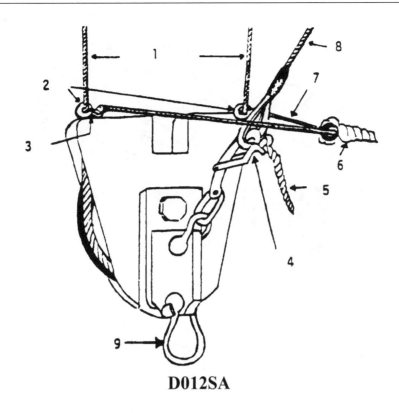

**D012SA**

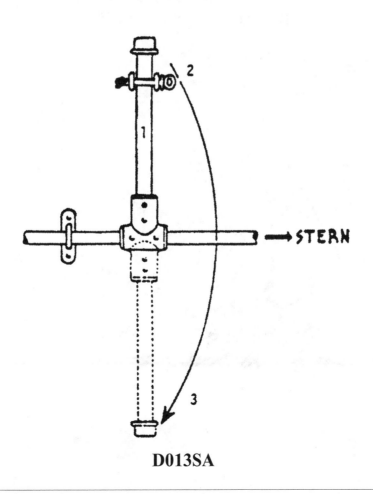

**D013SA**

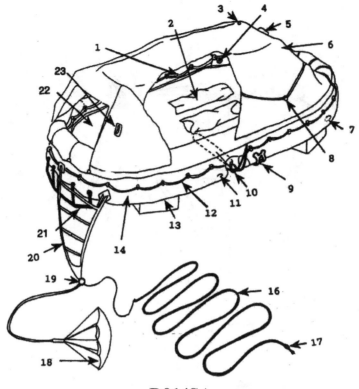

**D014SA**
**(Illustrations revised in 2006)**

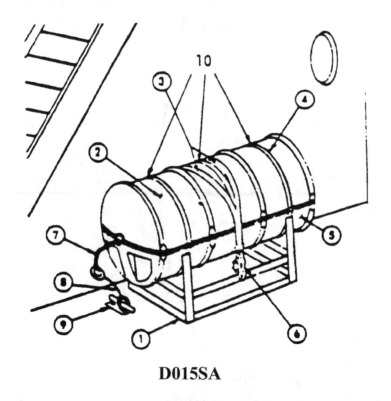

**D015SA**

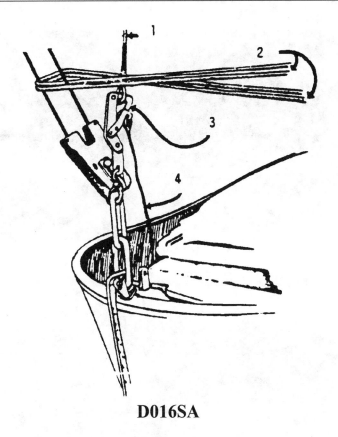

**D016SA**

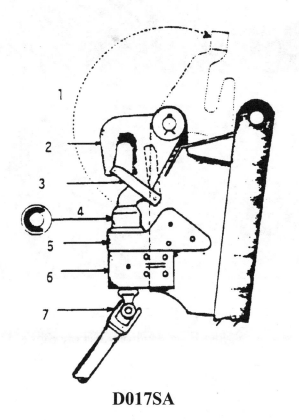

**D017SA**

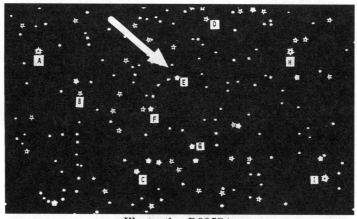

**Illustration D005SA**

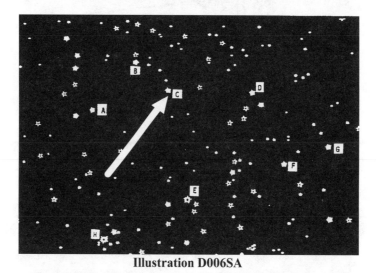

**Illustration D006SA**

**Illustration D007SA**

| ILLUSTRATION | ITEM | DESCRIPTION |
|---|---|---|
| D005SA | Letter E | Polaris (Pole Star) |
| D006SA | Letter C | Polaris (Pole Star) |
| D007SA | Letter F | Polaris (Pole Star) |

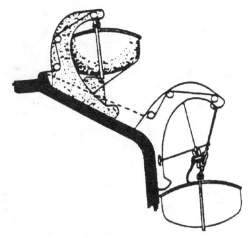

**Illustration D008SA**

| ITEM | DESCRIPTION |
|------|-------------|
| Gravity Davit | Lifeboat deployed |

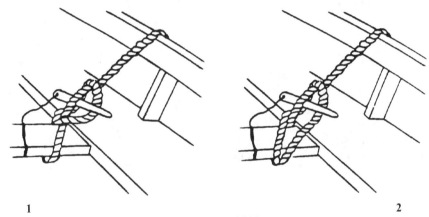

1                                                                          2

**Illustration D009SA**

| ITEM | DESCRIPTION |
|------|-------------|
| Number 1 | Sea painter, incorrectly rigged |
| Number 2 | Sea painter, correctly rigged |

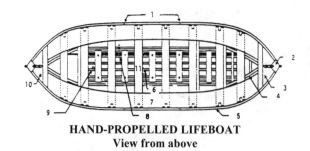

**HAND-PROPELLED LIFEBOAT**
View from above

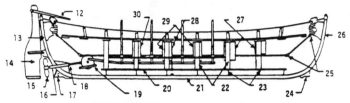

**HAND-PROPELLED LIFEBOAT**
Profile view
**Illustration D010SA**

| ITEM | DESCRIPTION |
|---|---|
| Number 1 | Row lock sockets |
| Number 2 | Bresthook |
| Number 3 | Bow sheet |
| Number 4 | Foot rest |
| Number 5 | Gunwale |
| Number 6 | Bilge pump |
| Number 7 | Side bench |
| Number 8 | Releasing lever |
| Number 9 | Drain plug |
| Number 10 | Stern sheet |
| Number 11 | Thwart |
| Number 12 | Tiller |
| Number 13 | Stern post |
| Number 14 | Rudder (unbalanced rudder) |
| Number 15 | Propeller |
| Number 16 | Stern tube |
| Number 17 | Keel rest (aft) |
| Number 18 | Stuffing box |
| Number 19 | Hand propelling unit & reversing gear |
| Number 20 | Footings |
| Number 21 | Keel (bar keel) |
| Number 22 | Stanchions |
| Number 23 | Floors |
| Number 24 | Keel rest (forward) |
| Number 25 | Universal joints |
| Number 26 | Stem |
| Number 27 | Tanks (equipment) |
| Number 28 | Bilge pump |
| Number 29 | Tanks (water) |
| Number 30 | Tank (provisions) |

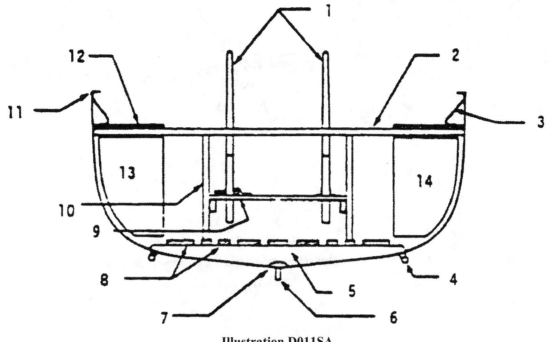

**Illustration D011SA**

| ITEM | DESCRIPTION |
|------|-------------|
| Number 1 | Hand propelling levers |
| Number 2 | Thwart |
| Number 3 | Bracket |
| Number 4 | Grab rail |
| Number 5 | Floor |
| Number 6 | Keel (bar keel) |
| Number 7 | Limber hole |
| Number 8 | Footings |
| Number 9 | Releasing gear rod |
| Number 10 | Stanchion |
| Number 11 | Gunwale |
| Number 12 | Side bench |
| Number 13 | Tank (air) |
| Number 14 | Tank (air) |

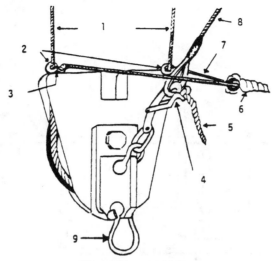

**Illustration D012SA**

| ITEM | DESCRIPTION |
|---|---|
| Number 1 | Falls (wire lifeboat) |
| Number 2 | Hooks (sister) |
| Number 3 | Mousing |
| Number 4 | Tricing pendant trip hook (McCluney) |
| Number 5 | Tripping line |
| Number 6 | Frapping line |
| Number 7 | Strap (wire) |
| Number 8 | Tricing pendant |
| Number 9 | Shackle |

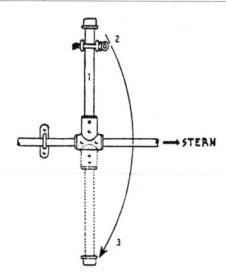

**Illustration D013SA**

| ITEM | DESCRIPTION |
|---|---|
| Number 1 | Rottmer releasing gear lever |
| Number 2 | Rottmer releasing gear lever (closed position) |
| Number 3 | Rottmer releasing gear lever (open position) |

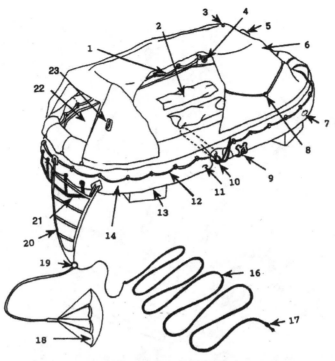

**Illustration D014SA**
**(Illustration revised in 2006)**

| ITEM | DESCRIPTION |
|---|---|
| Number 1 | Internal Lifeline |
| Number 2 | Equipment Bags |
| Number 3 | Recognition Light (External) |
| Number 4 | Pressure Relief Valve |
| Number 5 | Heaving Line (With Quoit) |
| Number 6 | Canopy |
| Number 7 | Battery (Water Activated) |
| Number 8 | Rain Water Catchment Tube Assembly |
| Number 9 | Righting Strap |
| Number 10 | $CO_2$ Inflation System |
| Number 11 | Deflation Plug |
| Number 12 | External Lifelines |
| Number 13 | Ballast Bags |
| Number 14 | Buoyancy Tubes |
| Number 15 | [INTENTIONALLY LEFT BLANK] |
| Number 16 | Sea Painter (Operating Cord) |
| Number 17 | Weak Link |
| Number 18 | Sea Anchor (Drogue) |
| Number 19 | Towing Connection |
| Number 20 | Towing Bridle |
| Number 21 | Boarding Ladder |
| Number 22 | Inflatable Floor |
| Number 23 | Floating Sheath Knife |

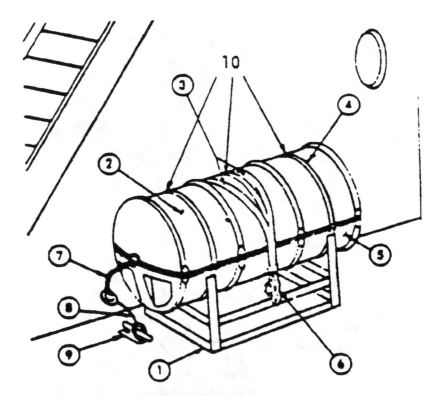

**Illustration D015SA**

| ITEM | DESCRIPTION |
|---|---|
| Number 1 | Liferaft cradle |
| Number 2 | Fiberglass container |
| Number 3 | Tie-down straps |
| Number 4 | Packing band |
| Number 5 | Fiberglass container gasket |
| Number 6 | Hydrostatic release |
| Number 7 | Operating cord (painter) |
| Number 8 | Weak link |
| Number 9 | Cleat |
| Number 10 | Packing bands |

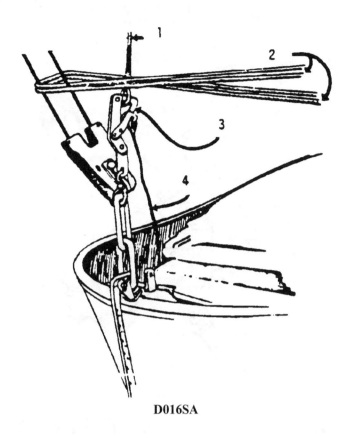

**D016SA**

| ITEM | DESCRIPTION |
|---|---|
| Number 1 | Tricing pendant |
| Number 2 | Frapping line |
| Number 3 | Tricing pendant trip hook (McCluney hook) |
| Number 4 | Tripping line |

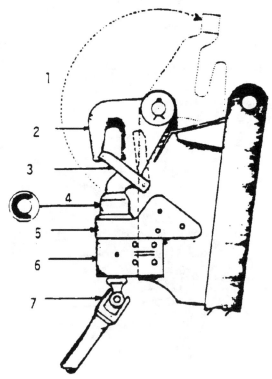

**Illustration D017SA**

| ITEM | DESCRIPTION |
|---|---|
| Number 1 | Hook (open position) |
| Number 2 | Hook (closed position) |
| Number 3 | Preventer bar |
| Number 4 | Hook lock |
| Number 5 | Upper bearing guide |
| Number 6 | lower bearing guide |
| Number 7 | Universal joint |

# LIFEBOATMAN
## STUDY GUIDE

## SAFETY OF LIFE AT SEA

### SOLAS REGULATIONS

**070001/DG01443**                              **McEWEN**

The Safety of Life at Sea Convention was developed by the _____.

A. U.S. Coast Guard
B. American Bureau of Shipping
⚓ C. International Maritime Organization
D. American Institute of Maritime Shipping

**070002/DG03770**                              **SOLAS IV/18**

SOLAS requires a lifesaving training manual be provided in each crew cabin or in the _____.

A. bridge
B. engineering control station
⚓ C. recreation and messrooms
D. fire control room

## SURVIVAL AT SEA

### MAINTENANCE OF BODY MOISTURE

**070003/DS01560**                              **WSM**

The most important reason for taking anti-seasickness pills as soon as possible after entering a liferaft is to _____.

A. assist in sleeping
B. reduce appetite by decreasing nausea
⚓ C. prevent loss of body moisture by vomiting
D. prevent impaired judgment due to motion-induced deliriousness

**070004/DS05408**                              **WSM**

One of the first actions to be taken by survivors when they have boarded an inflatable liferaft is to _____.

A. stream the sea anchor
⚓ B. take an anti-seasickness pill
C. open the pressure relief valve
D. drink at least one can of water

**070005/DS01511**                              **WSM**

Which step should normally be taken FIRST by those who have boarded a liferaft in an emergency?

A. Ration food and water supplies.
⚓ B. Take anti-seasickness pills, if available.
C. Determine position and closest point of land.
D. Check pyrotechnic supplies.

**070006/DS01429**                              **WSM**

When collecting condensation for drinking water, _____.

⚓ A. a sponge used to mop up and store condensation must be kept salt free
B. only condensation on the bottom of the canopy should be collected
C. it should be strained through a finely woven cloth
D. chlorine tablets should be used to make it drinkable

**070007/DS09195**                              **SAFETY AT SEA**

When using the rain water collection tubes on a liferaft, the first collection should be _____.

A. passed around so all can drink
⚓ B. poured overboard because of salt washed off the canopy
C. saved to be used at a later time
D. used to boil food

**070008/DS01540**                              **WSM**

Which statement concerning the sources of drinking water is FALSE?

⚓ A. Fresh water may be obtained from fish.
B. Lifeboat covers or canopies should be washed with rain before drinking water is collected.
C. Fresh water may be collected from condensation inside the liferaft.
D. Seawater should never be consumed.

**070009/DS00133**                              **SHIP'S MEDICINE CHEST**

You have abandoned ship and are in charge of a liferaft. How much water per day should you permit each occupant to drink after the first 24 hours?

A. 1 can
⚓ B. 1 pint
C. 1 quart
D. 1 gallon

**070010/DS09391**                              **SEATECH**

Once you have established the daily ration of drinking water in a survival situation, how should you drink it?

A. Small sips at regular intervals during the day
B. The complete daily ration at one time during the day
⚓ C. One-third the daily ration three times daily
D. Small sips only after sunset

**070011/DS01555**                              **WSM**

Seawater may be used for drinking _____.

A. at a maximum rate of two ounces per day
B. after mixing with an equal quantity of fresh water
C. if gathered during or immediately after a hard rain
⚓ D. under no conditions

**070012/DS01562**                    **SAFETY AT SEA**
Drinking salt water will _____.
A. protect against heat camps
B. prevent seasickness
C. be safe if mixed with fresh water
⚓ D. dehydrate you

**070013/DS09191  SAFETY AT SEA; SURVIVAL GUIDE**
After abandoning a vessel, water that is consumed within the first 24 hours will _____.
⚓ A. pass through the body with little absorbed by the system
B. help to prevent fatigue
C. quench thirst for only 2 hours
D. help to prevent seasickness

**070014/DS09197**                    **SAFETY AT SEA**
In the first 24 hours after abandoning a vessel, water should be given only to personnel who are _____.
A. thirsty
⚓ B. sick or injured
C. wet
D. awake

**070015/DS00979**                         **WSM**
When should you first have any food or water after boarding a lifeboat or liferaft?
A. After 12 hours
⚓ B. After 24 hours
C. Within 48 hours
D. Some food and water should be consumed immediately and then not until 48 hours later.

### WATER ENTRY PROCEDURES

**070016/DS01503**                         **MSRS**
If you have to jump in the water when abandoning ship, your legs should be _____.
A. spread apart as far as possible
B. held as tightly against your chest as possible
C. in a kneeling position
⚓ D. extended straight down and crossed at the ankles

**070017/DS02784**                         **WSM**
When abandoning ship and jumping into the water from a substantial height without a life jacket, you should _____.
A. dive head first, using your hands to break the surface of the water
B. hold your arms firmly at your sides and jump feet first
⚓ C. jump feet first, covering your nose and mouth with one hand and grasping the opposing upper arm with the other
D. jump feet first, holding your knees to your chest

**070018/DS07403**                         **MSRS**
If you must jump from a MODU, your posture should include _____.
⚓ A. holding down the life preserver against the chest with one arm crossing the other, covering the mouth and nose with a hand, and feet together
B. knees bent and held close to the body with both arms around legs
C. body straight and arms held tightly at the sides for feet first entry into the water
D. both hands holding the life preserver below the chin, with knees bent, and legs crossed

**070019/DS07395**                         **MSRS**
In evacuation from a MODU, an individual without the option of a survival craft or liferaft should enter the water on the leeward side, except when _____.
⚓ A. there is burning oil on the water
B. there is a rescue craft in the area
C. water temperature is below 40° F
D. a rigid survival craft is in the area

**070020/DS07397**                         **MSRS**
In evacuation from a MODU, an individual without the option of a survival craft or liferaft should enter the water on the leeward side, except when _____.
A. there is a rescue craft in the area
⚓ B. there is hydrogen sulfide present
C. water temperature is below 40° F
D. a rigid survival craft is in the area

**070021/DS07401**                         **MSRS**
In evacuation from a MODU, an individual without the option of a survival craft or liferaft should enter the water on the leeward side, except when _____.
A. there is a rescue craft in the area
B. water temperature is below 40° F
⚓ C. there is a severe list to the windward side of the MODU
D. a rigid survival craft is in the area

**070022/DS02063**                         **MSRS**
If there are a number of survivors in the water after abandoning ship, they should _____.
A. tie themselves to the unit so they won't drift with the current
⚓ B. form a small circular group to create a warmer pocket of water in the center of the circle
C. send the strongest swimmer to shore for assistance
D. form a raft by lashing their life preservers together

### RECOVERING SURVIVORS

**070023/DS07578**  MSRS

When a helicopter is lifting personnel from an enclosed lifeboat, the other individuals in the boat should _____.

A. enter the water in case the person being lifted slips from the sling
B. stand on the outside of the boat to assist the person being lifted
C. remove their life preservers to prepare for their transfer to the helicopter
⚓ D. remain seated inside to provide body weight for stability

**070024/DS04447**  MSRS

When a helicopter is lifting personnel from a survival craft, the other individuals in the craft should _____.

A. enter the water in case the person being lifted slips from the sling
B. stand on the outside of the craft to assist the person being lifted
C. remove their life preservers to prepare for their transfer to the helicopter
⚓ D. remain seated inside the craft to provide body weight for stability

**070025/DS09271**  MSRS

You are involved in an emergency landing of a helicopter on the water. You should inflate your life jacket _____.

A. upon entering the helicopter
B. prior to reaching the water
C. after reaching the water, but prior to exiting the helicopter
⚓ D. after exiting clear of the helicopter

**070026/DG01192**  AMSM

A person has fallen overboard and is being picked up with a lifeboat. If the person appears in danger of drowning, the lifeboat should make _____.

A. an approach from leeward
B. an approach from windward
⚓ C. the most direct approach
D. an approach across the wind

**070027/DG01270**  WSM

When a man who is conscious has fallen overboard is being picked up by a lifeboat, the boat should approach with the wind _____.

A. astern and the victim just off the bow
B. ahead and the victim just off the bow
C. just off the bow and the victim to windward
⚓ D. just off the bow and the victim to leeward

**070028/DG01487**  MMOH

You are approaching a disabled vessel in order to remove survivors from it. If your vessel drifts faster than the disabled vessel, how should you make your approach?

⚓ A. To windward of the disabled vessel
B. To leeward of the disabled vessel
C. Directly astern of the disabled vessel
D. At three times the drifting speed of the disabled vessel

**070029/DG01985**  CHAPMAN

You are on a 165 foot (50.3 meters) long vessel with a draft of 9 feet (2.7 meters) and twin screws. Which statement about rescuing a survivor in the water with ship pickup is TRUE?

A. You should stop to windward of the man and drift down on him.
B. You should stop with the man on your weather beam and twist the ship up to him.
⚓ C. A pickup off the weather bow gives maximum maneuverability with the least possibility of injury to the man.
D. Ship pick up should never be used with a shallow draft vessel.

**070030/DG01265**  CHAPMAN

You are picking up an unconscious person that has fallen overboard in a fresh breeze. For safety reasons a small craft should approach with the _____.

A. victim to leeward
⚓ B. victim to windward
C. wind on your port side
D. wind on your starboard side

**070031/DG01728**  MFPFFS

You are trying to rescue survivors from a wrecked vessel on fire. You should approach _____.

A. to leeward of the wrecked vessel
B. at a speed of at most one-half that of the wrecked vessel
C. at a speed of at least that of the wrecked vessel
⚓ D. to windward of the wrecked vessel

**070032/DS08584**  MSRS

When transferring survivors from an enclosed lifeboat to a rescue vessel, personnel on board the boat should _____.

A. remove their life preservers to make it easier to climb on board the rescue vessel
B. climb on top of the boat while waiting for their turn to transfer to the rescue vessel
⚓ C. remain seated inside and make the transfer one person at a time
D. enter the water and swim over to the rescue vessel

**070033/DS04453**      **MSRS**

When transferring survivors from a survival craft to a rescue vessel, personnel on board the craft should _____.

A. remove their life preservers to make it easier to climb on board the rescue vessel

B. climb on top of the survival craft while waiting for their turn to transfer to the rescue vessel

⚓ C. remain seated inside the survival craft and make the transfer one person at a time

D. enter the water and swim over to the rescue vessel

**070034/DG01950**      **MERSAR**

You are proceeding to a distress site and expect large numbers of people in the water. Which statement is TRUE?

A. You should stop to windward of the survivors in the water and only use the ship's boats to recover the survivors.

B. If the survivors are in inflatable rafts you should approach from windward to create a lee for the survivors.

⚓ C. An inflatable liferaft secured alongside can be an effective boarding station for transfer of survivors from the boats.

D. Survivors in the water should never be permitted alongside due to the possibility of injury from the vessel.

**070035/DS02247**      **WHITTAKER**

When a rescue vessel approaches a survival craft in heavy seas, the person in charge of the survival craft should _____.

A. tie up to the rescue vessel

B. transfer only those personnel who are not seasick

⚓ C. wait for calmer weather before transferring personnel

D. transfer all personnel immediately

**070036/DG02074**      **MERSAR; *USCP**

You are proceeding to a distress site. The survivors are in liferafts. What will make your ship more visible to the survivors?

A. Steering a sinuous course

B. Steering a zig-zag course

⚓ C. Turning on all available deck lights at night

D. Dumping debris over the side to make a trail to your vessel

**070037/DG02104**      **MERSAR; *USCP**

You are proceeding to a distress site where the survivors are in liferafts. Which action will assist in making your vessel more visible to the survivors?

A. Steering a zigzag course with 5 to 10 minutes on each leg

B. Steering a sinuous course

C. Dumping debris over the side to make a trail to your vessel

⚓ D. Making smoke in daylight

## LIFESAVING EQUIPMENT - LIFEBOATS

**LIFEBOAT DAVIT SYSTEMS**
**RADIAL DAVIT SYSTEMS**

**070038/DS01280**      **AMSM**

On which type davit does the davit head stay at the same height?

⚓ A. Radial

B. Sheath-screw

C. Quadrantal

D. Gravity

**070039/DG02706**      **AMSM**

Which type of davit is not considered to be a mechanical davit?

A. Sheath-screw boom

⚓ B. Radial

C. Crescent

D. Quadrantal

### MECHANICAL DAVIT SYSTEMS

**070040/DG02909**      ***46 CFR 160**

A mechanical davit is designed to automatically _____.

A. position the boat at the embarkation station

⚓ B. lift the boat off the inboard chocks

C. energize the winch for the falls

D. set the brake on the winch

**070041/DG04058**      **AMSM**

Your vessel is equipped with mechanical davits. When stowing the lifeboat after a drill while underway, you should _____.

A. leave the tricing pendants slack

⚓ B. ensure the falls are taut

C. leave the outboard part of the cradle in the down position

D. secure the inboard gripes only

## QUADRANTAL DAVIT SYSTEMS

**070042/DG02469**                                         **WSM**
While cranking out a quadrantal davit, slippage of the quadrant due to excessive wear or failure of the teeth in the quadrant will cause the _____.
A. davit arm to pivot on the traveling nut and the head to fall outboard
B. traveling nut to lock up in place on the worm gear
C. limit switch to engage and hold the traveling nut in position
D. winch brake to lock in position and prevent lowering the boat

## CRESCENT DAVIT SYSTEMS

**070043/DG02644**                                         **AMSM**
The boat is stowed on the davit rather than on a cradle with which type of davit?
A. Crescent
B. Sheath-screw boom
C. Quadrantal
D. Radial

**070044/DG02508**                                         **WSM**
What is required to launch a boat stowed in a crescent davit?
A. Hoist the boat clear of the cradle.
B. Release the outboard part of the cradle.
C. Rig the tricing lines.
D. Crank the crescent out.

## SHEATH-SCREW DAVIT SYSTEMS

**070045/DG02926**                                    **\*PUB 117; IKS**
Many sheath-screw davits have markings to indicate the maximum angle to which they should be cranked out. If the angle is exceeded, the davit _____.
A. may jam against the stops
B. will not automatically position the boat at the embarkation station
C. screw may come out of the sheath
D. will chafe against the falls and may cause their failure

**070046/DG02726**                                         **WSM**
The lifeboats on your vessel are stowed on cradles on deck and are handled by sheath-screw boom davits. Which of the following statements about launching a boat is TRUE?
A. The boat should be hoisted a few inches clear of the cradle before cranking out the davits.
B. The inboard gripes should be cast off before the outboard gripes.
C. The outboard section of the cradle must be released.
D. The tricing pendants will automatically bring the boat alongside at the embarkation deck.

**070047/DG04032**                                         **NVIC 6-81**
The pivot pin at the base of a sheath-screw boom davit must be _____.
A. inserted each time before the booms are cranked out
B. periodically removed for inspection and lubricated
C. replaced at each inspection for certification
D. in the locked position after the boat is cradled and griped down

**070048/DS01260**                                         **AMSM**
The type of davit on which you must turn a crank in order to swing the lifeboat out over the ship's side is a _____.
A. sheath-screw davit
B. gravity davit
C. radial davit
D. bruckner davit

## GRAVITY DAVIT SYSTEMS

**070049/DS01270**                                         **AMSM**
The most common type of davit found on merchant vessels today is the _____.
A. radial
B. sheath-screw
C. gravity
D. quadrantal

**070050/DS01290**                                         **AMSM**
Which davit type may be operated by one man?
A. Quadrantal
B. Gravity
C. Sheath-screw
D. Radial

**070051/DS01190**                                         **WSM**
What could be a result of insufficient lubrication of lifeboat winches and davits?
A. Moisture accumulation in winch motor damaging the electrical wiring
B. Freezing of gears in cold weather
C. Corroding of sheaves on the davits so they will not rotate
D. All of the above

**070052/DS05274**                                         **AMSM**
The type davits shown are _____. See DIAGRAM D008SA
A. round-bar davits
B. radial davits
C. gravity davits
D. quadrantal davits

## DAVIT EQUIPMENT - MANROPES

**070053/DS01240**                         ***46 CFR 199.155 (d)**

On open lifeboats, the purpose of the wire stretched between the davit heads is to _____.
A.  keep the movement of the davits at the same speed
B.  keep the davits from slipping when they are in the stowed position
C.  prevent vibration during lowering of the boat
⚓ D.  support the manropes

**070054/DG02607**                         ***46 CFR 199.155 (d)**

Which statement is TRUE concerning lifeboat installations on Great Lakes vessels?
A.  All davit installations shall have 3 lifelines fitted to a davit span.
B.  All vessels over 3,000 gross tons must be fitted with gravity davits.
⚓ C.  All lifelines shall be able to reach the water at the vessel's lightest draft with a 20° list.
D.  All of the above

## DAVIT EQUIPMENT - GRIPES

**070055/DS00553**                                    **AMSM**

Which statement is TRUE concerning lifeboat gripes?
A.  They must be released by freeing a safety shackle.
B.  They should not be released until the boat is in lowering position.
⚓ C.  They may be adjusted by a turnbuckle.
D.  They are normally used only with radial davits.

## DAVIT EQUIPMENT - FRAPPING LINES

**070056/DS00000**                                    **AMSM**

Frapping lines _____.
A.  secure the lifeboat in the davits when in the stowed position
B.  bring the lifeboat close alongside the rail in the embarkation position
C.  give the occupants a safety line when the boat is being lowered from the embarkation level
⚓ D.  reduce the swinging of the lifeboat at the embarkation level

**070057/DS01310**                                    **AMSM**

Frapping lines are fitted to lifeboat davits to _____.
⚓ A.  reduce the swinging of the lifeboat as it is being lowered from the embarkation level
B.  secure the lifeboat in the davits when in the stowed position
C.  hold the lifeboat to the ship's side until the tricing lines are passed
D.  be used as a safety line in an emergency

**070058/DS01220**                                    **AMSM**

Lines passed around the falls to hold the boat while passengers are boarding are _____.
A.  life lines
⚓ B.  frapping lines
C.  tricing lines
D.  tripping lines

**070059/DS01200**                                    **AMSM**

What is TRUE concerning frapping lines?
⚓ A.  They are used to steady a lifeboat when lowered.
B.  They are normally attached to the davit span.
C.  They are needed only on radial davits.
D.  They are used to clear the puddings.

**070060/DS01095**                                    **AMSM**

When launching a lifeboat, frapping lines should be rigged _____.
A.  before the gripes are released
B.  before the boat is moved from the davits
⚓ C.  at the embarkation deck
D.  after the boat is in the water

**070061/DS01085**                                    **LBMAN**

When lowering lifeboats in heavy seas, a good practice is to rig frapping lines _____.
A.  on only the forward falls
B.  on only the after falls
⚓ C.  with a lead of about 45 degrees to the boat
D.  from the falls to the main deck of the vessel

**070062/DS04594**                                    **AMSM**

As shown, a frapping line is indicated by number _____. See DIAGRAM D016SA
A.  1
⚓ B.  2
C.  3
D.  4

## DAVIT EQUIPMENT - TRICING PENNANTS

**070063/DS01230**                                    **AMSM**

The purpose of the tricing pendants is to _____.
A.  control the fore and aft motion of a lifeboat during lowering
B.  control the outboard swing of a lifeboat during lowering
C.  provide suspensions for the manropes
⚓ D.  hold a lifeboat next to the embarkation deck while loading

**070064/DS01360**                                     **AMSM**

When lowering a boat with gravity davits, it will be pulled into the embarkation deck by the _____.
A.  falls
B.  tricing pendants
C.  frapping lines
D.  boat hooks

**070065/DS01105**                                     **AMSM**

In launching a lifeboat, when should the tricing pendants be released?
A.  Before the boat is lowered from the stowage position
B.  As soon as the boat-fall blocks clear the davit head
C.  After the limit switch is activated
D.  After all people have been embarked

**070066/DS01210**                                     **AMSM**

The tricing pendants should be released _____.
A.  before the gripes are removed
B.  before loading the passengers
C.  after loading the passengers
D.  after the boat is afloat

**070067/DS01115**                                     **AMSM**

When launching a lifeboat, the tricing pennants should be released _____.
A.  before the boat is lowered from the stowed position
B.  as the boat-fall blocks break clear of the davit head
C.  before the boat is lowered from the embarkation level
D.  after the boat is released into the water

**070068/DS04636**                                     **AMSM**

What will be released by pulling on line number 5? See DIAGRAM D012SA
A.  Frapping line
B.  Gripes
C.  Tricing pendant
D.  Lifeboat

**070069/DS05094**                                     **AMSM**

The mechanism that will release the tricing pendant, as shown, is _____. See DIAGRAM D012SA
A.  the fore and aft gripes
B.  the McCluney hook
C.  a quick release lever
D.  a 3/4" shackle

**070070/DS05312**                                     **AMSM**

As shown, the line indicated by number 4 is connected to the _____. See DIAGRAM D016SA
A.  releasing gear
B.  sea painter
C.  McCluney hook
D.  Fleming gear

## DAVIT EQUIPMENT - WINCHES & CONTROLS

**070071/DS01150**                       **AMSM; *46 CFR 160.15-3**

After the boat is at the top of the davit heads, the davit arms begin moving up the tracks and are stopped by the _____.
A.  hoist man
B.  limit switch
C.  brake handle
D.  preventer bar

**070072/DS01140**                                     **AMSM**

Limit switches are used on which davits?
A.  Sheath-screw davits
B.  Gravity davits
C.  Radial davits
D.  Quadrantal davits

**070073/DS01120**                       **AMSM; *46 CFR 160.15-3**

You will find a limit switch on a _____.
A.  liferaft cradle
B.  radial davit
C.  sheath-screw davit
D.  gravity davit

**070074/DS01535**                       **AMSM; *46 CFR 160.15-3**

Limit switches _____.
A.  control the descent rate of a lifeboat
B.  control the ascent rate of a lifeboat
C.  cut off power to the winch when the lifeboat nears the final stowed position
D.  cut off power to the winch when the lifeboat reaches the davit bumpers

**070075/DS01130**                       **AMSM; *46 CFR 160.15-3**

What is the purpose of the limit switch on gravity davits?
A.  To cut off the power when the davits hit the track safety stops
B.  To stop the davits from going too fast
C.  To cut off the power when the davits are about 12 inches or more from the track safety stops
D.  None of the above

**070076/DS02287**                                     **WHITTAKER**

The limit switches on a MODUs survival-craft winch system _____.
A.  stop the winch just before the craft reaches the final stowage position
B.  limit the amount of cable on the drum
C.  limit the ascent rate
D.  stop the winch in case the craft weighs too much

**070077/DS01110**            **AMSM**

Limit switches on gravity davits should be tested by _____.

A. the engineers, from a panel in the engine room
B. shutting off the current to the winch
C. pushing the switch lever arm while the winch is running
D. All of the above

**070078/DS00656**          **\*46 CFR 160.15-5 (b) (4); \*46 CFR 160.15-5**

The governor brake on a lifeboat winch shall be capable of controlling the speed of lowering a fully equipped lifeboat from a cargo ship at _____.

A. a safe speed only specified
B. not less than 120 feet per minute
C. not more than 120 feet per minute
D. not more than 90 feet per minute

**070079/DS01100**           **\*46 CFR 160.15-3 (g)**

The maximum speed of lowering for a lifeboat on gravity davits is controlled by the _____.

A. limit switches
B. emergency disconnect switch
C. governor brake
D. position of the counterweight on the brake handle

**070080/DS00606**           **\*46 CFR 160.15-2 (e)**

When lifeboat winches with grooved drums are fitted on a vessel the lead sheaves to the drums shall be located to provide fleet angles of not more than _____.

A. 4°
B. 8°
C. 12°
D. 16°

**070081/DS00616**           **\*46 CFR 160.15-3 (e)**

Winch drums for lifeboat falls shall have a diameter at the base of the groove equal to at least _____.

A. 6 times the diameter of the wire rope
B. 8 times the diameter of the wire rope
C. 12 times the diameter of the wire rope
D. 16 times the diameter of the wire rope

**070082/DS01273**        **WSM; \*46 CFR 160.15-5**

In launching a covered lifeboat, what would safely lower the lifeboat from inside the lifeboat cabin?

A. Frapping line
B. Tricing line
C. Rottmer release
D. Winch remote control wire

## DAVIT EQUIPMENT - BLOCKS & FALLS

**070083/DG02548**          **\*46 CFR 94.33-10**

What is the accepted standard for wire rope falls used in connection with the lifeboat gear?

A. Six by seven galvanized wire rope
B. Six by twenty-four improved plow steel wire rope
C. Six by thirty-seven preformed fiber-core wire rope
D. Six by nineteen regular-lay filler wire rope

**070084/DS01250**        **NICHOLL; \*46 CFR 160.15**

The falls on gravity davits are _____.

A. manila
B. nylon
C. wire
D. All of the above

**070085/DS01300**          **\*46 CFR 160.32-3 (a)**

Blocks and falls used as lifeboat gear must be designed with a minimum safety factor of _____.

A. 4, based on the breaking strength
B. 5, based on the maximum allowable stress
C. 6, based on the maximum working load
D. 8, based on the normal working load

**070086/DS03450**      **SOLAS REG, CHAP III; \*46 CFR 199.190 (j) (ii)**

According to the regulations for lifeboat falls, which action must be taken at 30-month intervals?

A. End-for-ended
B. Renewed
C. Inspected
D. Weight tested

**070087/DS03490**      **SOLAS REG, CHAP III; \*46 CFR 199.190 (j) (ii)**

According to the SOLAS regulations, lifeboat falls must be renewed at intervals of how many years?

A. 2.5
B. 3
C. 4
D. 5

**070088/DS03470**      **SOLAS REG, CHAP III; \*46 CFR 199.190 (j) (ii)**

According to the regulations for lifeboat falls, which action must be taken with the falls no later than 5-year intervals?

A. Proof tested
B. End-for-ended
C. Renewed
D. Weight tested

## LIFEBOAT EQUIPMENT - DISENGAGING APPARATUS

**070089/DS00713**                     **LBMAN; *46 CFR 160.33**
Preventer bars are fitted on lifeboat releasing gear to prevent _____.
A. the falls from unhooking if the releasing gear is operated accidentally
B. operation of the release lever until the boat is waterborne
C. the falls from rehooking after they have been released
⚓ D. accidental unhooking when the falls become slack

**070090/DS01545**                     **WSM; *46 CFR 160.33**
Preventer bars are fitted on lifeboat releasing hooks to prevent _____.
A. the falls from unhooking if the releasing gear is operated accidentally while the boat is being lowered
B. operation of the release lever until the boat is waterborne
C. the falls from rehooking after they have been released
⚓ D. accidental unhooking when the falls become slack

**070091/DS03144**                     **LBMAN; *46 CFR 160.33**
On a lifeboat equipped with Rottmer-type releasing gear, turning the releasing lever releases _____.
A. the painter
B. the after boat fall only if the boat is waterborne
C. both falls at the same time only if the boat is waterborne
⚓ D. both falls at the same time even if the boat has not reached the water

**070092/DS00072**                     **WHITTAKER**
To disengage a survival craft suspended from the cable above the water, you must pull the safety pin and _____.
A. pull the hook release handle
⚓ B. pull the hook release handle and use the ratchet bar
C. use the ratchet bar and depress the retainer
D. pull the hook release handle and depress the retainer

**070093/DS08047**                     **MSRS**
An "on-load" release system on a survival craft means the cable can be released _____.
A. only when the load is taken off the cable
B. only when there is a load on the cable
C. only when activated by the controls at the lowering station
⚓ D. at any time

**070094/DS08051**                     **MSRS**
The "off-load" release system on a survival craft is designed to be activated _____.
⚓ A. when there is no load on the cable
B. when there is a load on the cable
C. only when the doors are closed
D. when the engine is started

**070095/DS04744**                     **AMSM; *46 CFR 160.33**
You operate the lever shown when the lifeboat is _____. See DIAGRAM D013SA
A. in the secured position
B. at the embarkation deck
C. being lowered to sea level
⚓ D. waterborne

## LIFEBOAT EQUIPMENT

**070096/DS00836**                     **\*46 CFR 160.44-2 (a) (2);**
                                        **\*46 CFR 199.175 (b) (2)**
What size bilge pump is required for a lifeboat which has a capacity of 675 cubic feet?
A. 1
⚓ B. 2
C. 3
D. 4

**070097/DS01680**                     **WSM; *46 CFR 199.175 (b) (6)**
In an open lifeboat, the lifeboat compass is usually _____.
⚓ A. placed in a fixed bracket when being used
B. clamped to any position convenient for the coxswain to see it
C. permanently mounted on the lifeboat's centerline
D. mounted in the center of the boat to eliminate deviation

**070098/DS00773**                     **BOWD; *46 CFR 199.175 (b) (6)**
When using the lifeboat compass, you must be careful to _____.
A. set it on the centerline of the boat
B. apply the correction for compass error
C. keep metal objects away from it
⚓ D. All of the above

**070099/DS00733**                     **LBMAN; *46 CFR 199.175 (b) (13)**
Lifeboat hatchets should be _____.
A. kept in a locker
⚓ B. secured at each end of the boat with a lanyard
C. kept next to the boat coxswain
D. kept in the emergency locker on the ship and brought to the lifeboat when needed

**070100/DS00633**      AMSM; *46 CFR 199.175 (b) (20)

A sweep oar is an oar that is _____.

A. generally shorter than the others and is used to steer with

B. is longer than the others and is used as the stroke oar

C. is raised in the bow of the boat for the steersman to steer by

⚓ D. longer than the others used for steering

**070101/DS00613**      AMSM; *46 CFR 199.175 (b) (20)

The length of the steering oar in a lifeboat is _____.

A. shorter than the rowing oars

B. the same length as the rowing oars

⚓ C. longer than the rowing oars

D. unrelated to the length of the rowing oars

**070102/DS00866**      *46 CFR 199.175

The number of rowing oars that must be carried in a motor-propelled open lifeboat on a cargo vessel is _____.

A. determined by the Master

B. specified by the Coast Guard

⚓ C. specified by the manufacturer

D. None

**070103/DS00223**      AMSM

The steering oar in a lifeboat is _____.

A. shorter than the others

B. used for the stroke oar

C. used by the forward man in the boat to direct the bow

⚓ D. longer than the others and should be lashed to the stern

**070104/DS00643**      AMSM; *46 CFR 199.175 (b) (20)

The steering oar in a lifeboat is usually referred to as the _____.

A. bumpkin oar

B. stroke oar

⚓ C. sweep oar

D. becket oar

**070105/DS00846**      *46 CFR 199.175 (b) (21)

If a lifeboat is stowed 40 feet above the light water draft and 200 feet from the bow, how long must the sea painter be?

⚓ A. 80 feet

B. 160 feet

C. Sufficiently long enough to reach the water when the vessel has an adverse list of 15°

D. One third the length from the bow to where the lifeboat is stowed

**070106/DS10065**      *46 CFR 199.175 (b) (21)

What is the required minimum length of the painter for a lifeboat in ocean service?

A. 60 fathoms

B. the distance from the main deck to the light waterline

C. twice the distance from the main deck to the light waterline or 50 feet whichever is greater

⚓ D. two times the distance from the boat deck to the light waterline or 50 feet whichever is greater

**070107/DS10066**      LBMAN; *46 CFR 199.175 (b) (3)

Which item is of the most use in getting a lifeboat away from a moving vessel?

A. The falls

⚓ B. Sea Painter

C. Fleming Gear

D. Boat Hook

**070108/DS01330**      AMSM

How should the lifeboat sea painter be rigged?

A. Spliced into the ring on the stem post

B. Secured by a toggle around the outboard side of a forward thwart

⚓ C. Secured to the inboard side of a forward thwart and led inboard of the falls

D. Secured by a toggle to the stem post and led outboard of the falls

**070109/DS00603**      WSM; *46 CFR 199.175 (b) (21)

The painter which is to be attached to the thwart of a lifeboat should _____.

A. be fitted at the end with an approved safety shackle

B. have a long eye splice at the end, and a shackle and pin should be attached to the painter with a lanyard

⚓ C. have a long eye splice at the end, and a hardwood toggle should be attached to the thwart with a lanyard

D. be fitted with a swivel and quick-releasing pelican hook

**070110/DS00593**      AMSM; *46 CFR 199.175 (b) (21)

The sea painter is secured in the lifeboat by _____.

⚓ A. a turn around a forward thwart with a toggle pin thru the eye

B. a knot around a thwart

C. an eye splice placed over one of the hooks of the releasing gear

D. All of the above

**070111/DS00573**      AMSM; *46 CFR 199.175 (b) (21)

The sea painter of a lifeboat should be led _____.

⚓ A. forward and outside of all obstructions

B. forward and inside of all obstructions

C. up and down from the main deck

D. to the foremost point on the ship

**070112/DS02084       SEATECH; *46 CFR 199.175 (b) (21)**
The sea painter of a lifeboat should be secured _____.

A. to the bow of the lifeboat
B. to an inboard thwart in the forward one-third of the boat
C. as close as possible to amidships of the lifeboat
D. anywhere along the inboard side of the boat

**070113/DS05486       AMSM; *46 CFR 199.175 (b) (21)**
This illustration shows the correct method of securing a _____. See DIAGRAM D009SA

A. man-rope
B. frapping line
C. sea painter
D. lifeline

**070114/DS00393       AMSM; *46 CFR 199.175 (b) (27); *46 CFR 160.19**
A sea anchor is _____.

A. a heavy anchor with an extra long line used to anchor in deep water
B. a cone shaped bag used to slow down the wind drift effect
C. a pad eye to which the sea painter is made fast
D. made of wood if it is of an approved type

**070115/DS00403       AMSM; *46 CFR 199.175 (b) (27); *46 CFR 160.19**
Due to the shape of the sea anchor, the best way to haul it back aboard is by _____.

A. hauling in on the anchor line as you would any anchor
B. getting all hands to assist
C. its trip line
D. cutting the line, as you cannot haul it back in

**070116/DS00383       AMSM; *46 CFR 199.175 (b) (27); *46 CFR 160.19**
The purpose of the tripping line on a sea anchor is to _____.

A. aid in casting off
B. direct the drift of the vessel
C. aid in its recovery
D. maintain maximum resistance to broaching

**070117/DS00283       AMSM; *46 CFR 199.175 (b) (27)**
Spreading oil on the open sea has the effect of _____.

A. diminishing the height of the seas
B. lengthening the distance between successive crests
C. increasing the height of the seas
D. preventing the wave crests from breaking

**070118/DS00423       AMSM; *46 CFR 199.175 (b) (27); *46 CFR 160.19**
When you stream a sea anchor, you should make sure that the holding line is _____.

A. long enough to cause the pull to be more horizontal than downward
B. long enough to reach bottom
C. short enough to cause the pull to be downward
D. short enough to avoid tangling

**070119/DS01557       AMSM; *46 CFR 199.175 (b) (27); *46 CFR 160.19**
When a sea anchor for a lifeboat is properly rigged, it will _____.

A. completely stop the lifeboat from drifting
B. help to prevent broaching
C. prevent the lifeboat from pitching
D. None of the above

**070120/DS00363       AMSM; *46 CFR 199.175 (b) (27); *46 CFR 160.19**
You are in a lifeboat in a heavy sea. Your boat is dead in the water and unable to make way. To prevent broaching, you should _____.

A. take no action, broaching is recommended in a heavy sea
B. put out the sea anchor
C. put out the sea painter
D. fill the bottom of the boat with about one foot of water to make it ride better

**070121/DS10037       WHITTAKER**
Using a sea anchor with the survival craft will _____.

A. reduce your drift rate
B. keep the survival craft from turning over
C. aid in recovering the survival craft
D. increase your visibility

**070122/DS03186       WHITTAKER**
Using a sea anchor will _____.

A. reduce the drift rate of the liferaft
B. keep the liferaft from turning over
C. aid in recovering the liferaft
D. increase your visibility

**070123/DS01851       FVSM; *46 CFR 199.175 (b) (30)**
When using a hand held smoke signal from a lifeboat, you should activate the signal _____.

A. on the downwind side
B. on the upwind side
C. inside the boat
D. at the stern

**070124/DS00786    AMSM; *46 CFR 199.175 (b) (31), (30)**
Which statement is TRUE concerning distress signals in a lifeboat?
A. Hand held flares and orange smoke signals are required.
B. If hand-held rocket-propelled parachute flares are provided, they are the only distress signals required.
C. Two hand-held smoke signals shall be provided.
D. A Very pistol with twelve flares is required.

**070125/DS01910                                       AMSM**
Which visual distress signal is acceptable for daylight use only?
A. Hand-held red flare
B. Self-contained rocket-propelled parachute red flare
C. Hand-held orange smoke distress flare
D. Red aerial pyrotechnic flare

**070126/DS10040           LBMAN; *46 CFR 160.21-5 (b)**
What is the maximum length of time that distress flares are approved for?
A. 1 and 1/2 years
B. 2 years
C. 3 and 1/2 years
D. 5 years

**070127/DS09387           FVSM; *46 CFR 199.175 (b) (31);**
**          *46 CFR 160.28; *46 CFR 160.36; *46 CFR 160.37**
When should you use distress flares and rockets?
A. Only when there is a chance of their being seen by rescue vessels
B. At half-hour intervals
C. At one-hour intervals
D. Immediately upon abandoning the vessel

**070128/DS00763           AMSM; *46 CFR 199.175 (b) (32);**
**                                          *46 CFR 160.36**
Which item of lifeboat equipment would be most suitable for night signaling to a ship on the horizon?
A. A red parachute flare
B. A red hand-held flare
C. A flashlight
D. A lantern

**070129/DS10002                    *46 CFR 199.175 (b) 40**
A liferaft with a capacity of 8 people used in ocean service is required by regulations to carry _____.
A. 8 liters of fresh water
B. 12 units of provisions
C. 12 liters of fresh water
D. 24 units of provisions

**070130/DS00736                    *46 CFR 199.175 (b) (40);**
**                                          *46 CFR 160.26**
How many liters of water per person must be carried in lifeboats on a tankship sailing a coastwise route?
A. None
B. One
C. Two
D. Three

**070131/DS00726           *46 CFR 199.175 (b) (40) (ii);**
**                                          *46 CFR 160.58**
On an oceangoing vessel, for each person a lifeboat (without desalting kits) is certified to carry, the boat must be supplied with _____.
A. 2 pounds of condensed milk
B. a signaling whistle
C. 3 liters of water
D. a life preserver

**070132/DS00716    *46 CFR 199.175 (40); *46 CFR 160.26**
The required amount of water for each person in a lifeboat on an oceangoing vessel, on an international voyage, is _____.
A. 1 liter
B. 2 liters
C. 3 liters
D. 4 liters

**070133/DS00696        *46 CFR 199.175 (b) (40), (22), (29)**
For each person it is certified to carry, a lifeboat on an oceangoing passenger vessel must be provided with all of the following EXCEPT _____.
A. 3 liters of water
B. 1 unit of provisions
C. 1 seasickness kit
D. 1 life preserver

### LIFEBOAT CONSTRUCTION

**070134/DS02227                             WATERCRAFT**
When the survival craft is supplied with bottles of compressed air they are used for _____.
A. an air supply for personnel
B. additional flotation
C. priming the sprinkler system
D. filling the self righting bags

**070135/DS01464              WSM; *46 CFR 160.35**
What is NOT a function of the air supply of a covered lifeboat?
A. Provides air for engine combustion
B. Pressurizes water spray system
C. Provides air for passenger respiration
D. Prevents smoke and other noxious fumes from entering craft

**070136/DS01520**                                                      **WSM**
When operating the air supply system in a covered lifeboat the _____.
A. fuel supply valve should be closed
⚓ B. hatches, doors, and oar ports should be closed
C. air cylinder shut-off valve should be closed
D. engine should be shut off

**070137/DS01239**          **WATERCRAFT; *46 CFR 160.35**
With the air supply on, the air pressure in an enclosed lifeboat will be _____.
A. changing in relation to the speed of the craft
B. less than outside air pressure
⚓ C. greater than outside air pressure
D. equal to outside air pressure

**070138/DS00201**                                                      **WSM**
Your vessel is equipped with totally enclosed lifeboats. Which statement is TRUE when the boat is enveloped in flames?
A. The ventilators will automatically close by the action of fusible links.
B. The motor takes its air supply from outside the lifeboat to prevent asphyxiation of the crew.
C. A water spray system to cool the outside of the boat is operated by a high-volume manual pump.
⚓ D. An air tank will provide about ten minutes of air for the survivors and the engine.

**070139/DS02303**                                              **WATERCRAFT**
The air cylinder bottles in the survival craft should be refilled with _____.
A. oxygen
B. nitrogen
⚓ C. compressed air
D. nitrogen and oxygen

**070140/DS00493**                        **LBMAN; *46 CFR 160.35**
Why are lifeboats usually double-enders?
⚓ A. They are more seaworthy and less likely to be swamped or broach to.
B. They can go forward and backward more easily.
C. They require less space for stowing aboard ship.
D. There is no particular reason for this.

**070141/DS00743**                        **AMSM; *46 CFR 160.35**
In order for the automatic lifeboat drain to operate properly _____.
A. the cap should be removed to drain the boat when it is waterborne
⚓ B. the cage must be free of rubbish or the ball may not seat properly
C. there is an automatic ball check located in a siphon tube
D. the small lever to release the rubber ball float must be turned counterclockwise

**070142/DS01075**                        **AMSM; *46 CFR 160.35**
Prior to lowering the lifeboat, the most important item to check is the _____.
A. oars
B. sail
⚓ C. boat plug
D. life preservers

**070143/DS01065**                                                      **AMSM**
Upon hearing the abandon ship signal, you put on your life jacket and report to your station. After the cover is removed you board your open lifeboat. The FIRST thing to do is to _____.
A. release the gripes
B. release tricing pendants
⚓ C. put the cap on the drain
D. lift the brake handle

**070144/DS00543**                                                      **AMSM**
Aluminum lifeboats are subject to damage by electrolytic corrosion (the aluminum being eaten away). In working around boats of aluminum you must be very careful _____.
A. to keep the boats covered at all times
⚓ B. not to leave steel or iron tools lying in or near these boats
C. to keep an electric charge on the hull at all times
D. to rinse these boats regularly with salt water

**070145/DS01695**                        **NVIC 2-63; *46 CFR 160.35**
In order to prevent galvanic corrosion, an aluminum boat must be insulated from the davits and gripes. Which of the following is acceptable as an insulator?
⚓ A. Hard rubber
B. Canvas
C. Leather
D. Sponge rubber

**070146/DS00673**                        **AMSM; *46 CFR 160.35**
The grab rail of a metal lifeboat is normally located _____.
⚓ A. along the turn of the bilge
B. along each side of the keel
C. near the top of the gunwale
D. at the bow and at the stern

**070147/DS00533**                        **WSM; *46 CFR 160.35**
What is the purpose of limber holes?
A. To allow for air circulation
B. To allow for stress and strain in rough waters
C. To allow water in the boat to drain overboard
⚓ D. To allow water in the bilge to get to the boat drain

**070148/DS02255**                                          **WHITTAKER**
The survival capsule is manufactured with fire retardant
_____.

- A. foam
- B. marine plywood
- C. steel
- ⚓ D. fiberglass

**070149/DS00523**                                                  **WSM**
The bottom row of plating next to the keel of a lifeboat is known as the _____.
- A. sheer strake
- B. bilge strake
- ⚓ C. garboard strake
- D. keel rib

**070150/DS00213**                          **AMSM; *46 CFR 160.35**
Most lifeboats are equipped with _____.
- ⚓ A. unbalanced rudders
- B. balanced rudders
- C. contraguide rudders
- D. straight rudders

**070151/DS00663**                                                 **AMSM**
Stretchers are fitted in lifeboats to provide a _____.
- A. place for people to lie down
- B. means for rigging the sail
- ⚓ C. place for rowers to brace their feet
- D. suitable means for water to drain below the footings

**070152/DS02291**                                          **WHITTAKER**
The purpose for the bag or box on top of some survival craft is to _____.
- ⚓ A. right the craft in case of capsizing
- B. increase area for radar detection
- C. act as a sail in case of a power loss
- D. steady the craft in heavy seas

**070153/DS00783**                          **LBMAN; *46 CFR 160.35**
A person referring to the stern sheets of a lifeboat is speaking of _____.
- A. the line attached to the tack of the lugsail
- B. the emergency rudder
- C. a canvas awning
- ⚓ D. the aftermost seating

**070154/DS01550**                          **WSM; *46 CFR 160.35**
The purpose of a water spray system on a covered lifeboat is to _____.
- A. cool the lifeboat engine
- ⚓ B. keep the lifeboat from reaching combustion temperature while operating in a fire
- C. keep the lifeboat warm in a cold climate by applying heated water spray from the engine to the boat
- D. put out a fire inside the lifeboat

**070155/DS01329**                     **WATERCRAFT; *46 CFR 160.35**
The sprinkler system of an enclosed lifeboat is used to _____.
- ⚓ A. cool the craft in a fire
- B. cool the engine
- C. spray oil on the sea to calm it
- D. spray personnel during a fire

**070156/DS02305**                                    **WATERCRAFT**
With the sprinkler system and air system on and all hatches shut, the survival craft will provide protection from a _____.
- A. nuclear environment
- ⚓ B. fire and toxic environment
- C. hurricane
- D. drop greater than 10 feet

**070157/DS00683**                          **LBMAN; *46 CFR 160.35**
The purpose of air tanks in a lifeboat is to _____.
- A. make the boat float higher
- B. provide a stowage place for provisions
- C. add strength to the boat
- ⚓ D. keep the boat afloat if flooded

### LIFEBOAT PROPULSION SYSTEMS

**070158/DS00536**                          ***46 CFR 160.35-5 (a) (5) (i)**
A fully loaded motor-propelled lifeboat must be capable of attaining a speed of at least _____.
- A. 3 knots in smooth water
- ⚓ B. 6 knots in smooth water
- C. 3 knots in rough water
- D. 6 knots in rough water

**070159/DS00566**                          ***46 CFR 160.35-5 (a) (5) (i)**
Which statement is TRUE concerning a motor lifeboat?
- A. It is propelled by engine or hand-propelling gear.
- B. It has a sufficient fuel capacity, if motorized, for 48 hours of operation.
- ⚓ C. It must be able to maintain a loaded speed of 6 knots.
- D. All of the above

**070160/DS01183          WHITTAKER; *46 CFR 160.35**
The engine in a covered lifeboat is fueled with _____.

A. leaded gasoline
B. unleaded gasoline
⚓ C. diesel oil
D. liquefied gas

**070161/DS02257                    WHITTAKER**
The survival craft's engine is fueled with _____.
A. kerosene
B. unleaded gasoline
⚓ C. diesel oil
D. liquefied gas

**070162/DS00756          *46 CFR 160.35-5 (a) (5) (i)**
A motor lifeboat shall carry sufficient fuel to operate continuously for a period of _____.
A. 12 hours
B. 18 hours
⚓ C. 24 hours
D. 36 hours

**070163/DS00526          *46 CFR 160.35-5 (a) (5) (i)**
Motor-propelled lifeboats are required to have sufficient fuel to operate continuously at 6 knots for how many hours?
A. 6
B. 12
C. 18
⚓ D. 24

**070164/DS08053          MSRS; *46 CFR 160.35-5 (a) (5) (i)**
At a speed of 6 knots the fuel aboard a survival craft should last _____.
A. 8 hours
B. 12 hours
⚓ C. 24 hours
D. 48 hours

**070165/DS00746          *46 CFR 160.35-5 (a) (5) (i)**
The quantity of fuel required to be carried in a motor lifeboat is _____.
⚓ A. the quantity needed for 24 hours continuous operation
B. the quantity needed for 48 hours continuous operation
C. 55 gallons
D. 90 gallons

**070166/DS01506                    WSM**
Before hydraulic starting of an engine on a covered lifeboat, what need NOT be checked?
A. Fuel supply line valve
B. Pressure registered on the accumulator gauge
⚓ C. Cold-spark voltage readings test lamp
D. Engine stop control

**070167/DS02261                    WHITTAKER**
If the engine of a survival craft does not start, check to see _____.
⚓ A. that the fuel valve is open
B. if the air supply system is open
C. if the water sprinkler system is open
D. if the limit switch is on

**070168/DS02245                    WHITTAKER**
The backup system on an electric start survival craft is a _____.

A. hydraulic system
B. pneumatic system
C. spare battery
⚓ D. hand crank

**070169/DS02243                    WHITTAKER**
Aboard a survival craft, ether can be used to _____.
⚓ A. start the engine in cold weather
B. aid in helping personnel breathe
C. prime the sprinkler system
D. prime the air supply

**070170/DS08055                    MSRS**
When inspecting a survival craft, you should check to make sure that the _____.
A. sea anchor is deployed
B. hydraulic starting system has been drained
⚓ C. hydraulic pressure is within the specified range
D. steering controls are locked

**070171/DS01121                    AMSM**
As shown, number 1 operates the _____. See DIAGRAM D011SA
A. releasing gear
B. McCluney hook
C. sea painter
⚓ D. Fleming gear

**070172/DS03426                    AMSM**
In illustration D011SA, number 1 operates the _____. See DIAGRAM D011SA
A. releasing gear
B. sea painter
⚓ C. Fleming gear
D. McCluney hook

### LIFEBOAT MARKINGS

**070173/DS00203          AMSM; *46 CFR 199.176**
The number 2 lifeboat on a tanker would be _____.
⚓ A. forward most on the port side
B. forward most on the starboard side
C. abaft #1 lifeboat port side
D. abaft #1 lifeboat starboard side

**070174/DS00503**  AMSM; *46 CFR 199.176
Your vessel has lifeboats on both sides. Lifeboat No. 2 is located _____.
A. forward of lifeboat No. 4 on the starboard side
B. forward of lifeboat No. 4 on the port side
C. aft of lifeboat No. 1 on the starboard side
D. All of the above

**070175/DS00513**  AMSM; *46 CFR 199.176
Number 3 lifeboat would be _____.
A. the forward boat on the starboard side
B. behind boat number 1 on the port side
C. behind boat number 1 on the starboard side
D. behind boat number 2 on the port side

**070176/DS01460**  AMSM
Your vessel has 3 lifeboats on each side. The middle boat on the starboard side is designated as boat number _____.
A. 2
B. 2 STARBOARD
C. 3
D. 4

**070177/DS00676**  *46 CFR 97.37-37 (b)
Your vessel has 3 lifeboats on each side. The middle boat on the starboard side is designated as boat number _____.
A. 2
B. 2 STARBOARD
C. 3
D. 4

**070178/DS01465**  WSM
Your vessel has 3 lifeboats on each side. The middle lifeboat on the port side is designated as boat number _____.
A. 2
B. 2 PORT
C. 3
D. 4

**070179/DS01720**  WSM
Your vessel has 3 lifeboats on each side. The aftermost boat on the starboard side is designated as boat number _____.
A. 6
B. 5
C. 3
D. 3 STARBOARD

**070180/DS01494**  WSM
Your vessel has 3 lifeboats on each side. The aftermost boat on the port side is designated as boat number _____.
A. 6
B. 5
C. 3
D. 3 PORT

**070181/DS02185**  *46 CFR 108.645 (a) (3)
On offshore drilling units, all lifeboats are required to be marked with the _____.
A. name of the owner of the unit
B. number of persons allowed in the boat
C. drilling location of the unit
D. All of the above

**070182/DS02183**  *46 CFR 108.645 (a) (1)
On offshore drilling units, all lifeboats are required to be marked with the _____.
A. name and port of the unit
B. owner and port of the unit
C. drilling location
D. builder

**070183/DS01459**  WSM; *46 CFR 108.645; *46 CFR 199.176
Which data is NOT painted on the bow of a lifeboat?
A. Number of persons allowed
B. Name of the vessel
C. Weight of the boat
D. Port of registry

**070184/DS01421**  *46 CFR 160.33-3 (b)
The control lever for the mechanical disengaging apparatus in a lifeboat shall _____.
A. be painted bright red
B. be secured to a permanent part of the lifeboat structure
C. have the area surrounding the lever painted white
D. All of the above

**070185/DS00496**  *46 CFR 160.33-3 (b)
The lifeboat releasing gear lever should be marked with the words _____.
A. "DANGER, DO NOT TOUCH"
B. "DANGER, BOAT MAY DROP"
C. "DANGER, LEVER RELEASES BOAT"
D. "DANGER, LEVER DROPS BOAT"

**070186/DS01387**  *46 CFR 78.47
In painting a lifeboat following its overhaul, which parts must be painted bright red?
A. the top 2-1/2 inches of each side
B. the releasing gear lever
C. the fuel tanks
D. the thwarts

**070187/DS01690**                    *46 CFR 160.35 (c) (1)
The tops of the thwarts, side benches, and the footings of a lifeboat are painted which color?
⚓ A.  International orange
B.  Yellow
C.  White
D.  Red

## LIFEBOAT MANNING

**070188/DS00886**                    *46 CFR 199.100 (d)
What is the minimum number of deck officers, able seaman or certificated persons required to command each lifeboat on a vessel in ocean service?
⚓ A.  Two
B.  Three
C.  Four
D.  Five

**070189/DS00876**                    *46 CFR 199.100 (c) (1)
Which person may command a lifeboat in ocean service?
A.  Licensed deck officer
B.  Able seaman
C.  Certificated person
⚓ D.  All of the above

## EMERGENCY DRILLS TESTS & INSPECTIONS

**070190/DS00803**       *46 CFR 35.10-5; *46 CFR 97.13-15
The abandon ship signal on the ship's whistle is _____.
A.  6 short blasts and 1 long blast
B.  more than 6 short blasts
⚓ C.  more than 6 short blasts and 1 long blast
D.  1 long blast of at least 10 seconds

**070191/DS00843**                    *46 CFR 199.80 (b) (2)
The signal given to commence lowering the lifeboats is _____.
A.  3 short blasts of the ship's whistle
⚓ B.  specified on the muster list (station bill)
C.  3 long blasts of the ship's whistle
D.  1 long blast of the ship's whistle

**070192/DS10043**       *46 CFR 35.10-5; *46 CFR 97.13-15
When whistle signals are used for launching lifeboats, one short blast means _____.
A.  "use the float-free method only"
⚓ B.  "lower all boats"
C.  "raise all boats"
D.  "drill is over, secure all boats"

**070193/DS00823**             AMSM; *46 CFR 35.10-5 (a)
Traditionally, the signal for fire aboard ship is _____.
A.  more than 6 short blasts and 1 long blast on the whistle, and the same signal on the general alarm
⚓ B.  continuous sounding of the ship's whistle and the general alarm for at least 10 seconds
C.  1 short blast on the whistle
D.  alternating short and long blasts on the ship's whistle

**070194/DS00833**                    *46 CFR 35.10-5 (a)
While reading the muster list you see that "3 short blasts on the whistle and 3 short rings on the general alarm bells" is the signal for _____.
A.  abandon ship
⚓ B.  dismissal from fire and emergency stations
C.  fire and emergency
D.  man overboard

**070195/DS04242**                    *46 CFR 199.100 (c) (2)
A certificated lifeboatman assigned to command the lifeboat should _____.
A.  be the first individual to board the craft
B.  drain the hydraulic pressure before lowering the craft
⚓ C.  have a list of the persons assigned to the lifeboat
D.  All of the above

**070196/DG01033**                         *46 CFR 97.13-15;
                              *46 CFR 109.505; MFPFFS
Each crewmember has an assigned firefighting station. This assignment is shown on the _____.
A.  fire fighting plan
B.  shipping articles
C.  Certificate of Inspection
⚓ D.  muster list

**070197/DG01368**                    *46 CFR 199.80
Fire and abandon ship stations and duties may be found on the _____.
A.  crewman's duty list
B.  Certificate of Inspection
C.  shipping articles
⚓ D.  muster list

**070198/DG00717**    *46 CFR 97.13-15; *46 CFR 109.505
It is the responsibility of the Master to ensure that _____.
A.  the muster list is posted in each compartment
⚓ B.  temporary personnel and visitors are advised of emergency stations
C.  names of crew members are listed on the muster list
D.  no changes are made to the muster list

**070199/DG01358**  *46 CFR 199.80
Seeing that all hands are familiar with their duties, as specified in the muster list, is the responsibility of the _____.

⚓ A. Master
B. Chief Mate
C. safety officer
D. department heads

**070200/DG01285**  *46 CFR 109.501
Which information MUST be entered on the muster list?
A. Names of all crew members
B. Use and application of special equipment
C. Listing of approved emergency equipment
⚓ D. Duties and station of each person during emergencies

**070201/DG01348**  *46 CFR 97.13-15; *46 CFR 109.505
Preparation of muster lists and signing of same is the responsibility of the _____.
A. Chief Officer of the vessel
B. owner of the vessel
⚓ C. Master of the vessel
D. United States Coast Guard

**070202/DG00982**  *46 CFR 97.13-15; *46 CFR 109.505 (b)
The muster list must be posted in conspicuous locations and signed by the _____.
A. safety officer
B. Coast Guard Officer approving the bill
C. owner
⚓ D. Master

**070203/DS01319**  AMSM; *46 CFR 35.10
Where should muster lists be posted?
A. In crew's accommodation spaces
B. On the navigating bridge
C. In the engine room
⚓ D. All of the above

**070204/DG01165**  *46 CFR 109.501; *46 CFR 97.13-1
The Muster List ("Station Bill") shows each person's lifeboat station, duties during abandonment, basic instructions, and _____.
⚓ A. all emergency signals
B. instructions for lowering the lifeboats
C. the time each weekly drill will be held
D. work schedule

**070205/DS08734**  WHITTAKER
All personnel should be familiar with the lifeboats _____.
⚓ A. boarding and operating procedures
B. maintenance schedule
C. navigational systems
D. fuel consumption rates

**070206/DS00433**  *46 CFR 199.80 (b) (7)
If passengers are on board when an abandon ship drill is carried out, they should _____.
⚓ A. take part
B. watch
C. go to their quarters
D. stay out of the way and do what they want

**070207/DS02295**  WHITTAKER
All MODU personnel should be familiar with the survival craft's _____.
⚓ A. boarding and operating procedures
B. maintenance schedule
C. navigational systems
D. fuel consumption rates

**070208/DG03710**  SOLAS IV/18; *46 CFR 199.180 (g)
A new crewman reports on board. He must be trained in the use of the ship's lifesaving appliances within what time period?
A. 2 months
B. 1 month
⚓ C. 2 weeks
D. Before sailing

**070209/DS01265**  *46 CFR 185.520 (a)
The Master of a small passenger vessel must conduct sufficient drills and give sufficient instruction as necessary _____.
A. At each crew change
B. Every week
C. Every month
⚓ D. To ensure that all crew members are familiar with their duties during emergencies

LIFEBOAT RADIO

**070210/DS00324**                    ***H.O. 102**
The national distress, safety, and calling frequency is channel _____.
A.  13
⚓ B.  16
C.  18
D.  22

**070211/DS03317**                    **MRT**
You are in a lifeboat broadcasting a distress message. What information would be essential to your rescuers?
A.  The nature of the distress
B.  The time of day
C.  Your radio call sign
⚓ D.  Your position by latitude and longitude

**070212/DS10049**                    **MRT**
You are in a survival craft broadcasting a distress message. What information would be essential to your rescuers?
A.  The nature of the distress
B.  The time of day
C.  Your radio call sign
⚓ D.  Your position by latitude and longitude

**070213/DS02773**                    ***46 CFR 109.321 (a)**
The required portable radio apparatus on an international voyage must be stowed in _____.
A.  the Master's quarters
B.  the ship's office
⚓ C.  the radio room, bridge, or protected location
D.  an unlocked cabinet next to the Muster List ("Station Bill")

**070214/DS02847**                    ***46 CFR 109.321 (b)**
The required portable radio shall be stored in the proper location and be _____.
A.  equipped with an approved carrying case
B.  equipped with spare batteries
⚓ C.  readily accessible for transfer to a lifeboat
D.  in a waterproof enclosure

## LIFEBOAT OPERATIONS

### LIFEBOAT LAUNCHING PROCEDURES

**070215/DS01593**                    ***46 CFR 199.175 (b) (4)**
When launching an open lifeboat by falls, the boathooks should be _____.
A.  secured forward and aft where readily available
B.  secured amidships where they will not hinder the personnel
⚓ C.  used for fending off
D.  used for picking up survivors in the water

**070216/DS01253**                    **WHITTAKER**
If there are no alternatives for escape, what is the maximum height that the survival craft could be dropped into the water?
A.  2 ft.
B.  6 ft.
⚓ C.  10 ft.
D.  14 ft.

**070217/DS00233**                    **WSM; MSRS**
Most enclosed lifeboats will right themselves after capsizing IF the _____.
A.  lower ballast tanks are filled with water
B.  fuel tanks are not less than half full
⚓ C.  passengers are strapped to their seats
D.  sea anchor is deployed to windward

**070218/DS02197**                    **WATERCRAFT**
A self-righting survival craft will return to an upright position provided that all personnel _____.
⚓ A.  are seated with seat belts on and doors shut
B.  are seated with seat belts on and doors open
C.  are to shift to one side to right it
D.  escape from the craft

**070219/DS02203**                    **WATERCRAFT**
Who is responsible for lowering the survival craft?
A.  Roustabout
B.  First man aboard
C.  Last man aboard
⚓ D.  Helmsman

**070220/DS02241**                    **WHITTAKER**
If the survival craft is not loaded to full capacity, the personnel should be _____.
A.  loaded more on the port side forward
B.  loaded equally on both sides with more forward
⚓ C.  loaded equally on both sides with more aft
D.  allowed to sit anywhere

**070221/DS01400**        **AMSM**

In rough weather, when a ship is able to maneuver, it is best to launch a lifeboat _____.

⚓ A. on the lee side
   B. on the windward side
   C. with the wind dead ahead
   D. with the wind from astern

**070222/DS10021**        **WHITTAKER**

During an abandonment or drill, the first person to arrive at the survival craft should _____.

   A. pass out food and water to personnel
   B. open the doors and start the sprinkler system
   C. activate the emergency release handle
⚓ D. open the doors and prepare the craft for boarding

**070223/DS00075**        **WHITTAKER**

If you must abandon a rig in VERY HEAVY SEAS, in a survival craft, when should you remove the safety pin and pull the hook release?

⚓ A. Immediately upon launching
   B. One to three feet before first wave contact
   C. Upon first wave contact
   D. Only when waterborne

**070224/DS01390**        **LBMAN**

Which sequence is correct when launching a lifeboat stowed in gravity davits?

   A. Release gripes, turn on emergency disconnect switch, release frapping lines
   B. Release tricing pennants, turn on emergency disconnect switch, release frapping lines
   C. Operate limit switches, release gripes, lift brake
⚓ D. Release gripes, lift brake, release tricing pennants

### LIFEBOAT RECOVERY PROCEDURES

**070225/DS01145**        **AMSM**

When hoisting a boat on gravity type davits using an electric motor driven winch, the davit arms should be brought up _____.

   A. to their final position with the winch operating at slow speed
   B. to the bar stop, and then hand cranked to their final position
⚓ C. until just before they make contact with the limit switch, and then hand cranked to their final position
   D. to the embarkation deck, and then hand cranked to their final position

**070226/DS01170**        **AMSM**

When operating gravity davits, the _____.

   A. gripes should be released after the boat is moving
⚓ B. davits should always be hand cranked the last 12 inches into the final stowed position
   C. boats are generally lowered by surging the falls around cruciform bitts
   D. tricing pendant should be tripped prior to releasing the gripes

**070227/DS09585**        **WHITTAKER**

While retrieving the survival craft, the engine should be stopped _____.

⚓ A. when the craft clears the water
   B. when the cable has been attached
   C. on approach to the platform
   D. at the embarkation deck

**070228/DS01125**        **AMSM**

What is the best procedure for picking up a lifeboat at sea while utilizing the lifeboat's sea painter?

   A. Place the lifeboat ahead and to windward of your vessel with the wind about broad on the bow of your ship.
⚓ B. Place the lifeboat ahead and to leeward of your ship with the wind about broad on the bow of your ship.
   C. Place your ship to windward of the lifeboat with the wind on the quarter to allow your ship to drift down to the lifeboat.
   D. Place the lifeboat ahead and to windward of your ship with the wind about broad on the quarter of your ship.

**070229/DS01155**    **LBMAN; *46 CFR 199.175 (b) (21)**

When picking up a lifeboat at sea with way on the ship, the sea painter should be secured _____.

⚓ A. well forward in the lifeboat
   B. about amidships in the lifeboat
   C. well aft in the lifeboat
   D. only after the falls have been attached

**070230/DS02285**        **WATERCRAFT**

When retrieving the survival craft, the helmsman should instruct the crewman to _____.

   A. check the fuel level
   B. open the doors
   C. take the life preservers off
⚓ D. check that hooks are fully locked in place

**070231/DS02281**                                    **WHITTAKER**

When retrieving the survival craft, the winch operator should stop the winch and check _____.
A.  that all personnel are seated in the craft
⚓ B.  that the cable has not jumped any grooves on the drum
C.  which way the wind is blowing
D.  the hydraulic fluid level before lifting

### LIFEBOAT RIDING & LANDING PROCEDURES

**070232/DS08848**                                          **MSRS**

Enclosed lifeboats which have been afloat over a long period of time require _____.
A.  frequent opening of hatches to permit entry of fresh air
⚓ B.  regular checks of bilge levels
C.  use of ear plugs to dampen engine noise
D.  frequent flushing of the water spray system with fresh water

**070233/DS09273**                                          **MSRS**

After being launched from MODUs, totally enclosed survival craft which have been afloat over a long period require _____.
A.  frequent opening of hatches to permit entry of fresh air
⚓ B.  regular checks of bilge levels
C.  use of ear plugs to dampen engine noise
D.  frequent flushing of the water spray system with fresh water

**070234/DS09454**                              **SURVIVAL GUIDE**

If water is rising in the bilge of a lifeboat, you should FIRST _____.
A.  abandon the survival craft
B.  check for cracks in the hull
C.  shift all personnel to the stern
⚓ D.  check the bilge drain plug

**070235/DS02625**                                    **WHITTAKER**

If help has not arrived in 10-12 hours after you abandon ship in a lifeboat, you should _____.
A.  go in one direction until the fuel runs out
B.  plot course for the nearest land
C.  take a vote on which direction you should go
⚓ D.  shut down the engines and set the sea anchor

**070236/DS02215**                                    **WHITTAKER**

If help has not arrived in 10-12 hours after you abandon a MODU in a survival craft, you should _____.
A.  go in one direction until the fuel runs out
B.  plot a course for the nearest land
C.  take a vote on which direction you should go
⚓ D.  shut down the engine(s) and set the sea anchor

**070237/DS04701**                                          **FVSM**

After you activate your emergency position indicating radio beacon, you should _____.
A.  turn it off for five minutes every half-hour
B.  turn it off and on at five-minute intervals
C.  turn it off during daylight hours
⚓ D.  leave it on continuously

**070238/DG00966**                                    **CHAPMAN**

When a boat turns broadside to heavy seas and winds, thus exposing the boat to the danger of capsizing, the boat has _____.
⚓ A.  broached
B.  pitchpoled
C.  trimmed
D.  yawed

**070239/DG01036**                                    **CHAPMAN**

What is meant by the term "broaching to"?
A.  Having the vessel head toward the sea
B.  Running before a sea
⚓ C.  Being turned broadside to the sea
D.  Having the vessel filled with water

**070240/DG01056**                                    **CHAPMAN**

In which situation could a vessel most easily capsize?
A.  Running into head seas
⚓ B.  Running in the trough
C.  Running with following seas
D.  Anchored with your bow into the seas

**070241/DS01613**                                    **WHITTAKER**

Steering a motor lifeboat broadside to the sea could cause it to _____.
⚓ A.  capsize
B.  run smoother
C.  run faster
D.  sink

**070242/DG01828**                          **CHAPMAN; KNIGHTS**

Your vessel is broken down and rolling in heavy seas. You can reduce the danger of capsizing by _____.
A.  constantly shifting the rudder
B.  moving all passengers to one side of the boat
⚓ C.  rigging a sea anchor
D.  moving all passengers to the stern

**070243/DS02217**                                    **WHITTAKER**

Steering a survival craft broadside to the sea could cause it to _____.
⚓ A.  capsize
B.  run smoother
C.  run faster
D.  sink

**070244/DG00926**                                        **CRENSHAW**

Usually the most gentle way of riding out a severe storm on a larger vessel is _____.

A. head on at slow speeds
B. hove to
⚓ C. running before the seas
D. to rig a sea anchor

**070245/DG00335**                                **MMOH; NICHOLS**

You are steaming in a heavy gale and find it necessary to heave to. Under most circumstances, this is best done by _____.

A. stopping the engines and drifting beam to the seas
B. going slow astern and taking the seas on the quarter
⚓ C. taking the sea fine on the bow and reducing the speed to the minimum to hold that position
D. maintaining speed and taking the sea broad on the bow

**070246/DG01016**                                        **CHAPMAN**

Your vessel is off a lee shore in heavy weather and laboring. Which action should you take?

⚓ A. Put the sea and wind about two points on either bow and reduce speed.
B. Heave to in the trough of the sea.
C. Put the sea and wind on either quarter and proceed at increased speed.
D. Put the bow directly into the sea and proceed at full speed.

**070247/DG00946**                                            **MMOH**

Which measure should NOT be taken to reduce the pounding of a vessel in a head sea?

⚓ A. Add ballast in the after peak.
B. Add ballast forward.
C. Alter course.
D. Reduce speed.

**070248/DG01046**                                        **CHAPMAN**

In a following sea, a wave has overtaken your vessel and thrown the stern to starboard. To continue along your original course, you should _____.

⚓ A. use more right rudder
B. use more left rudder
C. increase speed
D. decrease speed

**070249/DG01066**                                        **CHAPMAN**

If your propeller is racing in rough weather, you should _____.

⚓ A. decrease your engine speed
B. ignore it
C. increase your engine speed
D. stop your engine until the rough weather passes

**070250/DG01026**                                        **CHAPMAN**

When making way in heavy seas you notice that your vessel's screw is being lifted clear of the water and racing. One way to correct this would be to _____.

A. increase speed
⚓ B. decrease speed
C. move more weight forward
D. shift the rudder back and forth several times

**070251/DG01076**                                        **CHAPMAN**

You are underway in heavy weather and your bow is into the seas. To prevent pounding, you should _____.

A. change course, in order to take the seas at an 85 degree angle from the bow
⚓ B. decrease speed
C. increase speed
D. secure all loose gear

**070252/DG00986**                                        **CHAPMAN**

When running before a heavy sea, moving weights aft will affect the handling of a vessel by _____.

A. reducing rolling
B. increasing rolling
⚓ C. reducing yawing
D. increasing yawing

**070253/DG01006**                                **CHAPMAN; KNIGHTS**

Which action reduces the yawing of a vessel in a following sea?

A. Increasing GM
B. Pumping out tanks aft
C. Shifting weights to the bow
⚓ D. Shifting weights to the stern

**070254/DG00996**                                        **CHAPMAN**

With a following sea, a vessel will tend to _____.

A. heave to
B. pound
C. reduce speed
⚓ D. yaw

**070255/DG00956**                                        **CHAPMAN**

When a vessel is swinging from side to side off course due to quartering seas, the vessel is _____.

A. broaching
B. pitchpoling
C. rolling
⚓ D. yawing

**070256/DS01295**                                          **WSM**

If you must land on a beach with an oar-propelled lifeboat through a heavy surf, the recommended method is to _____.

A. keep the bow directly in toward the beach, and tow the sea anchor off the stern

B. ride in on the back of a large breaker

⚓ C. keep the bow into the seas with the sea anchor out over the bow, and row to meet the breaking waves

D. head directly into the beach by staying between the crests of the waves

**070257/DS00353**                                          **LBMAN**

When a sea anchor is used in landing stern first in a heavy surf, sternway is checked by _____.

A. slacking the tripping line and towing the sea anchor from the stern

⚓ B. slacking the tripping line and towing the sea anchor by the holding line

C. towing with the tripping line and leaving the holding line slack

D. towing the apex end forward with the tripping line

**070258/DS01234**                                          **AMSM**

When landing a lifeboat through heavy surf with a strong current running parallel to the beach (from right to left when facing from seaward) the recommended procedure is to _____.

A. approach while coming to the left to take advantage of the current

B. drop an anchor outside the surf line, then pay out anchor line over the bow while the seas carry the boat toward the beach

C. approach slow enough so that the boat can be brought around to meet breaking seas on the bow

⚓ D. rig a drogue with tripping line over the bow, back ashore with drogue tripped between breakers

**070259/DS01305**                                          **AMSM**

When backing a motor propelled lifeboat (right-hand propeller) with the rudder amidships, the stern will back _____.

A. straight

⚓ B. to port

C. to starboard

D. None of the above

**070260/DS02265**                        **USCGA BOATING SKILLS & SEAMANSHIP**

A right-handed propeller will cause the survival craft to _____.

A. walk the stern to starboard in reverse

⚓ B. walk the stern to port in reverse

C. run faster than a left-handed propeller

D. right itself if capsized

**070261/DS01353**                        **USCGA BOATING SKILLS & SEAMANSHIP**

In heavy seas the helmsman should steer the motor lifeboat _____.

⚓ A. into the seas

B. broadside to the seas

C. in the same direction as the seas

D. in a series of figure-eights

**070262/DS01285**                                          **AMSM**

You have abandoned ship and find yourself aboard a lifeboat in a heavy sea. Your boat is able to make way through the water. To prevent broaching, you should _____.

A. put the sea on your stern and run as fast as the boat will go

B. take no action to prevent broaching as this is a recommended maneuver in a heavy sea

⚓ C. head the boat into the swells to take them at a 30 to 40 degree angle on either bow and run as slow as possible without losing steerage

D. place everyone as far forward in the boat as possible to keep the bow heavy

**070263/DS02221**                        **USCGA BOATING SKILLS & SEAMANSHIP**

In heavy seas the helmsman should steer the survival craft _____.

⚓ A. into the seas

B. broadside to the seas

C. in the same direction as the seas

D. in a series of figure-eights

**070264/DS02223**                        **RGIT COXSWAIN'S MANUAL**

Knowing the compass heading that is 90° to the side of a MODU will enable the operator of a survival craft to initially steer _____.

A. into the wind

⚓ B. away in fire and smoke

C. directly to the standby boat

D. directly to the nearest land

**070265/DS01414**                        **AMSM; SAFETY AT SEA; SURVIVAL GUIDE**

What should be used to steer an open lifeboat if the rudder becomes lost or damaged?

A. Sea anchor

⚓ B. Steering oar

C. Spare rudder

D. Daggerboard

**070266/DS00123**                                                    **WSM**

If you are forced to abandon ship in a lifeboat, you should _____.

A. remain in the immediate vicinity
B. head for the nearest land
C. head for the closest sea-lanes
D. vote on what to do, so all hands will have a part in the decision

**070267/DS02271**                                              **WHITTAKER**

When abandoning ship, after launching the motor lifeboat you should _____.

A. plot a course for the nearest land
B. take a vote on which direction you should go
C. stay in the immediate area
D. go in one direction until fuel runs out

**070268/DS02213**                                        **WHITTAKER; MSRS**

When abandoning a MODU, after launching the survival craft you should _____.

A. plot a course for the nearest land
B. take a vote on which direction you should go
C. stay in the immediate area
D. go in one direction until fuel runs out

**070269/DS02267**                                              **WHITTAKER**

During the towing of a survival craft, a lookout should be on station to _____.

A. release the towline in an emergency
B. help the helmsman steer
C. look for food and water
D. check the water level in the bilge

**070270/DG03300**                                                **CHAPMAN**

You are heading into the sea during rough weather. Having too much weight forward can cause your small boat to _____.

A. broach
B. plunge into the wave
C. rise rapidly over the wave
D. list

## LIFEBOAT OAR COMMANDS

**070271/DS01165**                                                   **AMSM**

When in command of a lifeboat under oars, the command "Backwater" means to _____.

A. lift oars to vertical position, trim blades fore and aft with handles resting on footings
B. complete the stroke, come to "Oars", raise oars smartly to vertical, rest handles on footing, trim blades fore and aft
C. row in astern motion
D. complete stroke, stop rowing, dip blade about halfway into water, hold water to stop the way on the boat

**070272/DS01225**                                                   **AMSM**

If the coxswain of your lifeboat gives the command "HOLD WATER" you should _____.

A. complete the stroke, raise your oar slightly, swinging the oar slightly forward, and place it in the boat
B. lift the oar in a vertical position
C. complete the stroke and hold the oar out of the water
D. dip the blade of your oar into the water vertically and hold it perpendicular to the keel line

**070273/DS01489**                                                   **AMSM**

The boat command that means complete the stroke and level the oars horizontally with the blades trimmed fore and aft is _____.

A. "Oars"
B. "Up oars"
C. "Way enough"
D. "Hold water"

**070274/DS01195**                                                    **WSM**

The command "Oars" means to _____.

A. lift the oars to a vertical position
B. complete the stroke and bring the oars horizontal, blades feathered
C. place the oars in the boat with blades forward
D. place the oars in the rowlocks directly from the boated position

**070275/DS01185**                                                   **AMSM**

If the steersman of your lifeboat gives the command "Way enough", you should _____.

A. complete the stroke, hold your oar out from the boat and level with the water
B. dip the blade of your oar into the water and leave it there
C. lift your oar to a vertical position
D. complete the stroke, raise your oar slightly, swing it forward, and place it in the boat

## LIFEBOAT NAVIGATION

**070276/NG00279**                                          **BOWD; *BOWD 2**

As a vessel changes course to starboard, the compass card in a magnetic compass _____.

A. remains aligned with compass north
B. also turns to starboard
C. first turns to starboard then counterclockwise to port
D. turns counterclockwise to port

**070277/NG00873**                    BOWD; *BOWD 2
Compass error is equal to the _____.
A. deviation minus variation
B. variation plus compass course
⚓ C. combined variation and deviation
D. difference between true and magnetic heading

**070278/NG00853**                    BOWD; *BOWD 2
The standard magnetic compass heading differs from
the true heading by _____.
⚓ A. compass error
B. latitude
C. variation
D. deviation

**070279/NG01514**                    BOWD; *BOWD 2
The compass error of a magnetic compass that has no
deviation is _____.
A. zero
⚓ B. equal to variation
C. eliminated by adjusting the compass
D. constant at any geographical location

**070280/NG01811**                    BOWD; *BOWD 2
To find a magnetic compass course from a true course
you must apply _____.
A. deviation
⚓ B. deviation and variation
C. variation
D. magnetic anomalies (local disturbances)

**070281/NG00883**                    BOWD; *BOWD 2
When changing from a compass course to a true course
you should apply _____.
A. variation
B. deviation
⚓ C. variation and deviation
D. a correction for the direction of current set

**070282/NG01333**                    BOWD; *BOWD 2
If a magnetic compass is not affected by any magnetic
field other than the Earth's, which statement is TRUE?
⚓ A. Compass error and variation are equal.
B. Compass north will be true north.
C. Variation will equal deviation.
D. There will be no compass error.

**070283/NG00973**                    BOWD; *BOWD 2
The heading of a vessel is indicated by what part of the
compass?
A. Card
B. Needle
⚓ C. Lubber's line
D. Gimbals

**070284/NG01379**                    BOWD; *BOWD 2
The lubber's line on a magnetic compass indicates
_____.
A. compass north
⚓ B. the direction of the vessel's head
C. magnetic north
D. a relative bearing taken with an azimuth circle

**070285/NG01303**                    BOWD; *BOWD 2
Compass deviation is caused by _____.
A. magnetism from the earth's magnetic field
B. misalignment of the compass
⚓ C. magnetism within the vessel
D. a dirty compass housing

**070286/NG00754**                    BOWD; *BOWD 2
Deviation in a compass is caused by the _____.
A. vessel's geographic position
B. vessel's heading
C. earth's magnetic field
⚓ D. influence of the magnetic materials of the vessel

**070287/NG01293**                    BOWD; *BOWD 2
Deviation is caused by _____.
A. changes in the earth's magnetic field
B. nearby magnetic land masses or mineral deposits
⚓ C. magnetic influence inherent to that particular
vessel
D. the magnetic lines of force not coinciding with the
lines of longitude

**070288/NG01233**                    BOWD; *BOWD 2
Deviation is the angle between the _____.
A. true meridian and the axis of the compass card
B. true meridian and the magnetic meridian
⚓ C. magnetic meridian and the axis of the compass
card
D. axis of the compass card and the degaussing
meridian

**070289/NG01263**                    BOWD; *BOWD 2
The compass deviation changes as the vessel changes
_____.
A. geographical position
B. speed
⚓ C. heading
D. longitude

**070290/NG01253**                    BOWD; *BOWD 2
The horizontal angle between the magnetic meridian
and the north-south line of the magnetic compass is
_____.
⚓ A. deviation
B. variation
C. compass error
D. dip

**070291/NG00983**          BOWD; *BOWD 2
Error may be introduced into a magnetic compass by
_____.
A.  making a structural change to the vessel
B.  a short circuit near the compass
C.  belt buckles
⚓ D.  All of the above

**070292/NG02280**          BOWD; *BOWD 2
Which would influence a magnetic compass?
A.  Electrical wiring
B.  Iron pipe
C.  Radio
⚓ D.  All of the above

**070293/NG01419**          BOWD; *BOWD 2
The MOST important feature of the material used for
making the binnacle of a standard magnetic compass is
that it is _____.
⚓ A.  nonmagnetic
B.  weatherproof
C.  corrosion resistant
D.  capable of being permanently affixed to the vessel

**070294/NG02300**          BOWD; *BOWD 2
When a magnetic compass is not in use for a prolonged
period of time it should _____.
⚓ A.  be shielded from direct sunlight
B.  be locked into a constant heading
C.  have any air bubbles replaced with nitrogen
D.  have the compensating magnets removed

**070295/NG01203**          BOWD; *BOWD 2
If the compass heading and the magnetic heading are
the same then _____.
A.  the deviation has been offset by the variation
B.  there is something wrong with the compass
C.  the compass is being influenced by nearby metals
⚓ D.  there is no deviation on that heading

**070296/NG01213**          BOWD; *BOWD 2
If the magnetic heading is greater than the compass
heading, the deviation is _____.
⚓ A.  east
B.  west
C.  north
D.  south

**070297/NG01223**          BOWD; *BOWD 2
The difference between magnetic heading and compass
heading is called _____.
A.  variation
⚓ B.  deviation
C.  compass error
D.  drift

**070298/NG01363**          BOWD; *BOWD 2
True heading differs from magnetic heading by
_____.
A.  deviation
⚓ B.  variation
C.  compass error
D.  northerly error

**070299/NG00764**          BOWD; *BOWD 2
Magnetic variation changes with a change in
_____.
A.  the vessel's heading
B.  sea conditions
C.  seasons
⚓ D.  the vessel's position

**070300/NG01353**          BOWD; *BOWD 2
The difference in degrees between true north and
magnetic north is called _____.
⚓ A.  variation
B.  deviation
C.  drift
D.  compass error

**070301/NG01313**          BOWD; *BOWD 2
Variation in a compass is caused by _____.
A.  worn gears in the compass housing
⚓ B.  magnetism from the earth's magnetic field
C.  magnetism within the vessel
D.  lack of oil in the compass bearings

**070302/NG01343**          BOWD; *BOWD 2
Variation is a compass error that you _____.
A.  can correct by adjusting the compass card
B.  can correct by adjusting the compensating magnets
C.  can correct by changing the vessel's heading
⚓ D.  cannot correct

**070303/NG00774**          BOWD; *BOWD 2
Variation is not constant; it is different with every
change in _____.
A.  speed
B.  vessel heading
⚓ C.  geographical location
D.  cargo

**070304/NG00784**          BOWD; *BOWD 2
Variation is the angular measurement between
_____.
A.  compass north and magnetic north
B.  compass north and true north
⚓ C.  magnetic meridian and the geographic meridian
D.  your vessel's heading and the magnetic meridian

**070305/NG00809**                     **BOWD; \*BOWD 2**

The compass rose on a nautical chart indicates both variation and _____.

A. deviation
⚓ B. annual rate of variation change
C. precession
D. compass error

**070306/DS01454**                                  **BOWD**

You are in a lifeboat when you sight the stars indicated in illustration D005SA. You will be heading due north when you head for Polaris which is indicated by what letter? See DIAGRAM D005SA

A. A
B. C
⚓ C. E
D. I

**070307/DS01491**                                  **BOWD**

You are in a lifeboat when you sight the stars shown. You will be heading almost due north when you head for Polaris which is marked by what letter? See DIAGRAM D006SA

⚓ A. C
B. D
C. E
D. G

**070308/DS01427**                                  **BOWD**

You are in a lifeboat when you sight the stars as shown. You will be heading due north when you head for Polaris which is indicated by which letter? See DIAGRAM D007SA

A. E
⚓ B. F
C. G
D. H

**070309/NG00923**                     **BOWD; \*BOWD 2**

A magnetic compass card is marked in how many degrees?

A. 90
B. 180
⚓ C. 360
D. 400

**070310/NG02040**                     **BOWD; \*BOWD 2**

A vessel heading NNE is on a course of _____.

⚓ A. 022.5°
B. 045.0°
C. 067.5°
D. 090.0°

**070311/NG02030**                     **BOWD; \*BOWD 2**

A vessel heading NE is on a course of _____.

A. 022.5°
⚓ B. 045.0°
C. 067.5°
D. 090.0°

**070312/NG02020**                     **BOWD; \*BOWD 2**

A vessel heading ENE is on a course of _____.

A. 022.5°
B. 045.0°
⚓ C. 067.5°
D. 090.0°

**070313/NG02010**                     **BOWD; \*BOWD 2**

A vessel heading ESE is on a course of _____.

⚓ A. 112.5°
B. 135.0°
C. 157.5°
D. 180.0°

**070314/NG02000**                     **BOWD; \*BOWD 2**

A vessel heading SE is on a course of _____.

A. 112.5°
⚓ B. 135.0°
C. 157.5°
D. 180.0°

**070315/NG01890**                     **BOWD; \*BOWD 2**

A vessel heading SSE is on a course of _____.

A. 112.5°
B. 135.0°
⚓ C. 157.5°
D. 180.0°

**070316/NG01880**                     **BOWD; \*BOWD 2**

A vessel heading SSW is on a course of _____.

⚓ A. 202.5°
B. 225.0°
C. 247.5°
D. 270.0°

**070317/NG01870**                     **BOWD; \*BOWD 2**

A vessel heading SW is on a course of _____.

A. 202.5°
⚓ B. 225.0°
C. 247.5°
D. 270.0°

**070318/NG01860**                     **BOWD; \*BOWD 2**

A vessel heading WSW is on a course of _____.

A. 202.5°
B. 225.0°
⚓ C. 247.5°
D. 271.0°

**070319/NG01850**    **BOWD; \*BOWD 2**

A vessel heading WNW is on a course of _____.
- A. 270.0°
- ⚓ B. 292.5°
- C. 315.0°
- D. 337.5°

**070320/NG01840**    **BOWD; \*BOWD 2**

A vessel heading NW is on a course of _____.
- A. 274.5°
- B. 292.5°
- ⚓ C. 315.0°
- D. 337.5°

**070321/NG01830**    **BOWD; \*BOWD 2**

A vessel heading NNW is on a course of _____.
- A. 274.5°
- B. 292.0°
- C. 315.5°
- ⚓ D. 337.5°

**070322/NG00893**    **BOWD; \*BOWD 2**

One point of a compass is equal to how many degrees?
- A. 7.5
- ⚓ B. 11.25
- C. 17.5
- D. 22.5

**070323/NG00903**    **CHAPMAN**

Eight points of a compass are equal to how many degrees?
- A. 45
- ⚓ B. 90
- C. 180
- D. 360

**070324/NG00913**    **BOWD; \*BOWD 2**

How many points are there in a compass card?
- A. 4
- B. 8
- C. 24
- ⚓ D. 32

---

**LIFESAVING EQUIPMENT - LIFERAFTS**

LIFERAFT STOWAGE

**070325/DS01324**    **AMSM**

A hydrostatic release mechanism for a liferaft _____.
- A. must be wet before it will release
- B. should be kept in a watertight cover except in an emergency
- C. will inflate the raft in its cradle if operated manually
- ⚓ D. must be submerged to a certain depth to release automatically

**070326/DS02083**    **\*46 CFR 108.530 (c) (7)**

On offshore drilling units each inflatable liferaft that is not intended for davit launching must be stowed so as to float free or be _____.
- ⚓ A. equipped with a hydrostatic release
- B. stowed in approved racks
- C. located above the main deck area
- D. replaced every 12 months

**070327/DS01355**    **AMSM; \*46 CFR 160.62**

As a vessel sinks to a depth of 15 feet, the hydrostatic trip releases the liferaft container from its cradle by _____.
- A. breaking the weak link
- ⚓ B. releasing the tie-down strap
- C. pulling the operating cord
- D. releasing the $CO_2$ canister

**070328/DS04786**    **AMSM; \*46 CFR 160.62**

Which number indicates the hydrostatic release? See DIAGRAM D015SA
- A. 3
- ⚓ B. 6
- C. 7
- D. 10

**070329/DS01335**    **AMSM; \*46 CFR 160.73**

What prevents an inflated liferaft from being pulled under by a vessel which sinks in water over 100 feet in depth?
- A. The hydrostatic release
- B. Nothing
- C. A Rottmer release
- ⚓ D. The weak link in the painter line

**070330/DS01493**                          **AMSM; *46 CFR 160.73**
A new liferaft has been installed on your vessel. The operating cord should be _____.
⚓ A.  attached to the raft stowage cradle or to a secure object nearby with a weak link
B.  checked to see that it's unattached
C.  coiled neatly on the raft container
D.  faked on deck and lead through a chock

## LIFERAFT EQUIPMENT

**070331/DS01196          MIL; *46 CFR 199.175 (b) (16), (17)**
The knife on an inflatable liferaft will always be located _____.
A.  in one of the equipment bags
⚓ B.  in a special pocket near the forward entrance
C.  on a cord hanging from the canopy
D.  in a pocket on the first aid kit

**070332/DS01284AMSM; LBMAN; *46 CFR 160.51-7 (b) (8)**
The operating cord on an inflatable liferaft also serves as a _____.
A.  lifeline
⚓ B.  painter
C.  drogue
D.  marker

**070333/DS01304          AMSM; *46 CFR 160.51-7 (b) (8)**
The painter of an inflatable liferaft should be _____.
A.  free running on the deck
B.  faked out next to the case
⚓ C.  secured to a permanent object on deck
D.  stowed near the raft

**070334/DS09377                          SAFETY AT SEA**
After abandoning ship, you should deploy the sea anchor from a liferaft to _____.
A.  keep the liferaft from capsizing
B.  navigate against the current
C.  keep personnel from getting seasick
⚓ D.  stay in the general location

**070335/DS01404                          *46 CFR 94.20-25, 160**
Signaling devices which are required on inflatable liferafts include _____.
A.  a rocket shoulder rifle
B.  an oil lantern
⚓ C.  red flares
D.  an air horn

**070336/DS01376                          *46 CFR 199.175 (b) (31);**
                                          ***46 CFR 160.51-7**
Which distress signal is required for a liferaft in ocean service and could be effectively used to attract the attention of aircraft at night?
A.  The water light
B.  Smoke marker
⚓ C.  Red flares
D.  Orange dye marker

**070337/DS10024                          *46 CFR 199.175 (b) (30)**
Signaling devices required on inflatable liferafts include a(n) _____.
A.  Very pistol
⚓ B.  orange smoke signal
C.  air horn
D.  lantern

## LIFERAFT CONSTRUCTION

**070338/DS01346                          LBMAN; *46 CFR 160.51**
The canopy of an inflatable liferaft should _____.
⚓ A.  go into place as the raft is inflated
B.  be put up after everyone is aboard
C.  be put up only in severe weather
D.  be used as a sail if the wind is blowing

**070339/DS01236          AMSM; *46 CFR 160.51-5 (e) (8)**
Inflatable liferafts are provided with _____.
A.  a portable radio
B.  an oil lantern
C.  canned milk
⚓ D.  a towing connection

**070340/DS01246                          LBMAN; *46 CFR 160.51**
Inflatable liferafts are provided with _____.
A.  a Very pistol
⚓ B.  a towing connection
C.  a portable radio
D.  canned milk

**070341/DS03194                          WSM**
Generally, what is used to inflate liferafts?
⚓ A.  non-toxic gas
B.  Oxygen
C.  Hydrogen
D.  Helium

**070342/DS01266                          WSM; *46 CFR 160.51**
A life line must be connected to the liferaft _____.
A.  at the bow
B.  at the stern
C.  in the middle
⚓ D.  all around

**070343/DS01206**                    **AMSM; *46 CFR 199.175**
Inflatable liferafts are provided with a _____.
A.  knife
B.  towing connection
C.  lifeline
⚓ D.  All of the above

**070344/DS01286**                    **LBMAN; *46 CFR 160.51**
The inside light in an inflatable liferaft is turned on _____.
⚓ A.  automatically as the liferaft inflates
B.  with a switch near the boarding handle
C.  at night because the light has a photosensitive switch
D.  by screwing the bulb in after the raft is inflated

**070345/DS01276**                    **WSM; *46 CFR 160.51-7 (b) (5)**
The lights on the outside of the canopy on an inflatable liferaft operate _____.
A.  by turning the globe clockwise
B.  by a switch at each light
C.  by a light sensor
⚓ D.  automatically when the raft is inflated

**070346/DS01326**                    **MIL; *46 CFR 160.51-4 (b)**
All inflatable liferafts have _____.
A.  safety straps from the overhead
B.  built in seats
C.  releasing hooks at each end
⚓ D.  water stabilizing pockets

**070347/DS01256**                    **WSM; *46 CFR 160.51-4 (b)**
The water pockets located on the underside of inflatable liferafts _____.
A.  stow rainwater; these 4 spaces do not take up valuable space
⚓ B.  act as stabilizers by filling with sea water as soon as the raft is inflated and upright
C.  hold the freshwater required by regulation to be provided in the raft when packed
D.  None of the above

**070348/DS01356**                    ***46 CFR 160.51-4 (b); LBMAN**
What is placed on the underside of an inflatable liferaft to help prevent it from being skidded by the wind or overturned?
⚓ A.  Water pockets
B.  A keel
C.  Strikes
D.  Sea anchor

**070349/DS10038**                    **MIL; *46 CFR 160.51-4 (b)**
Water pockets on the underside of an inflatable liferaft are for _____.
A.  catching rain water
⚓ B.  stability
C.  easy drainage
D.  maneuverability

**070350/DS01296**                    **LBMAN; *46 CFR 160.51**
Hand holds or straps on the underside of an inflatable liferaft are provided _____.
⚓ A.  to right the raft if it capsizes
B.  to carry the raft around on deck
C.  for crewmen to hang on to
D.  to hang the raft for drying

### LIFERAFT MANNING

**070351/DS03989**                    ***46 CFR 199.201 (a) (5);**
                                       ***46 CFR 199.261 (a) (4)**
Inflatable liferafts on vessels on an international voyage must be able to carry at least _____.
A.  2 persons
B.  4 persons
⚓ C.  6 persons
D.  8 persons

### LIFERAFT TESTS AND INSPECTION

**070352/DS00936**                    **LBMAN; *46 CFR 199.190 (g) (3);**
                                       ***46 CFR 160.51-6**
If your vessel is equipped with inflatable liferafts, how should they be maintained?
A.  Have your crew check them annually.
B.  They do not need any maintenance.
⚓ C.  Have them sent ashore to an approved maintenance facility annually.
D.  Have them serviced by the shipyard annually.

**070353/DS00976**                    ***46 CFR 199.190 (g) (3) (i)**
Inflatable liferafts carried on passenger vessels must be annually _____.
A.  overhauled by the ship's crew
B.  sent to the Coast Guard for servicing
C.  sent to the steamship company shore repair facility
⚓ D.  sent to a Coast Guard approved service facility

**070354/DS01264**                    **LBMAN; *46 CFR 199.190 (g) (3);**
                                       ***46 CFR 160.51-6**
The operating cord on an inflatable liferaft should be renewed by _____.
A.  removing the top half of the shell, cutting the line at its source, and renewing completely
B.  cutting the line where it enters the case and replacing that portion
C.  leaving the original line and tying another one to it so the two lines will take the strain
⚓ D.  an approved servicing facility ashore

**070355/DS00926**                                        **WSM**

Inflatable liferafts must be overhauled and inspected at a U.S. Coast Guard approved service facility every _____.

   A. six months
⚓ B. twelve months
   C. eighteen months
   D. twenty-four months

**070356/DS10022**                    **\*46 CFR 199.190 (g) (1) (ii)**

Inflatable liferafts shall be serviced at an approved servicing facility every 12 months or not later than the next vessel inspection for certification. However, the total elapsed time between servicing cannot exceed _____.

   A. 12 months
   B. 15 months
⚓ C. 17 months
   D. 18 months

**070357/DS02081**                          **\*46 CFR 109.310 (g)**

On offshore drilling units, each inflatable liferaft must be serviced every _____.

⚓ A. 12 months
   B. 24 months
   C. 36 months
   D. 48 months

**070358/DS04079**                          **\*46 CFR 199.190 (g) (1)**

Your cargo vessel's Certification of Inspection expires 30 April 2002. One of your inflatable liferafts was last serviced in January 2002. The raft must be reinspected no later than _____.

⚓ A. 3-Jan
   B. 3-Jun
   C. 4-Apr
   D. 7-Jan

## LIFERAFT OPERATIONS

### LIFERAFT LAUNCHING PROCEDURES

**070359/DS01385**                                        **AMSM**

An inflatable liferaft is hand-launched by _____.

   A. pulling a cord
   B. cutting the wire restraining bands
   C. removing the rubber packing strip
⚓ D. throwing the entire container overboard

**070360/DS01345**                                        **AMSM**

An inflatable liferaft can be launched by _____.

   A. the float-free method ONLY
   B. breaking the weak link on the painter
⚓ C. throwing the entire container overboard and then pulling on the operating cord to inflate the raft
   D. removing the securing straps

**070361/DS01314**                                  **AMSM; LBMAN**

Under normal conditions a liferaft is released from its cradle by _____.

   A. cutting the restraining strap
   B. unscrewing the turnbuckle on the back of the cradle
   C. lifting one end of the raft
⚓ D. pushing the plunger on the center of the hydrostatic release

**070362/DS01395**                                        **AMSM**

After you have thrown the liferaft and stowage container into the water, you inflate the liferaft by _____.

⚓ A. pulling on the painter line
   B. forcing open the container which operates the $CO_2$
   C. hitting the hydrostatic release
   D. using the hand pump provided

**070363/DS01242**                                        **LBMAN**

The bosun has thrown the liferaft into the water before abandoning the vessel. The operating cord _____.

⚓ A. serves as a sea painter
   B. detaches from the liferaft automatically
   C. is used to rig the boarding ladder
   D. is cut immediately as it is of no further use

**070364/DS01184**                                        **AMSM**

If an inflatable liferaft is to be released manually, where should the operating cord be attached before throwing the raft overboard?

   A. Do not attach the cord to anything but throw it overboard with the raft container.
⚓ B. Attach the cord to a fixed object on the ship.
   C. You should stand on the cord.
   D. Attach the cord to the special pad eye on the "raft davit launcher".

**070365/DS01194**                                        **AMSM**

Which operation should be done when launching an inflatable liferaft by hand?

   A. Open the liferaft casing.
   B. Turn the valve on the $CO_2$ cylinder to start inflation.
⚓ C. Make sure the operating cord is secured to the vessel before throwing it over the side.
   D. After inflation, detach operating cord from liferaft.

### LIFERAFT RECOVERY PROCEDURES

**070366/DS01204**                                        **LBMAN**

Generally, when lifting an inflatable liferaft back aboard ship you would use the _____.

⚓ A. towing bridle
   B. main weather cover
   C. external lifelines
   D. righting strap

### LIFERAFT RIDING & LANDING PROCEDURES

**070367/DS10053**                                              **AMSM**

An inflatable liferaft is thrown into the water from a sinking vessel. What should occur after the painter trips the $CO_2$ bottles to inflate the raft?

⚓ A.  The sea anchor should be deployed as soon you are away from the vessel.

    B.  The floor will automatically inflate.

    C.  If upside down, the craft will right itself.

    D.  The painter will detach from the raft.

**070368/DS00013**                                              **MIL**

Your liferaft is to leeward of a fire on the water and riding to its sea anchor. You should FIRST _____.

⚓ A.  boat the sea anchor

    B.  paddle away from the fire

    C.  splash water over the liferaft to cool it

    D.  get out of the raft and swim to safety

**070369/DS07062**                           **FVSM; SURVIVAL GUIDE**

You are aboard a liferaft in a storm. What should you do with your Emergency Position Indicating Radio Beacon?

⚓ A.  Bring it inside the liferaft and leave it on.

    B.  Bring it inside the liferaft and turn it off until the storm passes.

    C.  Leave it outside the liferaft and leave it on.

    D.  Leave it outside the liferaft but turn it off.

**070370/DS04785**                                              **FVSM**

What should you do with your emergency position indicating radio beacon if you are in a liferaft in a storm?

⚓ A.  Bring it inside the liferaft and leave it on.

    B.  Bring it inside the liferaft and turn it off until the storm passes.

    C.  Leave it outside the liferaft and leave it on.

    D.  Leave it outside the liferaft but turn it off.

**070371/DS10025**                                              **WSM**

The air spaces in the floor of an inflatable liferaft will provide protection against _____.

    A.  asphyxiation from $CO_2$

    B.  loss of air in the sides of the raft

    C.  rough seas

⚓ D.  cold water temperatures

**070372/DS00183**                                              **LBMAN**

Which statement is TRUE concerning an inflatable liferaft?

    A.  The floor may be inflated for insulation from cold water.

    B.  Crew members can jump into the raft without damaging it.

    C.  The raft may be boarded before it is fully inflated.

⚓ D.  All of the above

**070373/DS00163**                                              **MIL**

You are at sea in an inflatable liferaft. In high latitudes, the greatest danger is _____.

    A.  asphyxiation due to keeping the canopy closed

⚓ B.  hypothermia caused by cold temperature

    C.  collapse of the raft due to cold temperatures

    D.  starvation

**070374/DS00173**                                              **MIL**

While adrift in an inflatable liferaft in hot, tropical weather _____.

    A.  the canopy should be deflated so that it will not block cooling breezes

    B.  the pressure valve may periodically open to prevent excessive air pressure

⚓ C.  deflating the floor panels may help to cool personnel

    D.  the entrance curtains should never be opened

**070375/DS00103**                                              **MIL**

You have just abandoned ship and boarded a raft. After the raft is completely inflated you hear a whistling noise coming from a safety valve. You should _____.

⚓ A.  not become alarmed unless it continues for a long period of time

    B.  plug the safety valve

    C.  unscrew the deflation plugs

    D.  remove the safety valve and replace it with a soft patch

**070376/DS09383**                                      **SAFETY AT SEA**

Immediately after abandoning a vessel, lookouts should be posted aboard liferafts to look for _____.

⚓ A.  survivors in the water

    B.  food and water

    C.  land

    D.  bad weather

**070377/DS09385**                                         **MSRS**
When personnel are lifted by a helicopter from an inflatable liferaft, the personnel on the raft should _____.

⚓ A.  deflate the floor of the raft to reduce the danger of the raft overturning
B.  inflate the floor of the raft to provide for additional stability
C.  remove their life preservers to prepare for the transfer
D.  take in the sea anchor to prevent fouling of the rescue sling

**070378/DS00083**                                         **LBMAN**
If more than one raft is manned after the vessel has sunk, you should _____.
A.  go in a different direction in search of land
B.  spread out to increase the possibility of a search aircraft finding you
C.  reduce the number of rafts by getting as many people as possible into as few rafts as possible
⚓ D.  tie the rafts together and try to stay in a single group

**070379/DS00093**                                         **LBMAN**
If, for any reason, it is necessary to abandon ship while far out at sea, it is important that the crew members should _____.
A.  separate from each other as this will increase the chances of being rescued
B.  get away from the area because sharks will be attracted to the vessel
C.  immediately head for the nearest land
⚓ D.  remain together in the area because rescuers will start searching at the vessel's last known position

**070380/DS00073**                                         **MSRS 179**
A liferaft which has inflated bottom-up on the water _____.

⚓ A.  should be righted by standing on the carbon dioxide cylinder, holding the righting straps, and leaning backwards
B.  should be righted by standing on the life line, holding the righting straps, and leaning backwards
C.  will right itself when the canopy tubes inflate
D.  must be cleared of the buoyant equipment before it will right itself

**070381/DS00043**       **SAFETY AND SURVIVAL AT SEA**
If an inflatable liferaft is overturned, it may be righted by _____.
A.  filling the stabilizers on one side with water
B.  releasing the CO₂ cylinder
C.  pushing up from under one end
⚓ D.  standing on the inflating cylinder and pulling on the straps on the underside of the raft

**070382/DS09381**                            **SAFETY AT SEA**
If the liferaft capsizes, all personnel should leave the raft and _____.
A.  climb onto the bottom
B.  swim away from the raft
⚓ C.  right the raft using the righting strap
D.  inflate the righting bag

**070383/DS00003**                                         **MIL**
To turn over an inflatable liferaft that is upside down, you should pull on the _____.
A.  canopy
B.  manropes
C.  sea painter
⚓ D.  righting strap

**070384/DS01281**                                         **WSM**
You are in the process of righting an inflatable liferaft that has inflated in an upside down position. Which statement is TRUE?
A.  As the raft flips to the upright position, you will be thrown clear.
B.  After the raft is in the upright position on top of you, dive down to prevent your life preservers from fouling as you come out.
⚓ C.  Swim out from under the raft in a face up position to keep your life preservers clear of the raft.
D.  You should remove your life preservers before attempting to right an inflatable raft.

**070385/DS01394**                                         **WSM**
In each inflatable liferaft, what equipment is provided to make quick, emergency, temporary repairs to large holes in the raft?
A.  No equipment is provided.
B.  Glue and rubber patches
⚓ C.  Several various-sized sealing clamps
D.  Self-adhesive rubberized canvas patches

**070386/DS10023**                                         **MIL**
Puncture leaks in the lower tubes or bottom of an inflatable liferaft should FIRST be stopped by using _____.

⚓ A.  sealing clamps
B.  repair tape
C.  a tube patch
D.  sail twine and vulcanizing kit

**070387/DS00153**                                         **MIL**
If you reach shore in a liferaft, the first thing to do is _____.

⚓ A.  drag the raft ashore and lash it down for a shelter
B.  find some wood for a fire
C.  get the provisions out of the raft
D.  set the raft back out to sea so someone may spot it

**070388/DS10050**                                        *PUB 117 4-21
You have abandoned ship and after two days in a liferaft you can see an aircraft near the horizon apparently carrying out a search pattern. You should _____.

A.  switch the EPIRB to the homing signal mode
B.  use the voice transmission capability of the EPIRB to guide the aircraft to your raft
C.  turn on the strobe light on the top of the EPIRB
⚓ D.  use visual distress signals in conjunction with the EPIRB

DAVIT LAUNCHED LIFERAFTS

**070389/DS04455**                                                  MSRS
What is the primary advantage of a davit-launched liferaft in comparison to an inflatable liferaft?
A.  The davit-launched liferaft is easier to maintain.
B.  The davit-launched liferaft is made of fire-retardant material.
C.  The davit-launched liferaft has a built-in sprinkler system for fire protection.
⚓ D.  The davit-launched liferaft enables personnel to enter the raft without having to enter the water.

**070390/DS02093**                                        SAFETY AT SEA
The davit launched liferaft can be boarded _____.
A.  from the water only
⚓ B.  at the deck
C.  by jumping down onto it
D.  through the escape tube

**070391/DS07385**                                                  MSRS
To assure safe boarding and launching of a davit-launched liferaft from a MODU, preparation should include _____.
A.  load testing the davit arm and the painter system
⚓ B.  removing any side protective rails and checking that the overside and surface level are clear
C.  testing the spring loaded drum to assure it will retract the fall release hook
D.  testing to assure that the required lamps are functioning properly

**070392/DS02087**                                        SAFETY AT SEA
The davit aboard a MODU is used to _____.
A.  lower personnel down by a transfer basket
B.  lower food and water to personnel in a liferaft
⚓ C.  lower the liferaft down with its full complement
D.  move equipment around the deck

**070393/DS02091**                                        SAFETY AT SEA
To inflate a davit launched liferaft you _____.
A.  initially connect the compressed air nozzle to the inflation tube
⚓ B.  pull the inflation lanyard
C.  connect the hand pump to the inflation tube and pump it up
D.  connect the helium nozzle to the inflation tube

**070394/DS02105**                                        SAFETY AT SEA
If a davit-launched liferaft aboard a MODU cannot be launched because of damage to the davit, you should _____.
A.  inflate the liferaft on deck
⚓ B.  roll the liferaft over the side
C.  go to another liferaft station
D.  get a saw and cut the liferaft free

**070395/DS07391**                                                  MSRS
Personnel boarding a davit-launched liferaft from a MODU should be checked to assure they are not in possession of or wearing _____.
A.  oil stained shoes or clothing
⚓ B.  sharp objects that may puncture or damage the liferaft
C.  matches or cigarette lighters
D.  drugs or paraphernalia not approved by a medical doctor

**070396/DS09167**                                        SAFETY AT SEA
To release the davit cable of a davit launched liferaft, you must _____.
⚓ A.  pull the release lanyard
B.  pull the hydraulic release
C.  push the release button
D.  pull on the ratchet handle

**070397/DS07393**                                                  MSRS
When a davit-launched raft is lowered from a MODU, upon becoming waterborne, the raft is released by _____.
A.  activating the release lock of the hook
B.  pulling smartly on the knobbed cocking lanyard
⚓ C.  the effects of buoyancy removing the weight of the raft from the hook
D.  releasing the boarding flap and the bowsing lines

**070398/DS04457**                                                  MSRS
Prior to entering a davit-launched liferaft, you should make sure that _____.
⚓ A.  the liferaft is well ventilated of excess carbon dioxide
B.  all personnel have removed their life preservers to facilitate boarding
C.  the door flap has been cut away and stowed inside the raft
D.  All of the above

**070399/DS07387**                                    **MSRS**

Prior to boarding from a MODU, a davit-launched liferaft should be well ventilated of excess _____.

A.  hydrocarbon gas
B.  carbon monoxide gas
⚓ C.  carbon dioxide gas
D.  freon gas

LIFEFLOATS

**070400/DS03414**                          **\*46 CFR 160.027-2**

A rigid lifesaving device designed to support survivors in the water is a _____.

A.  rigid liferaft
⚓ B.  life float
C.  inflatable liferaft
D.  survival capsule

**070401/DS04000**                          **\*46 CFR 199.175**

On a rigid liferaft (SOLAS B pack) which is equipped with all of the required equipment you may NOT find a _____.

A.  bailer
B.  sponge
C.  whistle
⚓ D.  fishing kit

## MISCELLANEOUS LIFESAVING EQUIPMENT

LIFE PRESERVERS
PERSONAL FLOATATION DEVICE (PFD)

**070402/DS00333     SURVIVAL GUIDE; \*46 CFR 160.01**

Which statement is TRUE concerning life preservers (Type I personal flotation devices)?

A.  Buoyant vests may be substituted for life jackets.
⚓ B.  Life preservers are designed to turn an unconscious person's face clear of the water.
C.  Life preservers must always be worn with the same side facing outwards to float properly.
D.  Lightly stained or faded life jackets will fail in the water and should not be used.

**070403/DS00293**                          **\*46 CFR 160.006-2 (b)**

Which statement is TRUE concerning life jackets which are severely damaged?

⚓ A.  They should be replaced.
B.  They must be tested for buoyancy before being continued in use.
C.  They can be repaired by a reliable seamstress.
D.  They can be used for children.

**070404/DS00313          CHAPMAN; \*46 CFR 160.47**

Kapok life jackets should NOT be _____.

A.  stowed near open flame or where smoking is permitted
B.  used as seats, pillows, or foot rests
C.  left on open decks
⚓ D.  All of the above

**070405/DS01920      \*46 CFR 180.25-1; \*46 CFR 160.47**

Which statement is TRUE concerning life preservers?

A.  Buoyant vests may be substituted for life preservers.
⚓ B.  Kapok life preservers must have vinyl-covered pad inserts.
C.  Life preservers must always be worn with the same side facing outwards.
D.  Life preservers are not designed to turn a person's face clear of the water when unconscious.

**070406/DS03611**                          **\*46 CFR 109.225 (a)**

Each life jacket light that has a non-replaceable power source must be replaced _____.

A.  every 6 months after initial installation
B.  every 12 months after initial installation
C.  every 24 months after initial installation
⚓ D.  on or before the expiration date of the power source

**070407/DS01036**                          **\*46 CFR 199.70 (b) (3)**

Life preservers must be marked with the _____.

A.  stowage space assigned
⚓ B.  vessel's name
C.  vessel's home port
D.  maximum weight allowed

**070408/DS10034**                          **\*46 CFR 108.850 (b) (3)**

The light on a life jacket must be replaced _____.

A.  when the power source is replaced
B.  each year after installation
C.  every six months
⚓ D.  when it is no longer serviceable

**070409/DS10033**                          **\*46 CFR 180.78 (a) (2)**

The life jackets on all vessels shall be _____.

A.  inspected weekly
B.  worn at all times
⚓ C.  readily available
D.  tested yearly

**070410/DG00313**                    ***46 CFR 25.25-5**

With the exception of a Coast Guard approved commercial hybrid Personal Flotation Device (PFD), which type of life preserver must be carried for each person on board an uninspected passenger vessel?

⚓ A. Type I

B. Type II

C. Type III

D. None of the above

**070411/DS02219**        ***46 CFR 108.697; *46 CFR 160.53**

Each buoyant work vest must be _____.

⚓ A. U.S. Coast Guard approved

B. marked with the name of the vessel

C. equipped with a water light

D. All of the above

**070412/DS01066**        ***46 CFR 180.72 (c); *46 CFR 160.53**

Coast Guard approved buoyant work vests _____.

A. may be substituted for 10 percent of the required life preservers

B. should be stowed adjacent to lifeboats and emergency stations

C. may be used by boat crews and line handlers during lifeboat drills

⚓ D. should be used when carrying out duties near a weather deck's edge

**070413/DS01056**        ***46 CFR 180.72 (c); *46 CFR 160.53**

U.S.C.G. approved buoyant work vests are considered to be items of safety equipment and may be worn by members of the crew _____.

A. in lieu of life preservers during fire drills

B. in lieu of life preservers during boat drills

C. in lieu of life preservers during an actual emergency

⚓ D. when carrying out duties near a weather deck's edge

**070414/DS08662**        ***46 CFR 108.699; *46 CFR 160.53**

When may a work vest be substituted for a required life preserver?

A. To replace a damaged life preserver

B. For use during fire drills

C. For use during boat drills

⚓ D. At no time

**070415/DS01594**        ***46 CFR 35.03-10; *46 CFR 160.53**

Which statement is TRUE concerning buoyant work vests aboard tank vessels?

A. They may be worn while working on deck but not while working over the side.

⚓ B. They must be used only under supervision of a designated ship's officer.

C. They will be accepted for up to 10% of the required life preservers.

D. They may be worn during drills.

**070416/DS03052**                    ***46 CFR 180.78**

Which statement is TRUE concerning work vests on a small passenger vessel?

A. They may be worn during drills

B. They may be substituted for up to 10% of the required life jackets on board

C. They need not be an approved type

⚓ D. They must be stowed separately from approved life jackets

**IMMERSION SUITS**

**070417/DS00781**            **NVIC 5-86; *46 CFR 160.171-9**

How is the external flotation bladder of an immersion suit inflated?

A. It is inflated by a small $CO_2$ bottle that is automatically tripped when the front zipper is at the top of the zipper track.

B. It is inflated by a small $CO_2$ bottle that is manually tripped.

⚓ C. It is inflated by blowing through an inflation tube.

D. It inflates by sea water bleeding into the flotation bladder and reacting with a chemical therein.

**070418/DS09185**            **NPFVOA; *46 CFR 160.171-9**

The external flotation bladder of an immersion suit should be inflated _____.

A. only after two hours in the water

B. only after four hours in the water

C. before entry into the water

⚓ D. upon entry into the water

**070419/DS00849          NVIC 5-86; *46 CFR 160.171-9**

You are testing the external inflation bladder on an immersion suit and find it has a very slow leak. Which action should be taken?

A.  Replace the suit.

B.  Replace the inflation bladder.

⚓ C.  Take it out of service and repair in accordance with the manufacturer's instructions.

D.  Some leakage should be expected and a topping off tube is provided; no other action is necessary.

**070420/DS01006          *46 CFR 160.171-9 (h)**

An immersion suit must be equipped with a(n) _____.

A.  air bottle for breathing

B.  orange smoke canister

⚓ C.  whistle, light and retro reflective material

D.  sea dye marker

**070421/DS00856          NVIC 1-92; *46 CFR 160.171**

Which statement about immersion suits is TRUE?

A.  Immersion suits should be worn during routine work on deck to provide maximum protection.

B.  After purchasing, the suit should be removed from its storage bag and hung on a hanger where readily accessible.

⚓ C.  Immersion suits must have a PFD light attached to the front shoulder area.

D.  Small leaks or tears may be repaired using the repair kit packed with the suit.

**070422/DS10045          *46 CFR 160.171-9;**
**                        *46 CFR 160.171-11 (a) (4)**

Which is TRUE concerning immersion suits and their use?

A.  Only a light layer of clothing may be worn underneath.

⚓ B.  They provide sufficient flotation to do away with the necessity of wearing a life jacket.

C.  They should be tight fitting.

D.  A puncture in the suit will not appreciably reduce its value.

**070423/DS04262          *46 CFR 160.171-9 (m)**

Which statement about immersion suits is TRUE?

⚓ A.  Prior to abandonment, the suit allows body movement such as walking, climbing a ladder and picking up small objects.

B.  The immersion suit seals in body heat and provides protection against hypothermia for weeks.

C.  The suit is flameproof and provides protection to the wearer while swimming through burning oil.

D.  The wearer of the suit is severely restricted and requires twice the time to climb a ladder than without the suit

**070424/DS00965          *46 CFR 199.70 (c) (2)**

What statement about immersion suits is TRUE?

A.  Immersion suits should be worn while performing routine work on deck.

⚓ B.  No stowage container for immersion suits may be capable of being locked.

C.  During the annual maintenance, the front zipper should be lubricated using light machine oil or mineral oil.

D.  Any tear or leak will render the suit unserviceable and it must be replaced.

**070425/DS04254          *46 CFR 160.171-11 (b)**

Which statement about immersion suits is TRUE?

A.  The suit's oil resistance is such that it will be serviceable and be usable after exposure to gasoline or mineral spirits without needing to be specially treated.

B.  The suit seals in body heat and provides protection against hypothermia indefinitely.

C.  The suit is flameproof and provides protection to the wearer while swimming through burning oil.

⚓ D.  The suit must, without assistance, turn an unconscious person's mouth clear of the water within 5 seconds.

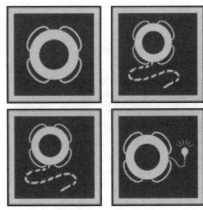

RING LIFEBUOYS

**070426/DS00648          *46 CFR 180.70 (b) (5)**

Ring life buoys used aboard a small passenger vessels on oceans or coastwise routes are required to be what color?

A.  White

B.  White or international orange

⚓ C.  Orange

D.  Any highly visible color easily seen from the air

**070427/DG00315**  ***46 CFR 180.70 (a) (1); *46 CFR 25.25-5 (d)**
A vessel must have one approved ring life buoy on board if its length is over how many feet?
A.  6 feet
B.  16 feet
⚓ C.  26 feet
D.  36 feet

**070428/DS02858**  ***46 CFR 180.70 (d)**
A 50-foot passenger vessel not limited to daylight operation is required to be equipped with at least _____.
⚓ A.  1 ring life buoy with a water light
B.  2 ring life buoys with a water light
C.  2 ring life buoys with 2 water lights
D.  3 ring life buoys with 2 water lights

**070429/DS03498**  ***46 CFR 199.630 (k)**
Your passenger vessel is 130 feet (40 m) long and is alternatively equipped for operating in river service. The number of ring life buoys required for the vessel is _____.
A.  2
⚓ B.  4
C.  6
D.  8

**070430/DS01096**  ***46 CFR 199.640 (i)**
What is the minimum number of ring life buoys required on board a 275-foot cargo vessel engaged in coastwise trade, under the alternatives for cargo vessels in a specified service?
⚓ A.  6
B.  8
C.  12
D.  14

**070431/DS03449**  ***46 CFR 199.640 (i)**
How many ring life buoys should a 700 foot cargo vessel, not subject to SOLAS, navigating the Great Lakes carry?
A.  12
⚓ B.  14
C.  18
D.  24

**070432/DG04059**  ***46 CFR 94.43-10 (a)**
A 750 foot passenger vessel operating on the Great Lakes, not subject to SOLAS regulations, is required to carry how many ring life buoys?
⚓ A.  24
B.  18
C.  12
D.  6

**070433/DS02153**  ***46 CFR 108.649 (a)**
On offshore drilling units each ring life buoy must be marked, in a contrasting color, with the unit's _____.
⚓ A.  name and port of registry
B.  owner and port of registry
C.  port of registry and identification number
D.  name and owner

## WATERLIGHTS

**070434/DG01388**  ***46 CFR 199.610 (b), 199.211 (b)**
If a passenger vessel navigating the Great Lakes is required to carry 8 life buoys, what is the allowable minimum number of these buoys that must have self-igniting lights attached?
A.  8
B.  6
⚓ C.  4
D.  2

**070435/DS00651**  ***46 CFR 180.70 (d)**
Small passenger vessels not limited to service during daylight hours must carry _____.
A.  a radar maintained in good operating condition
B.  a collision bulkhead
C.  a white 20 point anchor light
⚓ D.  at least one floating water light

LINE THROWING APPLIANCE

**070436/DS01146**  ***46 CFR 199.100**
Which vessel is NOT required to carry a rocket-type line throwing appliance?
⚓ A.  An oceangoing vessel of 140-GT
B.  A coastwise vessel of 550-GT
C.  An river-going vessel of 760-GT
D.  All of the above

**070437/DS03418**  ***46 CFR 199.170; *46 CFR 199.01**
Your 600-GT vessel must carry a line-throwing appliance if it is certificated for what type of service?
A.  river service
B.  Great Lakes service
⚓ C.  coastwise service
D.  None of the above

**070438/DS01116**      *46 CFR 160.40-4 (a)
Line throwing apparatus aboard ship must contain _____.

A. two rockets, one of which shall be the buoyant type
B. three rockets, one of which shall be the buoyant type
⚓ C. four rockets, two of which shall be the buoyant type
D. five rockets, two of which shall be the buoyant type

**070439/DS01176**      *46 CFR 199.170 (c)
Your vessel is required to have an impulse-projected line throwing appliance. The auxiliary line must _____.

A. be of a light color
B. be 250 meters in length
⚓ C. have a breaking strength of 9000 lbs
D. be made of synthetic material

**070440/DS01713**      MSRS
Line throwing equipment should NOT be operated _____.

A. during a rain storm
⚓ B. in an explosive atmosphere
C. near a liferaft canister
D. by other than licensed officers

**070441/DS03990**    *46 CFR 199.170; *46 CFR 199.180 (e)
What is a FALSE statement concerning the line throwing appliance on a vessel?
A. A drill on its use must be held once every three months.
B. The actual firing is at the discretion of the Master.
⚓ C. The auxiliary line must be of a light color.
D. The auxiliary line must be at least 1500 feet long.

**070442/DS10046**      MSRS
Which precaution should be taken when testing a line throwing gun?
⚓ A. Never remove the line from the rocket.
B. Fire it at an angle of approximately 90 degrees to the horizon.
C. Wear asbestos gloves.
D. All of the above

**070443/DS01164**      *46 CFR 199.180 (e)
A drill must be conducted in the use of the line throwing appliance at least once in every _____.
A. 2 months
⚓ B. 3 months
C. 4 months
D. 5 months

**070444/DS01700**      MSRS; *46 CFR 160.31;
     *46 CFR 160.40; *46 CFR 199.180 (e)
How often must the impulse-projected line throwing appliance be test fired?
A. Monthly
⚓ B. At the Master's discretion
C. Semiannually
D. Annually

**070445/DS01642**      MSRS
The Master or person in charge on a MODU shall insure that line throwing equipment is not operated _____.

A. during a rain storm
⚓ B. in an explosive atmosphere
C. near a lifeboat station
D. by other than senior rig personnel

**070446/DS10048**      *46 CFR 199.180 (e)
Which statement is TRUE concerning the testing of the line-throwing appliance?
A. It shall be fired at least once in every three months.
⚓ B. A drill in its use shall be held once in every 3 months.
C. Drills shall be held quarterly and it shall be fired annually.
D. No drills are required.

**070447/DS02141**      *46 CFR 109.213 (e)
How often is a drill on the use of the line throwing appliance required to be held on a mobile offshore drilling unit?
A. Once a month
B. Once a year
C. Once a week
⚓ D. Once every three months

**070448/DS04575**      MSRS
What precaution should be taken when testing a line throwing gun?
A. Wear asbestos gloves.
B. Fire it at an angle of approximately 90 degrees to the horizon.
⚓ C. Never remove the line from the rocket.
D. All of the above

### EMERGENCY POSITION INDICATING RADIOBEACON (EPIRB)

**070449/DS02137**                                                    **MRT**
Where would you find the FCC authorization for transmitting on your rig's EPIRB?
⚓ A. On the Ship Station License
B. On the side of the EPIRB transmitter
C. In the radio log
D. On the Certificate of Inspection

**070450/DS01599**                                    **SOLAS REG 7 (1.6.1)**
All self-propelled vessels on an international voyage must be equipped with how many Emergency Position Indicating Radio Beacons (EPIRB)?
⚓ A. One approved Category 1 EPIRB
B. Three approved Category 1 EPIRBs
C. One approved Class B EPIRB
D. Two approved Class B EPIRBs

**070451/DS00609**                                    **\*46 CFR 180.64**
Which small passenger vessel(s) is/are NOT required to carry a Category 1 406 MHz EPIRB?
A. A coastwise vessel whose route does not take it more than three miles from shore
B. A vessel operating on lakes, bays, sounds, and rivers
C. A vessel operating within three miles from the coastline of the Great Lakes
⚓ D. All of the above

**070452/DS00267**                                    **\*46 CFR 199.510**
Which type of EPIRB must each ocean-going ship carry?
A. Class A
B. Class B
C. Class C
⚓ D. Category 1

**070453/DS00257**                                    **\*46 CFR 199.610 (a)**
Which vessel greater than 100-GT is NOT required to have an EPIRB.
A. A sailing vessel
B. A fishing vessel
⚓ C. A non self-propelled vessel in tow
D. A towing vessel

**070454/DS04330**                                    **\*46 CFR 180.64**
Which vessel is required to carry a Category I, 406 MHz EPIRB installed to automatically float free and activate? (small passenger vessel regulations)
A. A vessel operating within 3 miles from the coastline in the Gulf of Mexico.
B. A vessel operating on the ocean within 5 miles from the coastline.
⚓ C. A vessel operating beyond 3 miles from the coastline of the Great Lakes.
D. A vessel operating exclusively on inland waters.

**070455/DS09397**            **MRT; \*PUB 117 1996 Ed. 4-14**
CATEGORY I EPIRB's transmit on frequencies that are monitored by _____.
⚓ A. orbiting satellites in space
B. commercial radio stations
C. private, commercial, and military aircraft
D. Both A & C

**070456/DS00473**                                    **\*46 CFR 180.64**
Each small passenger vessel that operates on the high seas, or beyond 3 miles from the coastline of the Great Lakes must have a Category 1 406 MHz EPIRB that _____.
A. is in good operating condition and is stowed near its charger
⚓ B. will float free and clear of a sinking vessel and automatically activate
C. is protected against all physical hazards
D. All of the above

**070457/DS03091**                                                    **MSRS**
When will the float-free emergency position indicating radio beacon be activated after abandoning ship?
⚓ A. Immediately after floating free
B. After about one hour when the salt water activates the battery
C. Only when keyed by the radar of another vessel
D. Only when daylight activates the photovoltaic cell

**070458/DS00227**                                                    **\*PUB 117**
The Emergency Position Indicating Radio beacon on a cargo vessel must be stowed _____.
A. in an inside passageway
B. in an approved bracket
C. so that it is accessible from the bridge of the vessel
⚓ D. so that it will float free if the vessel sinks

**070459/DS04174**                                    **\*46 CFR 109.208**
Each EPIRB shall be tested using the integrated test circuit and output indicator every _____.
A. week
B. two weeks
⚓ C. month
D. quarter

**070460/DS03062**                    ***46 CFR 185.728**
The Master of a vessel shall make sure the EPIRB is tested _____. (small passenger vessel regulations)
A. daily
B. weekly
C. every two weeks
⚓ D. monthly

**070461/DS00287**                    ***46 CFR 97.15-65**
The Master shall insure that the Emergency Position Indicating Radio beacon (EPIRB) is _____.
A. secured inside the wheelhouse
B. tested annually
⚓ C. tested monthly
D. secured in the emergency locker

**070462/DS00277**                    ***46 CFR 199.190 (e) (2)**
The vessel's Emergency Position Indicating Radio beacon (EPIRB) must be tested _____.
A. weekly
⚓ B. monthly
C. every 2 months
D. every 3 months

**SHIP'S DISTRESS SIGNALS**

**070463/DS00704**                                    **MRT**
Which radiotelephone transmission may be sent over channel 16?
A. Distress signal MAYDAY
B. Call to a particular station
C. A meteorological warning
⚓ D. All of the above

**LIFESAVING EQUIPMENT OPERATION**

**070464/DS00753**                                    **AMSM**
How should signal flares be used after you have abandoned ship and are adrift in a liferaft?
A. Immediately use all the signals at once.
B. Use all the signals during the first night.
C. Employ a signal every hour after abandoning ship until they are gone.
⚓ D. Use them only when you are aware of a ship or plane in the area.

**070465/DS09205**                                    **FVSM**
When you are firing a pyrotechnic distress signal, it should be aimed _____.
A. horizontally and directly abeam of your vessel
B. at the vessel whose attention you want to attract
C. into the wind
⚓ D. at greater than 60 degrees above the horizon

**070466/DS08783**                                    **FVSM**
When using a hand held smoke signal aboard a survival craft, you should activate the signal _____.
⚓ A. on the downwind side of the craft
B. on the upwind side of the craft
C. inside the craft
D. at the stern of the craft

**LIFESAVING/EMERGENCY EQUIPMENT**
**TESTS & INSPECTIONS**

**070467/DS00596**                    ***46 CFR 199.180 (d) (4)**
The Master of a cargo or tank vessel shall be responsible that each lifeboat, except those free-fall launched, is lowered to the water with crew and maneuvered at least once every _____.
A. week
B. month
⚓ C. three months
D. year

**070468/DS02088**                    ***46 CFR 199.180 (d) (5)**
If the OCMI has NOT granted an extension, free-fall lifeboats must be lowered into the water and launched with the assigned crew at least once every _____.
A. 3 months
⚓ B. 6 months
C. year
D. 2 years

**070469/DS02157**                    ***46 CFR 109.301 (e) (2)**
On offshore drilling units, each EPIRB or SART must be tested once every _____.
A. day
B. week
⚓ C. month
D. year

**070470/DS00556**                    ***46 CFR 199.190 (f) (1)**
All lifeboats, rescue boats, and rigid-type liferafts shall be stripped, cleaned, and thoroughly overhauled at least once every _____.
A. 6 months
⚓ B. year
C. 18 months
D. two years

**070471/DS02103*46 CFR 199.190 (f) (1); *46 CFR 97.15-45 (c)**
All lifeboats, rescue boats, and rigid-type liferafts shall
be stripped, cleaned, and thoroughly overhauled at least
once every _____.

⚓ A. year
B. 18 months
C. two years
D. 30 months

**070472/DS02193          *46 CFR 109.217 (e)**
On offshore drilling units, the lifeboats' fuel tanks must
be emptied and the fuel changed at least once every

_____.

⚓ A. 12 months
B. 24 months
C. 36 months
D. 48 months

**070473/DS01513          *46 CFR 199.190 (f) (2)**
Limit switches, winches, falls, etc. must be thoroughly
inspected at least every _____.
A. 2 months
B. 4 months
C. 6 months
⚓ D. year

## RULES & REGULATIONS FOR VESSEL INSPECTION

### PART 15 - MANNING REQUIREMENTS

**070474/DG01671**          ***46 CFR 15.501 (b)**
The number of certificated able seamen and lifeboatmen required on a vessel is determined by the _____.

A. International Maritime Organization
B. Corps of Engineers
⚓ C. Coast Guard
D. American Bureau of Shipping

**070475/DG03631**          ***46 CFR 15.501**
The number of certificated able seamen and lifeboatmen required on board is listed in the _____.

⚓ A. Certificate of Inspection
B. American Bureau of Shipping code
C. Muster List ("Station Bill")
D. Safety of Life at Sea Convention

**070476/DG00661**          ***46 CFR 15.501**
The number of certificated lifeboatmen required for a vessel is found on the _____.

⚓ A. Certificate of Inspection
B. Muster List ("Station Bill")
C. lifeboats
D. Register or Enrollment

### PART 91 - INSPECTION AND CERTIFICATION

**070477/DG02810ENCY. NAUT. KNOW.; *46 CFR 91.20-15**
Which document lists all the lifesaving equipment required for a vessel?

⚓ A. Certificate of Inspection
B. American Bureau of Shipping Classification Certificate
C. International Convention for the Safety of Life at Sea Certificate
D. Certificate of Registry

**070478/DG02601**          ***46 CFR 91.25; PETEX**
To determine the number of inflatable liferafts required on a vessel, you should check the _____.

A. Load Line Certificate
B. SOLAS Certificate
C. Stability Letter
⚓ D. Certificate of Inspection

### PART 108 - DESIGN AND EQUIPMENT

**070479/DS01643**          ***46 CFR 108.525 (a) (1) (i)**
On a MODU with lifeboats stowed in two different locations, if all the lifeboats are lost in one location then the remaining lifeboats must accommodate what percentage of the persons permitted on board?
A. 50%
B. 75%
C. 90%
⚓ D. 100%

**070480/DS02085**          ***46 CFR 108.525 (a) (2)**
An offshore drilling unit must have enough inflatable liferafts to accommodate at least what percentage of the persons allowed?
A. 20%
B. 30%
C. 50%
⚓ D. 100%

### PART 109 - OPERATIONS

**070481/DS02195**          ***46 CFR 109.323**
Who is charged with appointing persons to be in command of the lifeboats and (or) liferafts on a mobile offshore drilling unit?
A. Rig superintendent
B. Tool Pusher
C. Company man
⚓ D. Designated person in charge

### PART 160 - LIFESAVING EQUIPMENT

**070482/DS00682**          ***46 CFR 160.10-3**
How are lifelines attached to a life float?
A. By serving
B. By splicing one end of the line around the apparatus
⚓ C. Securely attached around the outside in bights no longer than three feet
D. With an approved safety hook or shackle

**070483/DS00649**          ***46 CFR 160.10-4 (f)**
The lifeline of a life float or buoyant apparatus shall _____.

A. be at least 3/8 inch diameter and properly secured around the sides and ends of the device
B. be festooned in bights not longer than three feet long
C. have a seine float in each bight unless the line is an inherently buoyant material
⚓ D. All of the above

**070484/DS00612**                    ***46 CFR 160.21-5 (b)**
The service life of distress signals must be not more than _____.
- A. forty two months from the date of manufacture
- B. thirty six months from the date of the last inspection
- C. twenty four months from the date of approval
- D. twelve months from the date of purchase

**070485/DS03016**                    ***46 CFR 160.21-5 (b)**
Hand held red flares expire 42 months from the date of manufacture. Floating orange smoke distress signals expire after how many months?
- A. 18 months
- B. 24 months
- C. 42 months
- D. 60 months

**070486/DS03056**                    ***46 CFR 160.21-5 (b)**
The service use of pyrotechnic distress signals measured from the date of manufacture shall be limited to a period of _____.
- A. 24 months
- B. 36 months
- C. 42 months
- D. 60 months

**070487/DS04070**          ***46 CFR 160.035-3 (m); WSM**
Motor-propelled lifeboats are required to be fitted with which of the following?
- A. Compartments for the storage of canned drinking water
- B. Ballast tanks to prevent the boat from capsizing
- C. An air starter on the diesel engine
- D. Auxiliary mechanical propulsion (Fleming gear)

**070488/DS10019**                    ***46 CFR 160.57-5 (c)**
By regulation, orange smoke distress signals will expire not more than how many months from the date of manufacture?
- A. 24 months
- B. 36 months
- C. 42 months
- D. 54 months

**070489/DG02030**          ***46 CFR 160; *46 CFR 199**
Safety equipment on board vessels must be approved by the _____.
- A. U.S. Coast Guard
- B. Safety Standards Bureau
- C. Occupational Safety and Health Administration (OSHA)
- D. National Safety Council

## PART 180 - LIFESAVING EQUIPMENT AND ARRANGEMENTS

**070490/DS01086**                    ***46 CFR 180.15 (d)**
Required lifesaving equipment on existing vessels may be continued in use on the vessel if _____.
- A. kept on board no more than 2 years
- B. inspected and serviced every 6 months
- C. destroyed if more than 5 years old
- D. maintained in good and serviceable condition

**070491/DS00567**                    ***46 CFR 180.25 (a)**
On small passenger vessels if an item of lifesaving equipment is carried but not required _____.
- A. the equipment must be approved by the Commandant
- B. it must be removed from the vessel as excess equipment
- C. it may remain aboard the vessel as excess equipment regardless of its condition
- D. it must be destroyed in the presence of a marine inspector

**070492/DS00627**                    ***46 CFR 180.68 (d) (e);
***46 CFR 160.37-6 (b); *46 CFR 160.21-5 (b)**
Distress flares and smoke signals for small passenger vessels _____.
- A. are not required aboard vessels on runs of less than 30 minutes duration
- B. must be Coast Guard approved and stowed in a portable, watertight container
- C. must be marked with an expiration date not more than 42 months from the date of manufacture
- D. All of the above

**070493/DS02859    *46 CFR 180.68 (a); *46 CFR 180.15 (f)**
For emergency communications, vessels operating on oceans, coastwise, or Great Lakes routes, on runs of more than 30 minutes shall carry in a portable watertight container at or near the operating station _____. (small passenger vessel regulations)
- A. six orange hand smoke distress signals
- B. six red hand flare distress signals
- C. one 3-cell flashlight
- D. six red hand flare distress signals and six orange hand smoke distress signals

**070494/DS02899** *46 CFR 180.68 (b); *46 CFR 180.15 (f)

All small passenger vessels operating on lakes, bays, sounds, or river routes on runs of more than 30 minutes are required to carry _____. (small passenger vessel regulations)

⚓ A. 3 red hand flare distress signals and 3 orange smoke hand distress signals

B. 8 red hand flare distress signals and 8 orange smoke hand distress signals

C. 6 red hand flare distress signals and 6 orange smoke hand distress signals

D. None of the above

**070495/DS02819** *46 CFR 180.68 (d)

Distress flares and smoke signals are not required on vessels operating on short runs. A "short run" is limited to _____. (small passenger vessel regulation)

A. water of less than 20 feet in depth

B. where land is always in sight

C. no more than 5 miles

⚓ D. about 30 minutes away from the dock

**070496/DS03059** *46 CFR 180.70

How many ring life buoys must a small passenger vessel, of less than 65 feet in length, carry?

⚓ A. 1

B. 2

C. 3

D. 4

**070497/DS02816** *46 CFR 180.70

When a lifeline is required to be attached to a ring life buoy it must be at least _____. (small passenger vessel regulations)

A. 30 feet long

⚓ B. 60 feet long

C. 90 feet long

D. 120 feet long

**070498/DS03019** *46 CFR 180.70 (d)

All vessels not limited to daylight service shall be fitted with a ring life buoy _____. (small passenger vessel regulations)

A. on the stern of the vessel

B. with a twenty fathom line attached

C. with no line attached

⚓ D. with a water light to be attached during nighttime operation

**070499/DS04232** *46 CFR 180.71 (a)

The number of approved adult life jackets that shall be carried is equal to _____. (small passenger vessel regulations)

A. 120% of the number of persons listed in the vessel's Certificate of Inspection

B. 90% of the number of persons listed in the vessel's Certificate of Inspection

C. 90% of the number of persons on board at the time

⚓ D. the number of persons on board at the time

**070500/DS03242** *46 CFR 180.71 (a), (b)

A vessel carrying passengers for hire shall have on board an approved life jacket _____. (small passenger vessel regulations)

A. for every passenger on board

⚓ B. for every person on board, plus 10% children's' life jackets

C. for every person on board, plus 10% additional on upper deck in box

D. or buoyant cushion for every person on board plus 10% for children

**070501/DS03202** *46 CFR 180.71 (a)

Which of these approved lifesaving devices must a small passenger vessel carrying passengers for hire carry for each person on board? (small passenger vessel regulations)

A. Buoyant cushion

⚓ B. Life jacket

C. Ring buoy

D. Buoyant vest

**070502/DS02976** *46 CFR 180.71 (b)

Aboard small passenger vessels the number of children's' life jackets carried must be at least what percentage of the total number of persons aboard?

A. 4%

B. 7.50%

⚓ C. 10%

D. 15%

**070503/DS03322** *46 CFR 180.71 (b)

If your vessel is certificated to carry 10 persons, including both adults and children, how many life jackets are you required to carry on board? (small passenger vessel regulations)

A. 11 adult

⚓ B. 10 adult and 1 child

C. 10 adult and 5 child

D. 10 adult

**070504/DS03284**                    ***46 CFR 180.71 (b)**
Unless the COI is endorsed for adults only, there shall be provided a number of approved life jackets suitable for children equal to at least _____. (small passenger vessel regulations)
A.  20% of the passengers carried
B.  10% of the total number of persons carried
C.  10% of the passengers carried
D.  20% of the total number of persons carried

**070505/DS02896**                    ***46 CFR 180.71 (b)**
Your vessel is certificated to carry 50 persons. You are required to have _____. (small passenger vessel regulations)
A.  50 adult life jackets
B.  40 adult life jackets and 10 child life jackets
C.  50 adult life jackets and 5 child life jackets
D.  50 adult life jackets and 2 child life jackets

**070506/DS02932**                    ***46 CFR 180.72 (b), (c)**
What is FALSE concerning the use of unicellular plastic foam work vests on small passenger vessels? (small passenger vessel regulations)
A.  They may be substituted for up to 50% of the required life jackets.
B.  They shall be of an approved type.
C.  They shall be stowed separately from required lifesaving equipment.
D.  They may be worn by crew members when working near or over the water.

**070507/DS03082**                    ***46 CFR 180.78**
On vessels subject to the provisions of 46 CFR Subchapter T, life jackets shall be _____.
A.  kept locked up at all times when underway
B.  stored in convenient places throughout the accommodation spaces
C.  inaccessible to passengers
D.  on the topmost deck of the vessel at all times

**070508/DS01950**                    ***46 CFR 180.78 (a) (2)**
The lifesaving equipment on all vessels shall be _____.
A.  inspected weekly
B.  stowed in locked compartments
C.  readily accessible
D.  tested yearly

**070509/DS02972**                    ***46 CFR 180.78 (b)**
Regulations require that approved buoyant work vests _____. (small passenger vessel regulations)
A.  may not be carried on inspected vessels
B.  may be substituted for 10% of the required life jackets
C.  shall be stowed in a place inaccessible to passengers
D.  shall be stowed separately from the required life jackets

**070510/DS03119**                    ***46 CFR 180.137 (f)**
Life floats and buoyant apparatus may be stowed in tiers, one above the other, to a height of not more than _____. (small passenger vessel regulations)
A.  3 feet
B.  4 feet
C.  5 feet
D.  6 feet

**070511/DS03018**                    ***46 CFR 180.175 (c)**
Each life float on an inspected vessel shall be fitted and equipped with _____. (small passenger vessel regulations)
A.  a lifeline, a painter, and one paddle
B.  a lifeline, a painter, and a water light
C.  two paddles, a light, and a lifeline
D.  two paddles, a light, a lifeline, a painter and pendants

**070512/DS08688**                    ***46 CFR 180.175 (c)**
Life floats must be equipped with _____. (small passenger vessel regulations)
A.  a sea anchor
B.  a signal mirror
C.  an EPIRB
D.  paddles

**070513/DS02938**                    ***46 CFR 180.175 (c)**
What equipment must be on a life float? (small passenger vessel regulations)
A.  Two paddles, a light, painter, lifeline and pendants
B.  Water-light, painter, and signal mirror
C.  Water-light and painter only
D.  Two paddles, painter, and six red flares

**070514/DS02978**                    ***46 CFR 180.175 (c)**
Which equipment is not required for a life float? (small passenger vessel regulations)
A.  Paddles
B.  Light
C.  Painter
D.  Compass

**070515/DS07648*46 CFR 180.175 (d); *46 CFR 180.15-5 (c)**
Buoyant apparatus are required to be fitted or equipped with all of the following equipment EXCEPT _____. (small passenger vessel regulations)
A. life lines
B. paddles
C. water lights
D. painters

**070516/DS03124 *46 CFR 180.175 (e) (1); *46 CFR 160.10**
On a life float or buoyant apparatus, the life line is _____. (small passenger vessel regulations)
A. secured around the sides and ends in bights of not longer than three feet
B. woven into a net and secured in the center of the float
C. used for securing unconscious persons to the sides
D. the lanyard for securing provisions

**070517/DS00734 *46 CFR 180.175 (e) (3) (i)**
On small passenger vessels painters fitted to life floats shall be at least _____.
A. 20.0 meters (65.5 feet) in length
B. 30.5 meters (100 feet) in length
C. 10 fathoms (60 feet) in length
D. 90 feet (27.5 meters) in length

**070518/DS00718 *46 CFR 180.175 (e) (3) (i) (ii)**
Painters fitted to life floats and buoyant apparatus with a capacity of 49 or less persons must _____.
A. be of manila rope or equivalent, not less than two inches in circumference and not less than four fathoms long
B. be 100 feet long and have a breaking strength of at least 1500 lbs.
C. be at least 100 feet long and have a breaking strength of 3,000 lbs.
D. be made of 90 feet of 3/8" nylon

**070519/DS02898 *46 CFR 180.175 (e) (3) (i)**
Painters on life floats shall be not less than _____. (small passenger vessel regulations)
A. 20 feet in length
B. 30 feet in length
C. 70 feet in length
D. 100 feet in length

**070520/DS00706 *46 CFR 180.175 (e) (3) (ii) (iii) (iv); *46 CFR 199.175 (b) (21)**
The painter on a life float or buoyant apparatus shall _____.
A. have a minimum breaking strength of 3,000 lbs. if the capacity of the lifesaving gear is 50 persons or greater
B. be resistant to ultraviolet sunlight deterioration
C. be stowed to pay out freely if the vessel sinks
D. All of the above

**070521/DS00699 *46 CFR 180.175 (e) (2)**
What is the minimum length of a life floats paddle on a small passenger vessel?
A. Three feet
B. Four feet
C. Five feet
D. Six feet

**070522/DS02822 *46 CFR 180.200 (c)**
Survival craft required on a steel small passenger vessel operating in cold water must _____.
A. have sufficient capacity for all persons on board the vessel in ocean service.
B. have sufficient capacity for at least 50% of all persons on board for vessels in ocean service
C. be only inflatable liferafts
D. international orange in color only for vessels in lakes, bays and sounds service

**070523/DS03022 *46 CFR 180.200 (c)**
Vessels operating in warm water whose routes are restricted to 20 miles from a harbor of safe refuge shall carry life floats or buoyant apparatus for not less than _____. (small passenger vessel regulations)
A. 25% of all persons on board
B. 50% of all persons on board
C. 75% of all persons on board
D. 100% of all persons on board

**070524/DS06402 *46 CFR 180.202 (a)**
Small passenger vessels in cold water ocean routes, that do not meet the standards for collision bulkheads or subdivision in subchapter S, must carry _____. (small passenger vessel regulations)
A. 100% inflatable buoyant apparatus
B. at least one hand fire pump
C. at least two EPIRBs
D. All of the above.

**070525/DS02942 *46 CFR 180.202 (a) (1)**
Vessels in ocean service shall carry _____. (small passenger vessel regulations)
A. life floats for 50% of all persons on board
B. buoyant apparatus for all persons on board
C. sufficient inflatable buoyant apparatus for all persons on board
D. life jackets for 50% of all persons on board

**070526/DS02902 *46 CFR 180.202 (a) (1)**
Vessels in ocean service shall carry sufficient life floats for _____. (small passenger vessel regulations)
A. 25% of all persons on board
B. 50% of all persons on board
C. 75% of all persons on board
D. 100% of all persons on board

**070527/DS05418**      *46 CFR 180.204

Small passenger vessels in coastwise service must carry approved _____.

A. life floats
B. inflatable buoyant apparatus
C. inflatable liferafts
⚓ D. Any of the above

**070528/DS02862**      *46 CFR 180.204 (a) (1)

A wooden small passenger vessel operating on a coastwise route in cold water shall carry sufficient inflatable buoyant apparatus for _____ or meet alternate requirements regarding collision bulkhead standards and the provision of life floats. (small passenger vessel regulations)

A. all persons aboard
⚓ B. 67% of the total number of persons permitted on board.
C. 50% of all persons aboard
D. 30% of all persons aboard

**070529/DS03435**      *46 CFR 180.204 (c)

Small wooden hull passenger vessels, whose routes are limited to coastwise warm water routes on the high seas, must carry approved life floats or buoyant apparatus _____.

A. for all persons on board
B. for not less than 67% of all persons permitted on board
⚓ C. for not less than 100% of all persons permitted on board
D. in place of ring life buoys

**070530/DS00749**      *46 CFR 180.208 (a) (1) Table; *46 CFR 180.200 (c)

Small passenger vessels on rivers routes in cold water must be provided with life floats of an aggregate capacity to accommodate _____.

⚓ A. at least 50% of all persons on board or meet certain construction standards
B. 25% of the crew and 50% of all passengers allowed to be carried
C. not less than 50% of all passengers on board at the time
D. All persons on board (100% of all passengers and crew)

**070531/DS00760**      *46 CFR 180.210 (a)

With certain exceptions a suitable rescue boat is required _____.

⚓ A. on most "T-Boats" more than 65 feet in length
B. on most "T-Boats" regardless of length
C. only on "K-Boats"
D. None of the above

PART 185 - OPERATIONS

**070532/DS02986**      *46 CFR 185.510 (a)

What must be mounted at a small passenger vessel's operating station for use by the Master and crew?

⚓ A. Emergency Instructions
B. A tide table for the area
C. Instructions on artificial respiration
D. The location of the first aid kit

**070533/DS03026**      *46 CFR 185.510 (a)

Who is required to prepare and post Emergency Instructions in a conspicuous place accessible to crew and passengers? (small passenger vessel regulations)

A. The builder of the vessel
⚓ B. The owner or Master of the vessel
C. The U.S. Coast Guard
D. The classification society

**070534/DS03058**      *46 CFR 185.604 (a) (2), (e), (g)

Life floats and buoyant apparatus shall be marked _____. (small passenger vessel regulations)

A. with the vessel's name
B. the number of persons capacity the device is equipped for
C. with the vessel's name on all paddles
⚓ D. All of the above

**070535/DS01269**      *46 CFR 185.604 (a) (1), (e)

Life floats and buoyant apparatus used aboard small passenger vessels shall be marked in clearly legible letters and numbers _____.

⚓ A. with the parent vessels name and the number of persons allowed
B. by a Coast Guard inspector after inspecting the equipment
C. by the American Bureau of Shipping (ABS), another recognized, authorized classification society or the vessels underwriters
D. by all of the above

**070536/DS03162**      *46 CFR 185.604 (b)

All life jackets and life buoys shall be marked with the vessel's name in letters at least _____. (small passenger vessel regulations)

A. 1/2 inch high
B. 1 inch high
⚓ C. Height not specified
D. 1-1/2 inches high

**070537/DS03122**                 ***46 CFR 185.604 (b) (2)**

All life jackets carried on board small passenger vessels are required to be marked _____. (small passenger vessel regulations)

⚓ A. with the vessel's name
   B. with the vessel's official number
   C. with the maximum weight to be held by the life preserver
   D. with the maximum serviceable life of the life preserver

**070538/DS02786**              ***46 CFR 185.604 (e), (g)**

Certain equipment aboard vessels, inspected under the small passenger vessel regulations, is required to be marked with the vessel's name. This includes _____. (small passenger vessel regulations)

   A. bunks, silverware, china, and glassware
   B. anchors, line, paint cans, and fuel drums
⚓ C. life jackets, life floats and paddles
   D. whistles, searchlights, navigation lights, and ship's bell

### PART 199 - LIFESAVING SYSTEMS FOR CERTAIN INSPECTED VESSELS

**070539/DS01940**                 ***46 CFR 199.70 (b) (2) (i)**

Life jackets should be stowed in _____.
   A. survival craft
   B. messrooms
⚓ C. readily accessible locations
   D. locked watertight containers

**070540/DG02598**                 ***46 CFR 199.70 (b) (v)**

Where, due to the arrangement of the vessel, lifejackets may become inaccessible, additional lifejackets shall be carried _____.
   A. for the people on bridge watch
   B. for the forward lifeboats
⚓ C. as determined by the OCMI
   D. for 50% of the crew of the vessel, not including those assigned to engineering duties

**070541/DS00636**                 ***46 CFR 199.155 (a)**

What is required by regulations concerning the stowage of lifeboats on cargo vessels?
⚓ A. Each lifeboat must have a launching appliance.
   B. Launching appliances must be of the gravity type.
   C. There may not be more than two launching appliances on the same deck.
   D. All of the above

**070542/DG02629**                 ***46 CFR 199.155 (d)**

Each open lifeboat carried on a vessel on an international voyage must have _____.
   A. hand-propelling gear
⚓ B. a davit span with at least 2 lifelines
   C. a mast and a sail
   D. a motor

**070543/DS01514**                 ***46 CFR 199.175**

"Thermal protective aids" are required for what percentage of the persons a survival craft is equipped to carry?
⚓ A. 10%
   B. 50%
   C. 75%
   D. 100%

**070544/DS01573**                 ***46 CFR 199.175 (b) (27)**

The searchlight on a survival craft must be capable of operating 3 hours continuously or 6 hours intermittently if operated in cycles of _____.
   A. 5 minutes on and 10 minutes off
   B. 10 minutes on and 5 minutes off
⚓ C. 15 minutes on and 5 minutes off
   D. 15 minutes on and 10 minutes off

**070545/DS01585**              ***46 CFR 199.175 (b) (40) (ii);**
                               ***46 CFR 160.58**

Up to two thirds of a survival crafts required drinking water may be produced by a manually-powered reverse osmosis desalinator if it can be done in _____.
   A. 12 hours
   B. 1 day
⚓ C. 2 days
   D. 4 days

**070546/DG03740**                 ***46 CFR 199.180 (g) (3)**

Instructions to the crew in the use of all the ship's lifesaving equipment shall be completed _____.
   A. before sailing
   B. within one week of sailing
   C. in one month and repeated quarterly
⚓ D. within any two month period

**070547/DS00624**                 ***46 CFR 199.190 (e) (2)**

Each EPIRB and SART for lifeboats shall be tested _____.
   A. weekly
   B. every 2 weeks
⚓ C. monthly
   D. every 3 months

**070548/DG02534**　　　　　　**\*46 CFR 199.640 (c)**

Great Lakes vessels, using liferafts, must have sufficient liferaft capacity on each side of the vessel to accommodate at least _____.

A.　50% of the persons on board

⚓　B.　100% of the persons on board

C.　100% of the persons normally assigned to those spaces

D.　150% of the crew

**070549/DG02679**　　　　　　**\*46 CFR 199.640 (d) (2)**

Great Lakes cargo vessels, having a liferaft stowed more than 100 meters from the bow or stern, must have at least how many liferafts?

A.　One

⚓　B.　Two

C.　Three

D.　Four

## DISTRESS & EMERGENCY SIGNALS

DISTRESS SIGNALS

**070550/RR04138**                                      **RULE 36**
BOTH INTERNATIONAL & INLAND A vessel may use any sound or light signals to attract the attention of another vessel as long as _____.
A.   white lights are not used
B.   red and green lights are not used
C.   the vessel signals such intentions over the radiotelephone
⚓ D.   the signal cannot be mistaken for a signal authorized by the Rules

**070551/RR04735**                                      **RULE 36**
BOTH INTERNATIONAL & INLAND One of the signals, other than a distress signal, that can be used by a vessel to attract attention is a(n) _____.
A.   red star shell
⚓ B.   searchlight
C.   burning barrel
D.   orange smoke signal

**070552/RR04113**                                      **RULE 36**
BOTH INTERNATIONAL & INLAND Which signal, other than a distress signal, can be used by a vessel to attract attention?
⚓ A.   Searchlight beam
B.   Continuous sounding of a fog signal apparatus
C.   Burning barrel
D.   Orange smoke signal

**070553/RR04733**                         **RULE 37; ANNEX IV**
BOTH INTERNATIONAL & INLAND A distress signal _____.
A.   consists of 5 or more short blasts of the fog signal apparatus
B.   consists of the raising and lowering of a large white flag
⚓ C.   may be used separately or with other distress signals
D.   is used to indicate doubt about another vessel's intentions

**070554/RR04102**                         **RULE 37; ANNEX IV**
BOTH INTERNATIONAL & INLAND A distress signal _____.
A.   consists of 5 or more short blasts of the fog signal apparatus
⚓ B.   may be used separately or with other distress signals
C.   consists of the raising and lowering of a large white flag
D.   is used to indicate doubt about another vessel's intentions

**070555/RR04182**                         **RULE 37; ANNEX IV**
BOTH INTERNATIONAL & INLAND Distress signals may be _____.
A.   red flares
B.   smoke signals
C.   sound signals
⚓ D.   Any of the above

**070556/RR04110**                         **RULE 37; ANNEX IV**
BOTH INTERNATIONAL & INLAND Continuous sounding of a fog whistle by a vessel is a signal _____.
A.   that the vessel is anchored
B.   to request the draw span of a bridge to be opened
⚓ C.   of distress
D.   that the vessel is broken down and drifting

**070557/RR04070**      **RULE 37; ANNEX IV**
BOTH INTERNATIONAL & INLAND You are underway and hear a vessel continuously sounding her fog whistle. This indicates the other vessel _____.
A. desires to communicate by radio
B. desires a pilot
⚓ C. is in distress
D. is aground

**070558/RR04098**      **RULE 37; ANNEX IV**
BOTH INTERNATIONAL & INLAND You can indicate that your vessel is in distress by _____.
A. displaying a large red flag
B. displaying three black balls in a vertical line
C. sounding four or more short rapid blasts on the whistle
⚓ D. continuously sounding the fog whistle

**070559/RR04125**      **RULE 37; ANNEX IV**
BOTH INTERNATIONAL & INLAND If you saw flames aboard a vessel but could see the vessel was not on fire, you would know that the _____.
A. crew was trying to get warm
⚓ B. vessel required immediate assistance
C. vessel was attempting to attract the attention of a pilot boat
D. vessel was being illuminated for identification by aircraft

**070560/RR04026**      **RULE 37; ANNEX IV**
BOTH INTERNATIONAL & INLAND Which is a distress signal?
A. Firing of green star shells
B. Sounding 5 short blasts on the whistle
C. Answering a one blast whistle signal with two blasts
⚓ D. A flaming barrel of oil on deck

**070561/RR04203**      **RULE 37; ANNEX IV**
BOTH INTERNATIONAL & INLAND If you hear the firing of a gun at one minute intervals from another vessel, this indicates that _____.
A. the gun is being used to sound passing signals
⚓ B. the vessel is in distress
C. all vessels are to clear the area
D. all is clear and it is safe to pass

**070562/RR04168**      **RULE 37; ANNEX IV**
BOTH INTERNATIONAL & INLAND When a vessel signals her distress by means of a gun or other explosive signal, the firing should be at intervals of approximately _____.
A. 10 minutes
⚓ B. 1 minute
C. 1 hour
D. 3 minutes

**070563/RR04227**      **RULE 37; ANNEX IV**
BOTH INTERNATIONAL & INLAND An orange flag showing a black circle and square is a _____.
A. signal indicating a course change
⚓ B. distress signal
C. signal of asking to communicate with another vessel
D. signal indicating danger

**070564/RR04057**      **RULE 37; ANNEX IV**
BOTH INTERNATIONAL & INLAND You see a vessel displaying the code flag "LIMA" below which is a red ball. The vessel is _____.
A. trolling
B. getting ready to receive aircraft
C. aground
⚓ D. in distress

**070565/RR04217**      **RULE 37; ANNEX IV**
BOTH INTERNATIONAL & INLAND A man aboard a vessel, signaling by raising and lowering his outstretched arms to each side, is indicating _____.
A. danger, stay away
B. all is clear, it is safe to pass
C. the vessel is anchored
⚓ D. a distress signal

**070566/RR04005**      **RULE 37; ANNEX IV**
BOTH INTERNATIONAL & INLAND Which signal is recognized as a distress signal?
A. Directing the beam of a searchlight at another vessel
⚓ B. A smoke signal giving off orange colored smoke
C. A whistle signal of one prolonged and three short blasts
D. International Code Signal "PAN" spoken over the radiotelephone

**070567/RR04248**      **RULE 37; ANNEX IV**
BOTH INTERNATIONAL & INLAND What is NOT a distress signal?
A. Red flares or red rockets
B. Continuous sounding of fog signaling apparatus
C. International Code Flags "November" over "Charlie"
⚓ D. Basket hanging in the rigging

**070568/RR04083**      **RULE 37; ANNEX IV; RULE 34 (d)**
BOTH INTERNATIONAL & INLAND All of the following are distress signals EXCEPT _____.
A. the continuous sounding of any fog signal apparatus
⚓ B. giving five or more short and rapid blasts of the whistle
C. firing a gun at intervals of about a minute
D. a barrel with burning oil in it, on deck

**070569/RR04446RULE 37; ANNEX IV; Lifesaving Signals**
BOTH INTERNATIONAL & INLAND Which is NOT
a distress signal?
A.  A continuous sounding with any fog signal
    apparatus
B.  A signal sent by radiotelephone consisting of the
    spoken word "Mayday"
C.  An International Code Signal of N.C.
⚓ D.  The firing of green star rockets or shells

**070570/RR04318RULE 37; ANNEX IV; Lifesaving Signals**
BOTH INTERNATIONAL & INLAND Which is NOT
a distress signal?
A.  Flames on a vessel
⚓ B.  Vertical motion of a white lantern at night
C.  Code flags "November" and "Charlie"
D.  Dye marker on the water

**070571/RR04269RULE 37; ANNEX IV; Lifesaving Signals**
BOTH INTERNATIONAL & INLAND All of the
following are distress signals under the Rules EXCEPT
_____.
⚓ A.  International Code Signal "AA"
B.  orange-colored smoke
C.  red flares
D.  the repeated raising and lowering of outstretched
    arms

### LIFESAVING SIGNALS

**070572/DS01054**                          AMSM; *H.O. 102
By day, the signal meaning, "This is the best place to
land" is a _____.
A.  vertical motion of a red flag
⚓ B.  vertical motion of a white flag or the arms
C.  white smoke signal
D.  white star rocket

**070573/DS00954**                              *H.O. 102
Which is the lifesaving signal for, "This is the best
place to land"?
A.  Red star rocket
B.  Orange smoke signal
⚓ C.  Green star rocket
D.  Horizontal motion of a flag

**070574/DS00994**                              *H.O. 102
The signal to guide vessels in distress, which indicates,
"This is the best place to land" is the _____.
A.  horizontal motion of a white flag
⚓ B.  letter K in Morse code given by light
C.  code flag S as a hoist
D.  firing of a white star signal

**070575/DS01014**                              *H.O. 102
Which signal would be used by a shore rescue unit to
indicate "Landing here highly dangerous"?
A.  The firing of a white star signal
⚓ B.  Horizontal motion with a white flag
C.  Vertical motion of a white light
D.  Code letter "K" by blinker light

**070576/DS10063**                              *H.O. 102
What does the lifesaving signal indicated by a
horizontal motion of a white light or white flare mean?
A.  "Landing here highly dangerous"
B.  "Negative"
C.  "Avast hauling"
⚓ D.  All of the above

**070577/DS01074**                      AMSM; *H.O. 102
Which one of the following signals is made at night by
a lifesaving station to indicate "Landing here highly
dangerous"?
⚓ A.  Horizontal motion of a white light or flare
B.  Vertical motion of a white light or flare
C.  White star rocket
D.  Vertical motion of a red light or flare

**070578/DS01004**                              *H.O. 102
The lifesaving signal used to indicate, "Landing here
highly dangerous" is _____.
A.  firing of a white star signal
⚓ B.  firing of a red star signal
C.  vertical motion of a red light
D.  code letter "K" given by light or sound signaling
    apparatus

**070579/DS00904**                              *H.O. 102
If you are on the beach and are signaling to a small boat
in distress that your present location is dangerous and
they should land to the left, you would _____.
A.  fire a green star to the left
B.  send the letter K by light and point to the left
C.  place an orange signal to your left as you signal
    with a white light
⚓ D.  send the code signal S followed by L

**070580/DS00934**                          MRT; *H.O. 102
The signal used with shore lifesaving equipment to
indicate, "Affirmative" is _____.
⚓ A.  vertical motion of the arms
B.  code signal "C" sent by light or sound signaling
    apparatus
C.  firing of a red star signal
D.  None of the above

**070581/DS01064**                                    **AMSM**
By day, the horizontal motion of a white flag, or arms extended horizontally, by a person on the beach indicates _____.
A. "Haul away"
B. "Tail block is made fast"
⚓ C. "Negative"
D. "Affirmative"

**070582/DS00964**                                    ***H.O. 102**
Which signal is used by a rescue unit to indicate, "Avast hauling"?
A. Firing of a green star signal
⚓ B. Firing of a red star signal
C. An orange smoke signal
D. Three white star rockets fired at one-minute intervals

**070583/DS01024**                                    ***H.O. 102**
The firing of a red star signal may mean _____.
A. "This is the best place to land"
B. "You are seen - assistance will be given as soon as possible"
C. "Tail block is made fast"
⚓ D. "Slack away"

**070584/DS00914**                                    ***H.O. 102**
What is the lifesaving signal for "You are seen - assistance will be given as soon as possible"?
A. Red star rocket
⚓ B. Orange smoke signal
C. Green star rocket
D. Vertical motion of a flag

**070585/DS01044**                          **AMSM; *H.O. 102**
What is the lifesaving signal for "You are seen - assistance will be given as soon as possible"?
A. Green star rocket
B. Red star rocket
⚓ C. Orange smoke signal
D. Horizontal motion of a flag

**070586/DS00924**                                    ***H.O. 102**
What is the lifesaving signal for "You are seen - assistance will be given as soon as possible"?
⚓ A. 3 white star signals
B. Horizontal motion with a white flag
C. Vertical motion of a white light
D. Code letter "K" by blinker light

**070587/DS00944**                                    ***H.O. 102**
The lifesaving signal indicating "You are seen - assistance will be given as soon as possible" is the _____.
A. vertical motion of white flags
B. vertical motion of a white light or flare
C. firing of a green star signal
⚓ D. None of the above

## LIFESAVING EQUIPMENT

### LIFEJACKET & WORK VESTS

**080001/DS02903*46 CFR 185.604 (b); *46 CFR 199.70 (b) (3)**
Life jackets should be marked with the _____.
A. maximum weight allowed
B. stowage space assigned
C. vessel's home port
⚓ D. vessel's name

**080002/DS02883**                    **\*46 CFR 199.70 (b) (2) (i)**
Life jackets should be stowed in _____.
A. survival craft
B. messrooms
⚓ C. readily accessible locations
D. locked watertight containers

**080003/DS02935**                    **\*46 CFR 160.006-2 (b)**
Which statement is TRUE concerning life jackets which are severely damaged?
⚓ A. They should be replaced.
B. They must be tested for buoyancy before being continued in use.
C. They can be repaired by a reliable seamstress.
D. They can be used for children.

**080004/DS03055**                    **\*46 CFR 160.06-2 (b)**
Which statement is TRUE concerning life jackets?
A. Buoyant vests may be substituted for life jackets.
⚓ B. Life jackets are designed to turn an unconscious person's face clear of the water.
C. Life jackets must always be worn with the same side facing outwards to float properly.
D. Lightly stained or faded life jackets will fail in the water and should not be used.

**080005/DS03057**                    **\*46 CFR 131.710**
Each buoyant work vest on an OSV must be _____.
⚓ A. Coast Guard Approved
B. marked with the name of the unit
C. equipped with a waterlight
D. All of the above

**080006/DS03053**                    **\*46 CFR 131.720 (c)**
On an OSV, when may a work vest be substituted for a required life jacket?
A. To replace a damaged life jacket
B. For use during fire drills
C. For use during boat drills
⚓ D. At no time

### IMMERSION SUITS

**080007/DS03003**                    **NVIC 5-86; WSM**
How is the external flotation bladder of an immersion suit inflated?
A. It is inflated by a small $CO_2$ bottle that is automatically tripped when the front zipper is at the top of the zipper track.
B. It is inflated by a small $CO_2$ bottle that is manually tripped.
⚓ C. It is inflated by blowing through an inflation tube.
D. It inflates by seawater bleeding into the inflation bladder and reacting with a chemical.

**080008/DS03051**                    **NVIC 5-86;**
**FISHING VESSEL SAFETY MANUAL**
The external flotation bladder on an immersion suit should be inflated _____.
A. only after two hours in the water
B. only after four hours in the water
C. before entry into the water
⚓ D. upon entry into the water

**080009/DS03035**                    **NVIC 5-86; WSM**
The external inflation bladder on an immersion suit should be inflated _____.
A. before you enter the water
⚓ B. after you enter the water
C. after one hour in the water
D. after you notice that your suit is losing buoyancy

**080010/DS03045**            **NVIC 5-86; *46 CFR 160.171-9**
You are testing the external flotation bladder of an immersion suit and find it has a very slow leak. Which action should be taken?
A. Replace the suit.
B. Replace the inflation bladder.
⚓ C. Contact the manufacturer for repair instructions.
D. Some leakage should be expected and a topping off tube is provided; no other action is necessary.

**080011/DS02970**                    *46 CFR 160.171-9

An immersion suit must be equipped with a/an

_____.

A. air bottle for breathing
B. orange smoke canister
⚓ C. whistle, light and retro reflective material
D. sea dye marker

**080012/DS03037**                         NPFVOA

An immersion suit should be equipped with a/an

_____.

A. air bottle for breathing
B. whistle and hand held flare
⚓ C. whistle, strobe light and reflective tape
D. whistle, hand held flare and sea dye marker

**080013/DS03001**                       NVIC 5-86;
                          *46 CFR 160.171-11 (b) (I); WSM

Which statement concerning immersion suits is TRUE?

A. Immersion suits should be worn during routine work on deck to provide maximum protection.
B. After purchasing, the suit should be removed from its storage bag and hung on a hanger where readily accessible.
⚓ C. Immersion suits must have a PFD light attached to the front shoulder area.
D. Small leaks or tears may be repaired using the repair kit packed with the suit.

**080014/DS02965**                      *46 CFR 160.171-9;
                          *46 CFR 160.171-11 (a) (4)

Which is TRUE concerning immersion suits and their use?

A. Only a light layer of clothing may be worn underneath.
⚓ B. They provide sufficient flotation to do away with the necessity of wearing a life jacket.
C. They should be tight fitting.
D. A puncture in the suit will not appreciably reduce its value.

**080015/DS04268**                    *46 CFR 160.171-9 (m)

Which statement about immersion suits is TRUE?

⚓ A. Prior to abandonment, the suit allows body movement such as walking, climbing a ladder and picking up small objects.
B. The immersion suit seals in body heat and provides protection against hypothermia for weeks.
C. The suit is flameproof and provides protection to the wearer while swimming through burning oil.
D. The wearer of the suit is severely restricted and requires twice the time to climb a ladder than without the suit.

**080016/DS04269**                    *46 CFR 160.171-9 (m)

Which statement about immersion suits is TRUE?

⚓ A. Prior to abandonment, the suit allows body movement such as walking, climbing a ladder and picking up small objects.
B. The immersion suit seals in body heat and provides protection against hypoglycemia for weeks.
C. The suit is flameproof and provides protection to the wearer while swimming through burning oil.
D. The wearer of the suit is severely restricted and requires 1.5 times more time to climb a ladder than without the suit.

**080017/DS03043**                   NVIC 5-86; WSM

Which statement concerning immersion suits is TRUE?

A. Immersion suits should be worn while performing routine work on deck.
⚓ B. After purchasing, the suit should be stowed in the storage bag in which it was received.
C. During the annual maintenance, the front zipper should be lubricated using light machine oil or mineral oil.
D. Any tear or leak will render the suit unserviceable and it must be replaced.

**080018/DS10047**                    *46 CFR 160.171-11 (b)

Which statement about immersion suits is TRUE?

A. The suit's oil resistance is such that it will be serviceable and be usable after exposure to gasoline or mineral spirits without needing to be specially treated.
B. The suit seals in body heat and provides protection against hypothermia indefinitely.
C. The suit is flameproof and provides protection to the wearer while swimming through burning oil.
⚓ D. The suit must, without assistance, turn an unconscious person's mouth clear of the water within 5 seconds.

**080019/DS04266**                    *46 CFR 160.171-11 (b)

Which statement about immersion suits is TRUE?

⚓ A. The suit must, without assistance, turn an unconscious person's mouth clear of the water within 5 seconds.
B. The immersion suit seals in body heat and provides protection against hypothermia for weeks.
C. The suit will still be serviceable after a brief (2-6 minutes) exposure to flame and burning.
D. The collar must be inflated before abandoning ship.

**080020/DS04270**      *****46 CFR 160.171-11 (b)**
Which statement about immersion suits is TRUE?
A. The primary color of the suit's exterior may be red, orange or yellow.
⚓ B. The suit must, without assistance, turn an unconscious person's mouth clear of the water within 5 seconds.
C. The suit is flameproof and provides protection to a wearer swimming in burning oil.
D. The suit may be stored in a machinery space where the ambient temperature is 160° F.

RIGID LIFERAFTS

**080021/DS03960**      *****46 CFR 160.027-2**
A rigid lifesaving device designed to support survivors in the water is a _____.
A. rigid liferaft
⚓ B. life float
C. inflatable liferaft
D. survival capsule

DISTRESS & EMERGENCY PROCEDURES

**080022/DS03143**      *****46 CFR 133.40**
The instructions for rescue boats and liferafts on an OSV must be approved by the _____.
A. lease operator
B. Minerals Management Service
⚓ C. Coast Guard
D. person-in-charge of the unit

**080023/DS03842**      *****46 CFR 180.25-10**
You must ensure that lifesaving equipment is _____.
A. locked up
⚓ B. readily accessible for use
C. inaccessible to passengers
D. on the topmost deck of the vessel at all times

**080024/DS03081**      **CHAPMAN**
A person who observes an individual fall overboard from an OSV should _____.
A. immediately jump into the water to assist the individual
⚓ B. call for help and keep the individual in sight
C. run to the radio room to send an emergency message
D. go to the control room for the distress flares

**080025/DS03078**      **SAFETY AT SEA; SURVIVAL GUIDE**
If you see an individual fall overboard, you should _____.
A. throw him/her a life buoy
B. hail "man overboard"
C. pass the word to the bridge
⚓ D. All of the above

**080026/DS04068**      **SURVIVAL GUIDE**
On board an OSV, the key to the most rapid and effective response to a man overboard situation is _____.
A. switching to hydraulic steering
B. a dedicated crew
C. good equipment
⚓ D. good communication

INFLATABLE LIFERAFTS

LIFERAFT CONSTRUCTION

**080027/DS03334**      **AMSM**
Inflatable liferafts are provided with _____.
A. a portable radio
B. an oil lantern
C. canned milk
⚓ D. a towing bridle

**080028/DS03335**      **AMSM; *****46 CFR 160.51-7**
Inflatable liferafts are provided with a _____.
A. jackknife
B. towing connection
C. lifeline
⚓ D. All of the above

**080029/DS03341**      **AMSM**
Inflatable liferafts are provided with a _____.
A. Very pistol
⚓ B. towing connection
C. portable radio
D. canned milk

**080030/DS03188**      **WSM**
The air spaces in the floor of an inflatable liferaft will provide protection against _____.
A. asphyxiation from $CO_2$
B. loss of air in the sides of the raft
C. rough seas
⚓ D. cold water temperatures

**080031/DS03204**                    **LBMAN; *46 CFR 160.51**
In accordance with SOLAS, the batteries that power interior lighting in inflatable liferafts can be made to last longer by _____.
A. unscrewing the bulb during the daylight
⚓ B. switching the light on only when necessary
C. taking no action as there is no way on saving power
D. taking no action as they shut off automatically in daylight

**080032/DS03203**                    **SURVIVAL AT SEA**
The inside light in an inflatable liferaft is turned on _____.
⚓ A. automatically as the liferaft inflates
B. with a switch near the boarding handle
C. at night because the light has a photosensitive switch
D. by screwing the bulb in after the raft inflates

**080033/DS03207**                                    **WSM**
The lights on the outside of the canopy of an inflatable liferaft operate _____.
A. by turning the globe clockwise
B. by a switch at the light
C. by a light sensor
⚓ D. automatically when the raft is inflated

**080034/DS03479**                                    **MIL**
A feature of an inflatable raft which helps keep people stationary in rough weather is _____.
A. lashings on the floor of the raft for the passenger's feet
B. straps from the overhead
⚓ C. lifelines on the inside of the raft
D. ridges in the floor of the raft

**080035/DS03231**                    **MIL; *46 CFR 160.51**
A lifeline must be connected to the liferaft _____.
A. at the bow
B. at the stern
C. in the middle
⚓ D. all around

**080036/DS03213**                    **MIL; *46 CFR 160.51-4 (b)**
A safety feature provided on all inflatable liferafts is _____.
A. overhead safety straps
B. built in seats
C. internal releasing hooks
⚓ D. water stabilizing pockets

**080037/DS03208**                                    **WSM**
Water pockets on the underside of an inflatable liferaft are for _____.
A. catching rain water
⚓ B. stability
C. easy drainage
D. maneuverability

**080038/DS03211**              ***46 CFR 160.51-4 (b); LBMAN**
What is placed on the underside of an inflatable liferaft to help prevent it from being skidded by the wind or overturned?
⚓ A. Ballast bags
B. A keel
C. Strikes
D. Sea anchor

**080039/DS03468**              **SAFETY AND SURVIVAL AT SEA**
Handholds or straps on the underside of an inflatable liferaft are provided _____.
⚓ A. to right the raft if it capsizes
B. to carry the raft around on deck
C. for crewmen to hang on to
D. to hang the raft for drying

**080040/DS03473**                                    **MIL**
In each inflatable rescue boat, what piece of equipment is provided to make quick, emergency, temporary repairs to a large hole in a raft?
A. No equipment is provided.
B. Glue and rubber patches
⚓ C. Several various-sized sealing clamps
D. Self-adhesive rubberized canvas patches

**080041/DS03478**                                    **MIL**
Puncture leaks in the lower tubes or bottom of an inflatable liferaft should FIRST be stopped by using _____.
⚓ A. sealing clamps
B. repair tape
C. a tube patch
D. sail twine and vulcanizing kit

**080042/DS03215**          **MIL; *46 CFR 199.175 (b) (16), (17);**
                                          ***46 CFR 160.51-7 (b) (8)**
The jackknife stored on an inflatable liferaft will always be located _____.
A. in one of the equipment bags
⚓ B. in a special pocket near the forward entrance
C. on a cord hanging from the canopy
D. in a pocket on the first aid kit

**080043/DS03469**  MIL; \*46 CFR 199.175 (b) (16), (17); \*46 CFR 160.51-7 (b) (8)

The knife on an inflatable liferaft will always be located _____.

A. in one of the equipment bags

⚓ B. in a special pocket on the exterior of the canopy

C. on a cord hanging from the canopy

D. in a pocket on the first aid kit

**080044/DS03467**  AMSM

An emergency sea anchor may be constructed by using _____.

A. a boat bucket

B. an air tank filled with water

C. an oar and canvas weighted down

⚓ D. All of the above

**080045/DS03457**  WHITTAKER

Using a sea anchor will _____.

⚓ A. reduce your drift rate

B. keep the liferaft from turning over

C. aid in recovering the liferaft

D. increase your visibility

**080046/DS03088**  CHAPMAN

Using a sea anchor with the survival craft will _____.

⚓ A. reduce your drift rate

B. keep the survival craft from turning over

C. aid in recovering the survival craft

D. increase your visibility

**080047/DS03456**  AMSM; \*46 CFR 199.175 (b) (27); \*46 CFR 160.19

When a sea anchor for a survival craft is properly rigged, it will _____.

A. completely stop the survival craft from drifting

⚓ B. help to prevent broaching

C. prevent the survival craft from pitching

D. prevent the survival craft from rolling

**080048/DS03453**  SAFETY AT SEA; SURVIVAL GUIDE

Your rescue craft is broken down and rolling in heavy seas. You can reduce the possibility of capsizing by _____.

A. shifting the rudder constantly

B. moving all personnel forward and low

C. moving all personnel aft

⚓ D. rigging a sea anchor

**080049/DS03894**  \*46 CFR 199.175

A liferaft with a capacity of 8 people used in ocean service is required by regulations to carry _____.

A. 8 liters of fresh water

B. 12 units of provisions

⚓ C. 12 liters of fresh water

D. 24 units of provisions

**080050/DS03472**  LBMAN

If you find an inflatable liferaft container with the steel bands still in place around its case, you should _____.

A. tell the Master

⚓ B. leave the bands in place

C. tell the Mate

D. remove the bands yourself

**080051/DS03251**  AMSM

A hydrostatic release mechanism for a liferaft _____.

A. must be wet before it will release

B. should be kept in a watertight cover except in an emergency

C. will inflate the raft in its cradle if operated manually

⚓ D. must be submerged to a certain depth to release automatically

**080052/DS03313**  AMSM; \*46 CFR 160.62

If the hydrostatic release mechanism for an inflatable liferaft is not periodically serviced and becomes inoperable, it will fail to _____.

A. set the water lights on immersion

B. release the dye marker from the liferaft

⚓ C. free the liferaft from the vessel

D. break the seal on the carbon dioxide cylinder

**080053/DS03497**  AMSM

What is the purpose of the hydrostatic release on an inflatable liferaft?

⚓ A. To release the raft from the cradle automatically as the ship sinks

B. To inflate the raft automatically

C. To test the rafts hydrostatically

D. None of the above

**080054/DS03294**  AMSM

What is the purpose of the liferaft hydrostatic release?

⚓ A. To release the liferaft from the cradle automatically as the ship sinks

B. To inflate the raft automatically

C. To test rafts hydrostatically

D. None of the above

**080055/DS03269**  AMSM

What is the purpose of the liferaft's hydrostatic release?

⚓ A. To release raft automatically as the ship sinks

B. To inflate the raft automatically

C. To test rafts hydrostatically

D. None of the above

**080056/DS03217**       **AMSM; *46 CFR 160.73**

Which of the devices listed will prevent an inflated liferaft from being pulled under by a vessel which sinks in water over 100 feet deep?

A. The hydrostatic release

B. A shear pin

C. A rottmer release

⚓ D. A weak link in the painter

**080057/DS03209**                  **WSM**

In the illustration shown, the floating sheath knife is indicated as item number _____. See DIAGRAM D014SA

A. 4

B. 8

C. 22

⚓ D. 23

**080058/DS03972**      **WATER SURVIVAL MANUAL**

The external recognition light can be seem up to two miles and is shown as item number _____. See DIAGRAM D014SA

⚓ A. 3

B. 5

C. 8

D. 23

**080059/DS03984**     **MIL; WSM; *46 CFR 160.51**

As shown in the illustration, item #8 would be a(n) _____. See DIAGRAM D014SA

A. recognition light

⚓ B. rain water catchment tube assembly

C. pressure relief valve

D. floating sheath knife

**080060/DS04316**      **WATER SURVIVAL MANUAL**

In the illustration shown, the righting strap is shown as item number _____. See DIAGRAM D014SA

A. 8

⚓ B. 9

C. 12

D. 16

**080061/DS03982**      **WATER SURVIVAL MANUAL**

In the illustration shown, the external lifelines are shown as item number _____. See DIAGRAM D014SA

A. 1

B. 8

⚓ C. 12

D. 16

**080062/DS03976**      **WATER SURVIVAL MANUAL**

In the illustration, which item number correctly identifies the ballast bags? See DIAGRAM D014SA

A. 2

B. 12

⚓ C. 13

D. 22

**080063/DS03970**      **WATER SURVIVAL MANUAL**

In the illustration, the sea painter is number _____. See DIAGRAM D014SA

A. 1

B. 12

⚓ C. 16

D. 18

**080064/DS04069**      **WATER SURVIVAL MANUAL**

In the illustration, the sea anchor is number _____. See DIAGRAM D014SA

A. 1

B. 12

C. 14

⚓ D. 18

**080065/DS05154**               **AMSM**

The sea anchor shown as item number 18 will NOT _____. See DIAGRAM D014SA

A. check the liferaft's way

B. keep the liferaft end on to the sea

C. reduce the possibility of capsizing or broaching

⚓ D. right the raft if it inflates inverted

**080066/DS04320**      **WATER SURVIVAL MANUAL**

In the illustration shown, the towing connection is shown as item number _____. See DIAGRAM D014SA

A. 7

B. 9

⚓ C. 19

D. 21

**080067/DS03979**      **WATER SURVIVAL MANUAL**

In the illustration shown, where would you find the knife? See DIAGRAM D014SA

⚓ A. 23

B. 21

C. 8

D. 4

**080068/DS03988**     **MIL; WSM; *46 CFR 160.51**

In the illustration shown, the weak link is item number _____. See DIAGRAM D015SA

⚓ A. 8

B. 6

C. 4

D. 1

## LIFERAFT INSPECTION

**080069/DS03488**                                         **WSM**
Who should inspect and test an inflatable liferaft?
A.   The person in charge
⚓ B.   An approved servicing facility
C.   Shipyard personnel
D.   A certificated lifeboatman

**080070/DS03489**                                        **AMSM**
If the hydrostatic release mechanism for an inflatable liferaft is not periodically serviced and becomes inoperative, it will NOT _____.
A.   set the water lights on immersion
B.   release the dye-marker from the liferaft
⚓ C.   free the liferaft from a sinking vessel
D.   break the seal on the carbon dioxide cylinder

## LIFERAFT OPERATIONS

**080071/DS03436**                                       **LBMAN**
After launching, an inflatable raft should be kept dry inside by _____.
A.   opening the automatic drain plugs
B.   draining the water pockets
C.   using the electric bilge pump
⚓ D.   using the bailers and cellulose sponge

**080072/DS03357**                                       **LBMAN**
What must be carried out in order to launch and inflate an inflatable liferaft?
A.   Pull on the hydrostatic release, pull on the sea painter.
⚓ B.   Push on the hydrostatic release, pull on the sea painter.
C.   Push on the hydrostatic release, push on the sea painter.
D.   Pull on the hydrostatic release, push on the sea painter.

**080073/DS03416**                            **\*46 CFR 199.180**
The instructions for the launching of lifeboats and liferafts must be approved by the _____.
A.   lease operator
B.   Minerals Management Service
⚓ C.   Coast Guard
D.   person-in-charge of the unit

**080074/DS03367**                              **AMSM; LBMAN;**
                                       **\*46 CFR 160.51-7 (b) (8)**
After a liferaft is launched, the operating cord _____.
⚓ A.   serves as a sea painter
B.   detaches automatically
C.   is used to rig the boarding ladder
D.   is cut immediately as it is of no further use

**080075/DS03406**                                        **AMSM**
After having thrown the liferaft and stowage container into the water, the liferaft is inflated by _____.
⚓ A.   pulling on the painter line
B.   forcing open the container which operates the $CO_2$
C.   hitting the hydrostatic release
D.   using the hand pump provided

**080076/DS03353**                                       **LBMAN**
An inflatable liferaft can be launched by _____.
A.   the float free method only
B.   kicking the hydrostatic release
⚓ C.   throwing the entire container overboard, then pulling on the operating cord to inflate the raft
D.   removing the securing straps

**080077/DS03366**                                        **AMSM**
An inflatable liferaft is floating in its container, attached to the ship by its painter, as the ship is sinking rapidly. Which action should be taken with respect to the liferaft container?
A.   Cut the painter line so that it will not pull the liferaft container down.
B.   Swim away from the container so that you will not be in danger as it goes down.
⚓ C.   Take no action as the pull on the painter will cause the liferaft to inflate and open the container.
D.   Manually open the container and inflate the liferaft with the hand pump.

**080078/DS03409**                                        **AMSM**
To launch a liferaft by hand, you should _____.
A.   cut the casing bands, throw the raft over the side and it will inflate by itself
B.   detach the operating cord, throw the liferaft over the side and it will then inflate
C.   cut the casing bands, throw the raft over the side and pull the operating cord
⚓ D.   throw the liferaft over the side and pull the operating cord

**080079/DS03365**                       **AMSM; \*46 CFR 131.530**
What is the correct procedure to follow when launching an inflatable liferaft by hand from an OSV?
A.   Connect the float free link to the vessel.
⚓ B.   Pull the painter from the container and make it fast to the cleat provided.
C.   Open the canopy relief valves.
D.   Remove the raft from the container to permit complete inflation.

**080080/DS03407**                    **AMSM**

The most important thing to remember when launching an inflatable liferaft by hand is to _____.

A. open the $CO_2$ inflation valve

B. open the raft container

⚓ C. ensure that the operating cord is secured to the vessel

D. inflate the raft on the vessel, then lower it over the side

**080081/DS03355**          **AMSM; *46 CFR 160.73**

The sea painter of an inflatable liferaft should be _____.

A. free running on deck

B. faked out next to the case

⚓ C. secured to a permanent object on deck via a weak link

D. stowed near the raft

**080082/DS03345**                    **AMSM**

When launching an inflatable liferaft, you should make sure that the operating cord is _____.

⚓ A. fastened to some substantial part of the vessel

B. not fastened to anything

C. secured to the hydrostatic release

D. fastened to the raft container

**080083/DS03439**                    **AMSM**

An inflatable liferaft should be manually released from its cradle by _____.

A. cutting the straps that enclose the container

B. removing the rubber sealing strip from the container

C. loosening the turnbuckle on the securing strap

⚓ D. pushing the button on the hydrostatic release

**080084/DS03363**                    **LBMAN**

What must be carried out in order to manually launch an inflatable liferaft not designed for float-free operation?

A. It will be easily launched by simply breaking the weak link.

⚓ B. Depress the hydrostatic release button.

C. It is easily launched by cutting the container securing straps.

D. It is only necessary to attach the weak link to the vessel.

**080085/DS03346**                    **WHITTAKER**

An inflatable liferaft is thrown into the water from a sinking vessel. Which action occurs automatically after the painter trips the $CO_2$ bottles to inflate the raft?

⚓ A. The sea anchor is deployed.

B. The floor inflates.

C. If upside down, the raft will right itself.

D. The painter detaches from the raft.

**080086/DS03417**                    **WSM**

Which statement is TRUE concerning an inflatable liferaft?

A. The floor may be inflated for insulation from cold water.

B. Crew members may jump into the raft without damaging it.

C. The raft may be boarded before it is fully inflated.

⚓ D. All of the above

**080087/DS03351**                    **LBMAN**

In good weather, you should deploy the sea anchor from the liferaft to _____.

A. keep the liferaft from capsizing

B. navigate against the current

C. keep personnel from getting seasick

⚓ D. stay in the general location

## RESCUE BOATS

### RESCUE BOAT EQUIPMENT

**080088/DS03556**          **\*46 CFR 199.175 (b) (6)**

The normal equipment of every rescue boat shall include _____.

⚓ A. compass

B. one 50 meter line

C. one can opener

D. All of the above

**080089/DS03559  \*46 CFR 133.175; SOLAS Regulation 47**

The rescue boat on an OSV is not required to carry a _____.

⚓ A. fishing kit

B. searchlight

C. sea anchor

D. radar reflector

**080090/DS03566**          **\*46 CFR 199.175 (b) (20);**
          **\*46 CFR 199.175 (b) (14); \*46 CFR 199.175 (b) (11)**

The normal equipment of every rescue boat shall include _____.

A. buoyant oars

B. one 50 meter line

C. one first aid kit

⚓ D. All of the above

**080091/DS03562**                              ***46 CFR 133.110***
The Master or person-in-charge of an OSV shall insure that each deck from which rescue boats are launched is _____.

A. surfaced with a nonskid texture
B. roped off to prevent unnecessary access
⚓ C. kept clear of any obstructions that would interfere with launching
D. posted with a list of persons assigned to the rescue boat

**080092/DS03097**                                         **WSM**
When retrieving the survival craft, the winch operator should stop the winch and check _____.

A. that all personnel are seated in the craft
⚓ B. that the cable has not jumped any grooves on the drum
C. which way the wind is blowing
D. the hydraulic fuel level before lifting

**080093/DS03095**                                         **WSM**
While retrieving the survival craft, the engine should be stopped _____.

⚓ A. when the craft clears the water
B. when the cable has been attached
C. on approach to the platform
D. at the embarkation

**080094/DS03558**              **AMSM; LBMN; *46 CFR 131.530**
Limit switches are located on the survival craft winch systems for OSVs to _____.

⚓ A. stop the winch just before the survival craft reaches final stowage position
B. limit the amount of cable on the drum
C. limit the ascent rate
D. stop the winch in case the craft's weight exceeds the load lift limit

**080095/DS03564**           **SEATECH; *46 CFR 199.175 (b) (21)**
The sea painter of a rescue boat should be led _____.

⚓ A. forward and outboard of all obstructions
B. forward and inboard of all obstructions
C. up and down from the main deck
D. to the foremost point on the vessel

### RESCUE BOAT OPERATIONS

**080096/DS03951**                                       **AMSM**
All personnel on board a vessel should be familiar with the rescue boat's _____.

⚓ A. boarding and operating procedure
B. maintenance schedules
C. navigational systems
D. fuel consumption rates

**080097/DS03569**                                   **WHITTAKER**
If help has not arrived in 10-12 hours after abandoning a vessel in a rescue boat, you should _____.

A. go in one direction until the fuel runs out
B. steer a course for the nearest land
C. steer a course for the nearest sea lane
⚓ D. shut down the engines if installed and put out the sea anchor

**080098/DS03586   SAFETY AT SEA; SURVIVAL GUIDE**
A person has fallen overboard and is being picked up with a rescue boat. If the person appears in danger of drowning, the rescue boat should be maneuvered to make _____.

A. an approach from leeward
B. an approach from windward
⚓ C. the most direct approach
D. an approach across the wind

**080099/DS03585   SAFETY AT SEA; SURVIVAL GUIDE**
When a man who has fallen overboard is being picked up by a rescue boat, the boat should normally approach with the wind _____.

A. astern and the victim just off the bow
B. ahead and the victim just off the bow
C. just off the bow and the victim to windward
⚓ D. just off the bow and the victim to leeward

**080100/DS03950   SAFETY AT SEA; SURVIVAL GUIDE**
You are picking up a conscious person that has fallen overboard. Recovery is easier if you approach with the _____.

⚓ A. victim to leeward
B. victim to windward
C. wind on your port side
D. wind on your starboard side

**080101/DS03588**                              ***46 CFR 131.530***
For the purpose of training and drills, if reasonable and practicable, rescue boats on an OSV must be launched with their assigned crew _____.

A. once a week
⚓ B. once a month
C. once a year
D. twice a year

## EMERGENCY & DISTRESS SIGNALS

### ABANDON SHIP SIGNAL

**080102/DS03770**          **\*46 CFR 35.10-5**
The abandon ship signal is _____.
- A. a continuous ringing of general alarm bells for at least 10 seconds
- B. a continuous ringing of the general alarm, and sounding of the ship's whistle
- ⚓ C. more than 6 short blasts and 1 long blast of the ship's whistle and the same signal on the general alarm bells
- D. a continuous sounding of the ship's whistle

**080103/DS03774**     **\*46 CFR 35.10-5; \*46 CFR 97.13-15**
The signal given to commence lowering the lifeboats is _____.
- A. 3 short blasts of the ship's whistle
- ⚓ B. 1 short blast of the ship's whistle
- C. 3 long blasts of the ship's whistle
- D. 1 long blast of the ship's whistle

**080104/DS03879**     **\*46 CFR 35.10-5; \*46 CFR 97.13-15**
The signal given to commence lowering the lifeboats is _____.
- ⚓ A. 1 short blast on the ship's whistle
- B. 3 short blasts on the ship's whistle
- C. 3 long blasts on the ship's whistle
- D. 1 long blast on the ship's whistle

**080105/DS03767**          **\*46 CFR 35.10-5**
When whistle signals are used for launching lifeboats, one short blast means _____.
- A. "use the float-free method only"
- ⚓ B. "lower all boats"
- C. "raise all boats"
- D. "drill is over, secure all boats"

### FIRE & EMERGENCY SIGNAL

**080106/DS03789**        **\*46 CFR 131.535**
The signal for a fire emergency on an OSV is _____.
- A. a 30 second on 30 second off alternating signal
- ⚓ B. the continuous blast of the ships whistle for not less than 10 seconds supplemented by the continuous ringing of the general alarm bells for not less than 10 seconds
- C. an intermittent ringing of the general alarm for not less than ten seconds
- D. announced over the PA system

**080107/DS03769**           **AMSM**
You hear the general alarm and ship's whistle sound for over 10 seconds. Traditionally, this is the signal for _____.
- A. abandon ship
- B. dismissal from fire and emergency stations
- ⚓ C. fire and emergency
- D. man overboard

**080108/DS03788**    **\*46 CFR 35.10-5; \*46 CFR 97.13-15**
When you hear three short blasts on the ship's whistle and the same signal on the general alarm bells, you _____.
- A. are required to be at your liferaft
- ⚓ B. are dismissed from drills
- C. should point to the man overboard
- D. should start the fire pump

**080109/DS03790**        **\*46 CFR 35.10-5 (a)**
While reading the muster list you see that "3 short blasts on the whistle and three short rings on the general alarm bell bells" is the signal for _____.
- A. abandon ship
- ⚓ B. dismissal from fire and emergency stations
- C. fire and emergency
- D. man overboard

## PRINCIPLES OF SURVIVAL AT SEA

### SURVIVAL PROCEDURES

**080110/DS03804**        **\*46 CFR 131.350**
All OSV personnel should be familiar with survival craft _____.
- ⚓ A. boarding and operating procedures
- B. maintenance schedule
- C. navigational systems
- D. fuel consumption rates

**080111/DS03810**           **WHITTAKER**
If help has not arrived in 10-12 hours after having abandoned an OSV in a survival craft, you should _____.
- A. go in one direction until the fuel runs out
- B. plot course for the nearest land
- C. take a vote on the direction in which to go
- ⚓ D. shutdown the engines and put out the sea anchor

**080112/DS03800**      **MSRS; AMSM; LBMN**
If you have to jump in the water when abandoning ship, your legs should be _____.
- A. spread apart as far as possible
- B. held as tightly against your chest as possible
- C. in a kneeling position
- ⚓ D. extended straight down and crossed at the ankles

**080113/DS03914**　　　　　　**MSRS; AMSM; LBMN**

If you must jump from a vessel, the correct posture includes _____.

⚓ A. holding down the life preserver against the chest with one arm crossing the other, covering the mouth and nose with a hand, and feet together

B. knees bent and held close to the body with both arms around legs

C. body straight and arms held tightly at the sides for feet first entry into the water

D. both hands holding the life preserver below the chin with knees bent and legs crossed

**080114/DS03799**　　　　　　**AMSM; LBMN**

With no alternative but to jump from an OSV, the correct posture should include _____.

⚓ A. holding down the lifejacket against the chest with one arm, crossing the other, covering the mouth and nose with a hand, and keeping the feet together

B. knees bent and held close to the body with both arms around legs

C. body straight and arms held tightly at the sides for a feet first entry into the water

D. both hands holding the lifejacket below the chin with knees bent and legs crossed

**080115/DS03776**　　　　　　**WSM**

If you continue to wear extra clothing when entering the water after abandoning your vessel, it will _____.

A. weigh you down

⚓ B. preserve body heat

C. reduce your body heat

D. make it more difficult to breathe

**080116/DS03926**　　　　　　**MSRS**

To keep injured survivors warm in the water after abandoning ship, they should _____.

⚓ A. be placed in the middle of a small circle formed by the other survivors in the water

B. float on their backs with their arms extended for maximum exposure to the air

C. remove their life preservers and hold on to the uninjured survivors

D. sip water at intervals of fifteen minutes

**080117/DS03922**　　　　　　**WSM**

You have abandoned ship and are in an inflatable raft that has just inflated. You hear a continuous hissing coming from a fitting in a buoyancy tube. What is the cause of this?

A. The saltwater is activating the batteries of the marker lights on the canopy.

B. The inflation pump is in automatic operation to keep the tubes fully inflated.

C. A deflation plug is partially open allowing the escape of $CO_2$.

⚓ D. Excess inflation pressure is bleeding off and should soon stop.

**080118/DS03794**　　　　　　**MSRS; AMSM; LBMN**

During an abandonment or drill, the first person to arrive at the survival craft should _____.

A. pass out food and water to personnel

B. open the doors and start the sprinkler system

C. activate the emergency release handle

⚓ D. open the doors and prepare the craft for boarding

**080119/DS03768　NVIC 2-92; SIU SURVIVAL MANUAL**

What is one of the FIRST actions you should take after abandoning and clearing away from a vessel?

⚓ A. Identify the person in charge.

B. Gather up useful floating objects.

C. Prepare for arrival of rescue units.

D. Arrange watches and duties.

**080120/DS03809**　　　　　　**SURVIVAL AT SEA**

Provided every effort is used to produce, as well as preserve body moisture content by avoiding perspiration, how long is it normally possible to survive without stored quantities of water?

A. Up to 3 days

⚓ B. 8 to 14 days

C. 15 to 20 days

D. 25 to 30 days

**080121/DS03936**　　**NVIC 2-92; LIFERAFT SURVIVAL;**
　　　　　　　　　　　　　　**SURVIVAL GUIDE**

After abandoning ship which action should be taken IMMEDIATELY upon entering a liferaft?

A. Open equipment pack.

B. Issue anti-seasickness medicine.

⚓ C. Get clear of the ship.

D. Dry the liferaft floor and inflate.

**080122/DS03939**　　**NVIC 2-92; LIFERAFT SURVIVAL**

You board an inflatable liferaft that has been hand launched from a sinking vessel. What should you do FIRST after everyone is onboard the liferaft?

⚓ A. Cut the painter.

B. Operate the radio equipment.

C. Open the equipment pack.

D. Ventilate the liferaft of $CO_2$.

**080123/DS03932** NVIC 2-92; WSM; SURVIVAL GUIDE
You have hand launched an inflatable liferaft. What should be one of your FIRST actions after all persons have boarded the liferaft?
A. Open the equipment pack.
B. Inflate the liferaft floor.
C. Decide on food and water rations.
⚓ D. Cut the sea painter and clear the vessel.

**080124/DS03956** AMSM
Your ship is sinking rapidly. A container containing an inflatable liferaft has bobbed to the surface upon functioning of the hydrostatic release. Which action should you take?
A. Cut the painter line so it will not pull the liferaft container down.
B. Swim away from the container so you will not be in danger as it goes down.
⚓ C. Take no action because the painter will cause the liferaft to inflate and open the container.
D. Manually open the container and inflate the liferaft with the hand pump.

**080125/DS03929** NVIC 2-29; SURVIVAL GUIDE; LIFERAFT SURVIVAL
What is one of the FIRST things you would do on boarding an inflatable liferaft?
A. Open equipment pack.
B. Post a lookout.
C. Issue anti-seasickness medicine.
⚓ D. Pick up other survivors.

**080126/DS03796** WSM
Which of the following steps should normally be taken first by those who have boarded a liferaft in an emergency situation?
A. Ration food and water supplies
⚓ B. Search for survivors
C. Determine position and closest point of land
D. Check pyrotechnic supplies

**080127/DS03930** NVIC 2-92; LIFERAFT SURVIVAL
You have abandoned your vessel. You are in a liferaft and have cleared away from your vessel. One of your FIRST actions should be to _____.
A. take measures to maintain morale
B. prepare and use radio equipment
C. identify the person in charge of liferaft
⚓ D. search for survivors

**080128/DS03806** SAFETY AND SURVIVAL AT SEA
A liferaft which has inflated bottom-up on the water _____.
⚓ A. should be righted by standing on the carbon dioxide cylinder, holding the righting straps and leaning backwards
B. should be righted by standing on the life line, holding the righting straps leaning backwards
C. will right itself when the canopy tube inflates
D. must be cleared of the buoyant equipment before it will right itself

**080129/DS03916** MIL
If an inflatable liferaft inflates upside down, you can right it by _____.
A. pushing up on one side
⚓ B. standing on the $CO_2$ bottle, holding the bottom straps, and throwing your weight backwards
C. getting at least three or four men to push down on the side containing the $CO_2$ cylinder
D. doing nothing; it will right itself after the canopy supports inflate

**080130/DS03952** SAFETY AND SURVIVAL AT SEA
If an inflatable liferaft is overturned, it may be righted by _____.
A. filling the stabilizers on one side with water
B. releasing the $CO_2$ cylinder
C. pushing up from under one end
⚓ D. standing on the inflating cylinder and pulling on the straps on the underside of the raft

**080131/DS03953** SHIP'S MANUAL OF INFLATABLE LIFERAFT
To turn over a liferaft that is floating upside down, you should pull on the _____.
A. canopy
B. manropes
C. sea painter
⚓ D. righting lines

**080132/DS03779** WSM
If more than one liferaft is manned after the vessel has sunk, _____.
A. each raft should go in a different direction in search of land
B. the possibility of a search aircraft finding you is increased by spreading out
C. reduce the number of liferafts by getting as many people as possible into as few rafts as possible
⚓ D. tie each of the rafts together and try to stay in a single group

**080133/DS03924**                                               **LBMAN**

If you are forced to abandon ship in a liferaft, your course of action should be to _____.

⚓ A. remain in the immediate vicinity
B. head for the nearest land
C. head for the closest sea-lanes
D. let the persons in the boat vote on what to do

**080134/DS03778**                                               **WSM**

When a ship is abandoned and there are several liferafts in the water, one of the FIRST things to be done is _____.

A. separate the rafts as much as possible to increase chances of detection
B. transfer all supplies to one raft
C. transfer all the injured to one raft
⚓ D. secure the rafts together to keep them from drifting apart

**080135/DS03912**                                               **WSM**

If you must enter water on which there is an oil fire, you should _____.

A. protect your life preserver by holding it above your head
⚓ B. enter the water on the windward side of the vessel
C. keep both hands in front of your face to break the water surface when diving head first
D. wear very light clothing

**080136/DS03129**                                               **WSM**

If water is rising in the bilge of a survival craft, you should first _____.

A. abandon the survival craft
B. check for cracks in the hull
C. shift all personnel to the stern
⚓ D. check the bilge drain plug

**080137/DS03920**                                               **LBMAN**

Inflatable liferafts are less maneuverable than lifeboats due to their _____.

A. shape
B. shallow draft
C. large sail area
⚓ D. All of the above

**080138/DS03918**                                               **MIL**

If your liferaft is to leeward of a fire on the water, you should FIRST _____.

⚓ A. cut the line to the sea anchor
B. paddle away from the fire
C. splash water over the liferaft to cool it
D. get out of the raft and swim to safety

**080139/DS03940**                                               **NORTON**

If you must swim through an oil fire, you should NOT _____.

A. wear as much clothing as possible
B. enter the water feet first
⚓ C. swim with the wind
D. cover eyes with one hand when entering the water

**080140/DS03819**                                               **\*46 CFR 131.530**

If there are a number of survivors in the water after abandoning an OSV and no rescue craft are in sight, they should _____.

A. tie themselves to the unit to avoid drifting with the current
⚓ B. group to form a small circle of survivors to create a warmer pocket of water in the center of the circle
C. send the strongest swimmer to shore for assistance
D. from a raft by lashing their life jackets together

**080141/DS03820   SAFETY AT SEA; SURVIVAL GUIDE**

Once the daily ration of drinking water in a survival situation has been established, the drinking routine should include _____.

A. small sips at regular intervals during the day
B. a complete daily ration at one time during the day
⚓ C. one-third the daily ration three times during the day
D. small sips only after sunset

**080142/DS03786**                                               **SAFETY AT SEA**

When using the rainwater collection tubes of a liferaft, the FIRST collection should be _____.

A. passed around so all can drink
⚓ B. poured overboard because of salt washed off the canopy
C. saved to be used at a later time
D. used to boil food

**080143/DS03826**                                   **SHIP'S MEDICINE CHEST**

You have abandoned ship and are in charge of a liferaft or survival craft. How much water per day should you permit each person to have after the first 24 hours?

A. 1 can
⚓ B. 1 pint
C. 1 quart
D. 1 gallon

**080144/DS03938**                          **NVIC 2-92; SURVIVAL GUIDE; LIFERAFT SURVIVAL**

You have abandoned ship in rough weather. After picking up other survivors in your liferaft, what should you do next?

⚓ A. Close up the entrances.
B. Top up the buoyancy tubes.
C. Prepare for the arrival of rescue units.
D. Decide on food and water rations.

**080145/DS03782**                                    **WSM**

You have abandoned ship in tropical waters. Which procedure should be used during a prolonged period in a liferaft?

A.  Wet clothes during the day to decrease perspiration.

B.  Get plenty of rest.

C.  Keep the entrance curtains open.

⚓ D.  All of the above

**080146/DS03942**                                    **89 MIL**

You have abandoned ship in tropical waters. Which procedure(s) should be used during a prolonged period in a raft?

A.  Wet clothes during the day to decrease perspiration.

B.  Get plenty of rest.

C.  Keep the entrance curtains open.

⚓ D.  All of the above

**080147/DS03814**                                    **WSM**

If you are forced to abandon ship in a rescue boat, you should _____.

⚓ A.  remain in the immediate vicinity

B.  head for the nearest land

C.  head for the closest sea-lanes

D.  vote on what to do, so all hands will have a part in the decision

**080148/DS03812**                        **SURVIVAL AT SEA**

If you have to abandon ship, and enter a liferaft, your main course of action should be to _____.

⚓ A.  remain in the vicinity of the sinking vessel

B.  head for the closest land

C.  head for the closest sea-lanes

D.  get a majority opinion

**080149/DS03816**                            **LBMAN; AMSM**

When abandoning an OSV, following the launching of the survival craft you should _____.

A.  plot a course for the nearest land

B.  take a vote on the direction in which to go

⚓ C.  stay in the immediate area

D.  go in one direction until fuel runs out

**080150/DS03061**                                **CHAPMAN**

When transferring survivors from a survival craft to a rescue vessel, personnel on board the craft should _____.

A.  remove their lifejackets to make it easier to climb on board the rescue vessel

B.  climb on top of the survival craft while waiting their turn to transfer to the rescue vessel

⚓ C.  remain seated inside the survival craft and make the transfer one person at a time

D.  enter the water and swim over to the rescue vessel

HELICOPTER PROCEDURES

**080151/DS03626**                        **MARINE SAFETY & RESCUE SYSTEMS**

When personnel are lifted by a helicopter from an inflatable liferaft, the personnel on the raft should _____.

⚓ A.  deflate the floor of the raft to reduce the danger of capsizing

B.  inflate the floor of the raft to provide for additional stability

C.  remove their lifejackets to prepare for the transfer

D.  take in the sea anchor to prevent fouling of the rescue sling

**080152/DS03629**                                    **MSRS**

When a helicopter is lifting personnel from a rescue boat, the other individuals in the boat should _____.

A.  enter the water in case the person being lifted slips from the sling

B.  stand on the outside of the boat to assist the person being lifted

C.  remove their lifejackets to prepare for their transfer to the helicopter

⚓ D.  remain seated inside to provide body weight for stability

EMERGENCY POSITION INDICATING RADIO BEACON (EPIRB)

**080153/DS00602**                            ***46 CFR 180.64**

What does "EPIRB" stand for?

A.  Emergency Position Indicating Radar Buoy

B.  Electronic Pulse Indicating Radio beacon

⚓ C.  Emergency Position Indicating Radio beacon

D.  None of the above

**080154/DS03594**                        **NPFVOA; *PUB 117**

After having activated the emergency position indicating radio beacon, you should _____.

A.  turn it off for 5 minutes every half-hour

B.  turn it off and on at 5 minute intervals

C.  turn it off during daylight hours

⚓ D.  leave it on continuously

**080155/DS03628**                    *46 CFR 199.510;
                    *46 CFR 199.01; *46 CFR 160.11

Each vessel in ocean and coastwise service must have an approved EPIRB. An EPIRB _____.
A. must be stowed in a manner so that it will float free if the vessel sinks
B. must be stowed where it is readily accessible for testing and use
C. is a devise that transmits a radio signal
⚓ D. All of the above

**080156/DS03592**        AMSM, LBMN; *46 CFR 131.890;
                    *46 CFR 133.60

When should the emergency position-indicating radio beacon be activated after abandoning an OSV?
⚓ A. Immediately
B. After one hour
C. Only when another vessel is in sight
D. Only after sunset

**080157/DS03613**                                **MRT**

You are in a survival craft broadcasting a distress message. What information would be essential to your rescuers?
A. The nature of the distress
B. The time of day
C. Your radio call sign
⚓ D. Your position by latitude and longitude

**080158/DS03598**                    NPFVOA; *PUB 117

If you have to abandon ship, the EPIRB can be used to _____.
A. hold the survival craft's head up into the seas
B. generate orange smoke
C. seal leaks in rubber rafts
⚓ D. send radio homing signals to searching aircraft

**080159/DS03599**                    **SURVIVAL GUIDE**

What should you do with your emergency position indicating radio beacon if you are in a lifeboat during storm conditions?
⚓ A. Bring it inside the liferaft and leave it on.
B. Bring it inside the liferaft and turn it off until the storm passes.
C. Leave it outside the liferaft and leave it on.
D. Leave it outside the liferaft and turn it off.

DISTRESS SIGNALS

**080160/DS03647**        *H.O. 102, RULE 36, INT. & INLAND

A distress signal _____.
A. consists of 5 or more short blasts of the fog signal apparatus
B. consists of the raising and lowering of a large white flag
⚓ C. may be used individually or in conjunction with other distress signals
D. is used to indicate doubt about another vessel's intentions

**080161/DS03651**                                *H.O. 102

Distress signals may be _____.
A. red flares
B. smoke signals
C. sound signals
⚓ D. Any of the above

**080162/DS03645**                *46 CFR 94.20-25, 160

Signaling devices which are required on inflatable liferafts include _____.
A. a rocket shoulder rifle
B. an oil lantern
⚓ C. red flares
D. an air horn

**080163/DS03666**                                **FVSM**

When you are firing a pyrotechnic distress signal, it should be aimed at _____.
A. straight overhead
B. at the vessel whose attention you are trying to get
C. into the wind
⚓ D. about 60 degrees above the horizon

**080164/DS03672**                    *46 CFR 133.175

Which item of the listed survival craft equipment would be the most suitable for night signaling to a ship on the horizon?
⚓ A. A red parachute flare
B. A red handheld flare
C. An orange smoke flare
D. A flashlight

**080165/DS03639** AMSM

Which condition represents the appropriate time for setting off distress flares and rockets?

⚓ A. Only when there is a chance of their being seen by rescue vessels
B. At half hour intervals
C. At one hour intervals
D. Immediately upon abandoning the vessel

**080166/DS03653** *H.O. 102

When a vessel signals her distress by means of a gun or other explosive signal, the firing should be at intervals of approximately _____.
A. 10 minutes
⚓ B. 1 minute
C. 1 hour
D. 3 minutes

**080167/DS03649** *H.O. 102

A man aboard a vessel, signaling by raising and lowering his outstretched arms to each side, is indicating _____.
A. danger, stay away
B. all is clear, it is safe to pass
C. all is clear, it is safe to approach
⚓ D. a distress signal

**080168/DS03646** RULE 36

One of the signals, other than a distress signal, that can be used by a rescue boat to attract attention is a/an _____.
A. red star shell
⚓ B. searchlight
C. burning barrel
D. orange smoke signal

**080169/DS03641** *46 CFR 199.175 (b) (30)

Signaling devices required on inflatable liferafts include a(n) _____.
A. Very pistol
⚓ B. orange smoke signal
C. air horn
D. lantern

**080170/DS03632** FVSM; *46 CFR 199.175 (b) (30)

When using a handheld smoke signal in a liferaft, you should activate the signal _____.
A. on the upwind side
B. inside the boat
C. at the stern
⚓ D. on the downwind side

**080171/DS03676** NVIC 5-86

You have abandoned ship and after two days in a liferaft you can see an aircraft near the horizon apparently carrying out a search pattern. You should _____.
A. switch the EPIRB to the homing signal mode
B. use the voice transmission capability of the EPIRB to guide the aircraft to your raft
C. turn on the strobe light on the top of the EPIRB
⚓ D. use visual distress signals in conjunction with the EPIRB

**080172/DS03655** *H.O. 102

You can indicate that your vessel is in distress by _____.
A. displaying a large red flag
B. displaying three black balls in a vertical line
C. sounding five or more short and rapid blasts on the whistle
⚓ D. continuously sounding the fog whistle

**080173/DS03648** *H.O. 102

All of the following are recognized distress signals under the Navigation Rules EXCEPT _____.
⚓ A. a green star signal
B. orange-colored smoke
C. red flares
D. the repeated raising and lowering of outstretched arms

## SURVIVAL CRAFT NAVIGATION

### SURVIVAL CRAFT NAVIGATION PROCEDURES

**080174/DS02387** *BOWD 2, TABLE 2

A magnetic compass card is marked in how many degrees?
A. 90
B. 180
⚓ C. 360
D. 400

**080175/DS02658** *BOWD 2

As a vessel changes course to starboard, the compass card in a magnetic compass _____.
A. first turns to starboard then counterclockwise to port
B. also turns to starboard
C. turns counterclockwise to port
⚓ D. remains aligned with compass north

**080176/DS02668**                          *BOWD 2
As a vessel changes course to starboard, the compass card in a magnetic compass _____.
⚓ A.  remains aligned with compass north
  B.  also turns to starboard
  C.  first turns to starboard then counterclockwise to port
  D.  turns counterclockwise to port

**080177/DS02687**                          *BOWD 2
As a vessel changes course to starboard, the compass card in a magnetic compass _____.
  A.  first turns to starboard then counterclockwise to port
  B.  also turns to starboard
⚓ C.  remains aligned with compass north
  D.  turns counterclockwise to port

**080178/DS02421**                    *BOWD 2, TABLE 2
How many degrees are there on a compass card?
⚓ A.  360°
  B.  380°
  C.  390°
  D.  420°

**080179/DS02779**                          *BOWD 2
Error may be introduced into a magnetic compass by _____.
  A.  making a structural change to the vessel
  B.  a short circuit near the compass
  C.  belt buckles
⚓ D.  All of the above

**080180/DS02794**                          *BOWD 2
Which would influence a magnetic compass?
  A.  Electrical wiring
  B.  Iron pipe
  C.  Radio
⚓ D.  All of the above

**080181/DS02835**                    *BOWD 2, TABLE 2
A vessel heading NNE is on a course of _____.
⚓ A.  022.5°
  B.  045.0°
  C.  067.5°
  D.  090.0°

**080182/DS02833**                    *BOWD 2, TABLE 2
A vessel heading NE is on a course of _____.
  A.  022.5°
⚓ B.  045.0°
  C.  067.5°
  D.  090.0°

**080183/DS02831**                    *BOWD 2, TABLE 2
A vessel heading ENE is on a course of _____.
  A.  022.5°
  B.  045.0°
⚓ C.  067.5°
  D.  090.0°

**080184/DS02823**                    *BOWD 2, TABLE 2
A vessel heading ESE is on a course of _____.
⚓ A.  112.5°
  B.  135.0°
  C.  157.5°
  D.  180.0°

**080185/DS02821**                    *BOWD 2, TABLE 2
A vessel heading SE is on a course of _____.
  A.  112.5°
⚓ B.  135.0°
  C.  157.5°
  D.  180.0°

**080186/DS02817**                          BOWD
A vessel heading SSE is on a course of _____.
  A.  112.5°
  B.  135.0°
⚓ C.  157.5°
  D.  180.0°

**080187/DS02807**                    *BOWD 2, TABLE 2
A vessel heading SSW is on a course of _____.
⚓ A.  202.5°
  B.  225.0°
  C.  247.5°
  D.  270.0°

**080188/DS02811**                    *BOWD 2, TABLE 2
A vessel heading SW is on a course of _____.
  A.  202.5°
⚓ B.  225.0°
  C.  247.5°
  D.  270.0°

**080189/DS02813**                          BOWD
A vessel heading WSW is on a course of _____.
  A.  202.5°
  B.  225.0°
⚓ C.  247.5°
  D.  271.0°

**080190/DS02815**                    *BOWD 2, TABLE 2
A vessel heading WNW is on a course of _____.
  A.  270.0°
⚓ B.  292.5°
  C.  315.0°
  D.  337.5°

**080191/DS02806**                    ***BOWD 2, TABLE 2**
A vessel heading NW is on a course of _____ .
- A.  274.5°
- B.  292.5°
- ⚓ C.  315.0°
- D.  337.5°

**080192/DS02805**                    ***BOWD 2, TABLE 2**
A vessel heading NNW is on a course of _____ .
- A.  274.5°
- B.  292.0°
- C.  315.5°
- ⚓ D.  337.5°

**080193/DS02694**                    ***BOWD 2**
The heading of a vessel is indicated by what part of the compass?
- A.  Card
- B.  Needle
- ⚓ C.  Lubber's line
- D.  Gimbals

**080194/DS02776**                    ***BOWD 2**
The lubber's line of a magnetic compass _____ .
- A.  always shows true north direction
- ⚓ B.  indicates the vessel's heading
- C.  is always parallel to the vessel's transom
- D.  is located on the compass card

**080195/DS02777**                    ***BOWD 2**
The lubber's line on a magnetic compass indicates _____ .
- A.  compass north
- ⚓ B.  the direction of the vessel's head
- C.  magnetic north
- D.  a relative bearing taken with azimuth circle

**080196/DS02803**                    ***BOWD 2**
When a magnetic compass is not in use for a prolonged period of time it should _____ .
- ⚓ A.  be shielded from direct sunlight
- B.  be locked into a constant heading
- C.  have any air bubbles replaced with nitrogen
- D.  have the compensating magnets removed

---

| LIFESAVING EQUIPMENT |
|---|

LIFESAVING EQUIPMENT - TESTS & INSPECTIONS

**080197/DS02127**                    ***46 CFR 160.51;**
                            ***46 CFR 199.201; *46 CFR 199.261**
On vessels on an international voyage, each inflatable liferaft shall have a carrying capacity of not less than

_____ .
- A.  50 percent of all persons on board
- B.  75 percent of all persons on board
- ⚓ C.  6 persons
- D.  10 persons

**080198/DS03849**                    ***46 CFR 199.178 (d)**
The capacity of any liferaft on board a vessel can be determined by _____ .
- A.  examining the Certificate of Inspection
- ⚓ B.  examining the plate on the outside of the raft container
- C.  referring to the Muster List ("Station Bill")
- D.  referring to the shipping articles

**080199/DS03870*46 CFR 131.565; *46 CFR 199.190 (e) (2)**
Each EPIRB required on an OSV shall be tested using the integrated test circuit and output indicator every

_____ .
- A.  week
- B.  two weeks
- ⚓ C.  month
- D.  two months

**080200/DS03830**          **LBMAN; *46 CFR 199.190 (g) (3);**
                            ***46 CFR 160.51-6**
Inflatable liferafts must be overhauled and inspected at a U. S. Coast Guard approved service facility every

_____ .
- A.  six months
- ⚓ B.  twelve months
- C.  eighteen months
- D.  twenty-four months

**080201/DS03829**                    ***46 CFR 199.190 (g) (1) (ii)**
Inflatable liferafts shall be serviced at an approved servicing facility every 12 months or not later than the next vessel inspection for certification. However, the total elapsed time between servicing cannot exceed

_____ .
- A.  12 months
- B.  15 months
- ⚓ C.  17 months
- D.  18 months

## LIFESAVING EQUIPMENT - REGULATIONS

**080202/DS03857**        ***46 CFR 126.220**
Where would you find a list of the lifesaving equipment onboard your supply boat?
A. Ship's Articles
B. Muster List ("Station Bill")
⚓ C. Certificate of Inspection
D. U.S. Coast Guard Regulations

**080203/DS03856**    ***46 CFR 133.70; *46 CFR 199.273 (c)**
The immersion suit requirements for OSV apply to units operating in the Atlantic Ocean _____.
A. above 20 degrees North and below 20 degrees South
B. above 25 degrees North and below 25 degrees South
C. above 30 degrees North and below 30 degrees South
⚓ D. above 32 degrees North and below 32 degrees South

**080204/DS02125**     **LBMAN; *46 CFR 199.190 (g) (3);
*46 CFR 160.51-6; *46 CFR 160.151-57**
Who should inspect and test an inflatable liferaft?
A. The Chief Mate
⚓ B. An approved servicing facility
C. Shipyard personnel
D. A certificated lifeboatman

**080205/DS03900**        ***46 CFR 180.78 (a) (2)**
The life jackets on all vessels shall be _____.
A. inspected weekly
B. worn at all times
⚓ C. readily available
D. tested yearly

**080206/DS03954**      **AMSM; *46 CFR 160.73-10 (b)**
The float free link attached to a sea painter on an inflatable liferaft has a breaking strength of _____.
A. 100-134 lbs for buoyant apparatus with a capacity of 10 persons or less
B. 200-268 lbs for buoyant apparatus with a capacity of 11 to 20 persons
C. 400-536 lbs for buoyant apparatus with a capacity of 21 persons or more
⚓ D. All of the above

## LIFESAVING EQUIPMENT - MARKINGS

**080207/DS03855**        ***46 CFR 31.05-1**
Which document will describe lifesaving equipment located aboard your vessel?
A. Muster List ("Station Bill")
⚓ B. Certificate of Inspection
C. Forecastle card
D. Clearance papers

**080208/DS03904**        ***46 CFR 108.850 (b) (3)**
The light on a life jacket must be replaced _____.
A. when the power source is replaced
B. each year after installation
C. every six months
⚓ D. when it is no longer serviceable

**080209/DS03854**        ***46 CFR 199.178 (d)**
According to the regulations, the capacity of a liferaft is required to be marked _____.
A. on the Muster List ("Station Bill")
⚓ B. at the liferaft stowage location
C. on the Certificate of Inspection
D. in the Operations Manual

**080210/DS03853MIL; *46 CFR 199.175 (b) (10), (15), (27);
*46 CFR 160.51-7 (b)**
Coast Guard Regulations (46 CFR) require inflatable liferafts to be equipped with _____.
A. a first aid kit
B. an instruction manual
C. a sea anchor
⚓ D. All of the above

**080211/DS03840**      **WSM; *46 CFR 160.51-7 (b) (8)**
The painter of the inflatable liferaft has a length of _____.
A. 25 feet
⚓ B. 100 feet
C. 200 feet
D. 400 feet

## LIFESAVING EQUIPMENT - TESTS & INSPECTIONS

**080212/DS03861**        ***46 CFR 185.604 (b);
*46 CFR 199.70 (b) (3)**
Coast Guard Regulations (46 CFR) require that life jackets shall be _____.
A. provided for each person onboard
B. provided for all personnel of watch
C. readily accessible to persons in the engine room
⚓ D. All of the above

**080213/DS03848**     ***46 CFR 133.70; *46 CFR 161.12**
Each personal flotation device light on an OSV that has a non-replacement power source must be replaced _____.
A. every six months after initial installation
B. every 12 months after initial installation
C. every 24 months after initial installation
⚓ D. on or before the expiration date of the power source

**080214/DS03896**                *46 CFR 199.70 (b) (3)
Life preservers must be marked with the _____.
A. stowage space assigned
⚓ B. vessel's name
C. vessel's home port
D. maximum weight allowed

**080215/DS03860**          *46 CFR 199.70 (b) (2) (i), (iv)
Lifejackets should be stowed in _____.
A. the forepeaks
B. the pumproom
⚓ C. readily accessible spaces
D. locked watertight containers

**080216/DS03852**        *46 CFR 133.70; *46 CFR 161.12
The light on a personal flotation device on an OSV
must be replaced _____.
A. when the power source is replaced
B. each year after installation
C. every six months
⚓ D. when it is no longer serviceable

**080217/DS03858**                *46 CFR 180.78 (a) (2)
Lifesaving equipment shall be stowed so that it will be
_____.
A. locked up
⚓ B. readily accessible for use
C. inaccessible to passengers
D. on the topmost deck of the vessel at all times

**080218/DS03862**      *46 CFR 180.72 (c); *46 CFR 160.53
In accordance with Coast Guard Regulations, Coast
Guard approved buoyant work vests _____.
A. should be stowed in engineering spaces in lieu of
   approved life jackets because they are less bulky
   and permit free movement in confined spaces
B. may be used as a substitute for approved life
   preservers during routine drills, but never during an
   emergency
⚓ C. should not be stowed where they could be confused
   with life jackets in an emergency
D. All of the above

**080219/DS03859**                *46 CFR 108.699;
                            *46 CFR 160.53; *46 CFR 97.34-10 (a)
When can a work vest be substituted for a lifejacket in
the total count of the required lifesaving gear?
A. When it is approved by the Coast Guard
B. When working near or over the water
C. When stowed away from the ring buoys
⚓ D. A work vest may never be counted as a lifejacket.

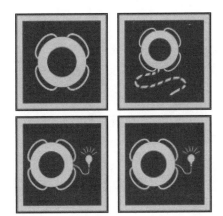

LIFESAVING EQUIPMENT - RING LIFEBUOYS

**080220/DS03863**                *46 CFR 133.70
On an OSV, how many ring buoys are required to have
a buoyant line attached?
A. One ring life buoy
⚓ B. One ring life buoy on each side of the OSV
C. Three ring life buoys
D. Two ring life buoys on each side of the OSV

**080221/DS03906**                *46 CFR 180.70
When a lifeline is required to be attached to a ring life
buoy it must be at least _____.
A. 30 feet long
⚓ B. 60 feet long
C. 90 feet long
D. 120 feet long

**080222/DS03864**                *46 CFR 133.70
Of the required ring life buoys for an OSV, how many
must be equipped with a waterlight?
A. 8
B. 4
⚓ C. 2
D. 1

**080223/DS03865**                *46 CFR 133.70
What is the minimum required number of ring life
buoys on an OSV certified for ocean service?
A. 4
⚓ B. 8
C. 12
D. 16

**LIFESAVING EQUIPMENT - DISTRESS SIGNALS**

**080224/DS03891     AMSM; *46 CFR 199.175 (b) (31), (30)**
Which statement is TRUE concerning distress signals in a survival craft?

⚓ A.  Hand held flares and orange smoke signals are required.
B.  If hand-held rocket-propelled parachute flares are provided, they are the only distress signals required.
C.  Two hand-held smoke signals shall be provided.
D.  A Very pistol with twelve flares is required.

**080225/DS03892                    *46 CFR 160.057-5 (c)**
By regulation, orange smoke distress signals will expire not more than how many months from the date of manufacture?
A.  24 months
B.  36 months
⚓ C.  42 months
D.  54 months

**080226/DS03866*46 CFR 199.175 (b) (30); *46 CFR 160.122**
Each distress signal and self-activated smoke signal must be replaced not later than the marked date of expiration, or not more than how many months from the date of manufacture?
A.  48 months
⚓ B.  42 months
C.  36 months
D.  30 months

**080227/DS03897          LBMAN; *46 CFR 160.021-5 (b)**
What is the maximum length of time that distress flares are approved for?
A.  1 and 1/2 years
B.  2 years
⚓ C.  3 and 1/2 years
D.  5 years

**LIFESAVING EQUIPMENT - EPIRB**

**080228/DS03886       *46†CFR†133.60; *46†CFR†199.510**
Which type EPIRB must each ocean-going OSV carry?
A.  Class A
B.  Class B
C.  Class C
⚓ D.  Category I

**080229/DS03883       *46 CFR 199.510; *46 CFR 199.01;**
**                          *46 CFR 199.610 (a) (1)**
Which vessel greater than 100-GT is NOT required to have an EPIRB.
A.  A sailing vessel
B.  A fishing vessel
⚓ C.  A non self-propelled vessel
D.  A towing vessel

**080230/DS03867                    *46 CFR 133.175**
Each OSV must carry _____.
A.  one category I 406 MHz satellite EPIRB
B.  at least one life buoy on each side of the vessel fitted with a buoyant life line
C.  at least 12 rocket parachute flares
⚓ D.  All of the above

**080231/DS03880            *46 CFR 133.60; *PUB 117**
The Emergency Position Indicating Radio beacon on an OSV vessel must be stowed _____.
A.  in an inside passageway
B.  in an approved bracket
C.  so that it is accessible from the pilothouse of the vessel
⚓ D.  so that it will float free if the vessel sinks

**080232/DS10020                    MRT; *PUB 117**
CATEGORY I EPIRB's transmit on frequencies that are monitored by _____.
⚓ A.  orbiting satellites in space
B.  commercial radio stations
C.  private, commercial, and military aircraft
D.  Both A & C

**080233/DS03887                    *46 CFR 97.15-65**
The Master shall insure that the Emergency Position Indicating Radio beacon (EPIRB) is _____.
A.  secured inside the wheelhouse
B.  tested annually
⚓ C.  tested monthly
D.  secured in the emergency locker

## LIFESAVING EQUIPMENT - TESTS & DRILLS

**080234/DS03955**　　　　*46 CFR 131.530 (7) (ii)*
The person-in-charge shall insure that each rescue boat on an OSV is lowered to the water, launched and operated at least once every _____.
A. week
B. two months
⚓ C. three months
D. six months

**080235/DS03868**　*46 CFR 133.135; *46 CFR 199.175 (39)*
The rescue boat on an OSV shall carry a tow line strong enough to tow the vessel's largest loaded liferaft at a speed of at least _____.
A. 1 knot
⚓ B. 2 knot
C. 5 knot
D. 10 knot

## LIFESAVING EQUIPMENT - LINE THROWING APPLIANCE

**080236/DS03907**　　　　　*46 CFR 160.040-4 (a)*
Line throwing apparatus aboard ship must contain _____.
A. two rockets, one of which shall be the buoyant type
B. three rockets, one of which shall be the buoyant type
⚓ C. four rockets, two of which shall be the buoyant type
D. five rockets, two of which shall be the buoyant type

**080237/DS03875**　　　　　*46 CFR 160.040-4 (c)*
The breaking strength of the service lines of the rockets used with an impulse-projected, rocket type line throwing appliances is _____.
A. 300 lbs
⚓ B. 500 lbs
C. 1000 lbs
D. 1500 lbs

**080238/DS03910**　　　　　*46 CFR 199.170 (c)*
Your vessel is required to have an impulse-projected line throwing appliance. The auxiliary line must _____.
A. be of a light color
B. be 250 meters in length
⚓ C. have a breaking strength of 9000 lbs
D. be made of synthetic material

**080239/DS03872**　　　　　*46 CFR 133.170 (a)*
For an OSV not on an international voyage, an approved substitute for an impulse projected type line throwing appliance is a _____.
A. spring-loaded line thrower
B. hand thrown buoyant line
⚓ C. shoulder type line throwing gun
D. heaving line

**080240/DS03876**　　　　　*46 CFR 97.15-25;
*46 CFR 160.31; *46 CFR 160.40; *46 CFR 199.180 (e)*
What is NOT a requirement for testing the line throwing appliance on a vessel?
A. A drill should be conducted every three months.
⚓ B. A regular service line must be used when it's fired.
C. A regular projectile must be used when it's fired.
D. The actual firing is at the discretion of the Master.

**080241/DS03065**　　　　　**CHAPMAN**
Which precaution should be taken when testing a line throwing gun?
⚓ A. Never remove the line from the rocket.
B. Fire it at an angle of approximately 90 degrees to the horizon.
C. Wear asbestos gloves.
D. All of the above

**080242/DS03909**　　　　　*46 CFR 199.180 (e)*
Which statement is TRUE concerning the testing of the line-throwing appliance?
A. It shall be fired at least once in every three months.
⚓ B. A drill in its use shall be held once in every 3 months.
C. Drills shall be held quarterly and it shall be fired annually.
D. No drills are required.

## FIRST AID

### FIRST AID & CPR

**080243/DS03692**　　　　**SHIP'S MEDICINE CHEST**
Before CPR is started, you should _____.
⚓ A. establish an open airway
B. treat any bleeding wounds
C. insure the victim is conscious
D. make the victim comfortable

**080244/DS03694**          **SHIP'S MEDICINE CHEST**
When administering artificial respiration, it is MOST important to _____.
A. monitor blood pressure
⚓ B. clear airways
C. use the rhythmic pressure method
D. know all approved methods

**080245/DS03698**          **SHIP'S MEDICINE CHEST**
You are attempting to administer CPR to a victim. When you blow into his mouth it is apparent that no air is getting into the lungs. What should you do?
A. Blow harder to force the air past the tongue.
B. Raise the victim's head higher than his feet.
C. Press on the victim's lungs so that air pressure will blow out any obstruction.
⚓ D. Re-tip the head and try again.

**080246/DS03686**          **SHIP'S MEDICINE CHEST**
When applying chest compressions on an adult victim during CPR, the sternum should be depressed about _____.
A. 1/2 inch or less
B. 1/2 to 1 inch
C. 1 to 1-1/2 inches
⚓ D. 1-1/2 to 2 inches

**080247/DS03688**          **SHIP'S MEDICINE CHEST**
You are administering chest compressions during CPR. Where on the victim's body should the pressure be applied?
⚓ A. Lower half of the sternum
B. Tip of the sternum
C. Top half of the sternum
D. Left chest over the heart

**080248/DS03712**          **SHIP'S MEDICINE CHEST**
The rescuer can best provide an airtight seal during mouth to mouth ventilation by pinching the victim's nostrils and _____.
A. cupping a hand around the patient's mouth
B. keeping the head elevated
⚓ C. applying his mouth tightly over the victim's mouth
D. holding the jaw down firmly

**080249/DS03684**          **SHIP'S MEDICINE CHEST**
The rescuer can best provide an airtight seal during mouth-to-mouth resuscitation by pinching the victim's nostrils and _____.
A. cupping a hand around the patient's mouth
B. keeping the head elevated
⚓ C. applying his mouth tightly over the victim's mouth
D. holding the jaw down firmly

**080250/DS03704**          **SHIP'S MEDICINE CHEST**
After a person has been revived by artificial respiration, he should be _____.
A. walked around until he is back to normal
B. given several shots of whiskey
⚓ C. kept lying down and warm
D. allowed to do as he wishes

**080251/DS03682**          **AMSM; MFPFFS**
At what rate would you render mouth to mouth or mouth to nose artificial respiration to an adult?
A. 4 to 6 times per minute
⚓ B. 12 to 15 times per minute
C. 20 to 30 times per minute
D. At least 30 times per minute

**080252/DS03689**          **SHIP'S MEDICINE CHEST**
Changing rescuers while carrying out artificial respiration should be done _____.
⚓ A. without losing the rhythm of respiration
B. only with the help of two other people
C. by not stopping the respiration for more than 5 minutes
D. at ten-minute intervals

**080253/DS03680**          **SHIP'S MEDICINE CHEST**
When administering artificial respiration to an adult, the breathing cycle should be repeated about _____.
⚓ A. 12 to 15 times per minute
B. 18 to 20 times per minute
C. 20 to 25 times per minute
D. as fast as possible

**080254/DS03678SHIP'S MEDICINE CHEST; RED CROSS**
When giving mouth-to-mouth rescue breathing to an adult, you should breathe at the rate of how many breaths per minute?
A. 4
B. 8
⚓ C. 12
D. 20

**080255/DS03700**          **SHIP'S MEDICINE CHEST;**
                                      **First Responder**
Sign(s) of respiratory arrest requiring artificial respiration is(are) _____.
A. vomiting
⚓ B. blue color and lack of breathing
C. irregular breathing
D. unconsciousness

**080256/DS03715**          **SHIP'S MEDICINE CHEST**
The necessity for administering artificial respiration may be recognized by the victim's _____.
A.  vomiting
⚓ B.  blue color and lack of breathing
C.  irregular breathing
D.  unconscious condition

**080257/DS03714**          **SHIP'S MEDICINE CHEST**
If someone suffers a heart attack and has ceased breathing, you should _____.
A.  immediately give a stimulant, by force if necessary
B.  make the victim comfortable in a bunk
⚓ C.  immediately start CPR
D.  administer oxygen

**080258/DS03716**          **SHIP'S MEDICINE CHEST**
In order to initiate CPR on a drowning victim, _____.
A.  start chest compressions before the victim is removed from the water
B.  drain water from the lungs before ventilating
⚓ C.  begin mouth-to-mouth ventilations
D.  do not tilt the head back since it may cause vomiting

**080259/DS03690**          **SHIP'S MEDICINE CHEST**
The MOST important element in administering CPR is _____.
A.  having the proper equipment for the process
⚓ B.  starting the treatment quickly
C.  administering of oxygen
D.  treating for traumatic shock

**080260/DS03709**          **SHIP'S MEDICINE CHEST**
When starting CPR on a drowning victim, you should _____.
A.  start chest compressions before the victim is removed from the water
B.  drain water from the lungs before ventilating
⚓ C.  begin mouth-to-mouth ventilations as soon as possible
D.  do not tilt the head back since it may cause vomiting

**080261/DS03708**          **SHIP'S MEDICINE CHEST**
If the patient vomits during mouth-to mouth resuscitation, the rescuer should FIRST _____.
A.  ignore it and continue mouth-to-mouth ventilation
B.  pause for a moment until the patient appears quiet again, then resume ventilation mouth-to-mouth
C.  switch to mouth-to-nose ventilation
⚓ D.  turn the patient's body to the side, sweep out the mouth and resume mouth-to-mouth ventilation

HYPERTHERMIA & HEAT STROKE

**080262/DS03719**          **SHIP'S MEDICINE CHEST**
Symptoms of heat stroke are _____.
A.  cold and moist skin, high body temperature
B.  cold and dry skin, low body temperature
C.  hot and moist skin, high body temperature
⚓ D.  hot and dry skin, high body temperature

HYPOTHERMIA & FROSTBITE

**080263/DS03725**          **SHIP'S MEDICINE CHEST**
A crew member has suffered frostbite to the toes of both feet. You should _____.
⚓ A.  immerse the feet in warm water
B.  warm the feet with a heat lamp
C.  warm the feet at room temperature
D.  rub the feet

**080264/DS03728**          **SHIP'S MEDICINE CHEST**
A crew member has suffered frostbite to the toes of the right foot. Which is NOT an acceptable first aid measure?
⚓ A.  Rub the toes briskly.
B.  Elevate the foot slightly.
C.  Rewarm rapidly.
D.  Give aspirin or other medication for pain if necessary.

**080265/DS10064**          **SHIP'S MEDICINE CHEST**
What is the proper treatment for frostbite?
A.  rubbing affected area with ice or snow
B.  rubbing affected area briskly to restore circulation
C.  wrapping area tightly in warm cloths
⚓ D.  warming exposed parts rapidly

**080266/DS03729**          **SHIP'S MEDICINE CHEST**
A crew member suffering from hypothermia should be given _____.
A.  a small dose of alcohol
⚓ B.  treatment for shock
C.  a large meal
D.  a brisk rub down

**080267/DS03724**          **SHIP'S MEDICINE CHEST**
Physical exertion on the part of a person who has fallen into cold water would _____.
A.  be the best thing to try if there was no rescue in sight
B.  increase survival time in the water
⚓ C.  increase the rate of heat loss from the body
D.  not affect the heat loss from the body

**080268/DS03736**          **RED CROSS**

The most effective treatment for warming a crew member suffering from hypothermia is _____.

A. running or jumping to increase circulation

B. raising body temperature rapidly by placing hands and feet in hot water

⚓ C. bundling the body in blankets to rewarm gradually

D. laying prone under heat lamps to rewarm rapidly

**080269/DS10062**          **SHIP'S MEDICINE CHEST**

What action should be taken for a patient suffering from heat exhaustion?

⚓ A. moved to a cool room and told to lie down

B. kept standing and encouraged to walk slowly and continuously

C. given a glass of water and told to return to work after 15 minutes of rest

D. None of the above are correct

### GENERAL FIRST AID

**080270/DS03751**          **SHIP'S MEDICINE CHEST**

A shipmate chokes suddenly, cannot speak, and starts to turn blue. You should _____.

⚓ A. perform the Heimlich maneuver

B. make the victim lie down with the feet elevated to get blood to the brain

C. immediately administer CPR

D. do nothing until the victim becomes unconscious

**080271/DS03748**          **SHIP'S MEDICINE CHEST**

A victim is coughing and wheezing from a partial obstruction of the airway. An observer should _____.

A. perform the Heimlich maneuver

B. immediately start CPR

C. give back blows and something to drink

⚓ D. allow the person to continue coughing and dislodge the obstruction on his own

**080272/DS03747**          **SHIP'S MEDICINE CHEST**

A person who gets battery acid in an eye should IMMEDIATELY wash the eye with _____.

A. boric acid solution

⚓ B. water

C. baking soda solution

D. ammonia

**080273/DS03749**          **SHIP'S MEDICINE CHEST**

If a person gets something in his or her eye and you see that it is not embedded, you can _____.

A. get them to rub their eye until the object is gone

B. remove it with a match or toothpick

C. remove it with a piece of dry sterile cotton

⚓ D. remove it with a moist, cotton-tipped applicator

**080274/DS03745**          **SHIP'S MEDICINE CHEST**

In reviving a person who has been overcome by gas fumes, what would you AVOID doing?

⚓ A. Giving stimulants

B. Prompt removal of the patient from the suffocating atmosphere

C. Applying artificial respiration and massage

D. Keeping the patient warm and comfortable

**080275/DS03755**          **SHIP'S MEDICINE CHEST**

To reduce mild fever the MOST useful drug is _____.

A. bicarbonate of soda

B. paregoric

⚓ C. aspirin

D. aromatic spirits of ammonia

**080276/DS03754**          **SHIP'S MEDICINE CHEST**

First aid means _____.

A. medical treatment of accident

B. setting of broken bones

⚓ C. emergency treatment at the scene of the injury

D. dosage of medications

**080277/DS03744**          **SHIP'S MEDICINE CHEST**

Which should NOT be a treatment for a person who has received a head injury and is groggy or unconscious?

⚓ A. Give a stimulant.

B. Elevate his head.

C. Stop severe bleeding.

D. Treat for shock.

**080278/DS03742**          **SHIP'S MEDICINE CHEST**

A rescuer can most easily determine whether or not an adult victim has a pulse by checking the pulse at the _____.

⚓ A. carotid artery in the neck

B. femoral artery in the groin

C. brachial artery in the arm

D. radial artery in the wrist

**080279/DS03756**          **SHIP'S MEDICINE CHEST**

Treatment of sunstroke consists principally of _____.

⚓ A. cooling, removing to shaded area, and lying down

B. bathing with rubbing alcohol

C. drinking ice water

D. All of the above

**080280/DS03757**　　　　**SHIP'S MEDICINE CHEST**
What are the symptoms of sun stroke?
A. Temperature falls below normal, pulse is rapid and feeble, skin is cold and clammy.
⚓ B. Temperature is high, pulse is strong and rapid, skin is hot and dry.
C. Temperature is high, pulse is slow and feeble, skin is clammy.
D. Temperature falls below normal, pulse is rapid, skin is clammy.

**080281/DS03738**　　　　**SHIP'S MEDICINE CHEST**
A crew member is unconscious and the face is flushed. You should _____ .
⚓ A. lay the crew member down with the head and shoulders slightly raised
B. administer a liquid stimulant
C. lay the crew member down with the head lower than the feet
D. attempt to stand the crew member upright to restore consciousness

**080282/DS03740**　　　　**SHIP'S MEDICINE CHEST**
The proper stimulant for an unconscious person is _____ .
A. tea
B. coffee
C. whiskey and water
⚓ D. ammonia inhalant

**LIFEBOATMAN**
**481XX-Deck Safety and Rules of the Road**
**Exam No. 330701**

1 - USCG 4102
BOTH INTERNATIONAL & INLAND A distress signal _____.
A.      consists of 5 or more short blasts of the fog signal apparatus
B.      consists of the raising and lowering of a large white flag
C.      may be used separately or with other distress signals
D.      is used to indicate doubt about another vessel's intentions

2 - USCG 313
Kapok life jackets should NOT be _____.
A.      stowed near open flame or where smoking is permitted
B.      used as seats, pillows, or foot rests
C.      left on open decks
D.      All of the above

3 - USCG 1940
Life jackets should be stowed in _____.
A.      survival craft
B.      messrooms
C.      readily accessible locations
D.      locked watertight containers

4 - USCG 781
How is the external flotation bladder of an immersion suit inflated?
A.      It is inflated by a small $CO_2$ bottle that is automatically tripped when the front zipper is at the top of the zipper track.
B.      It is inflated by a small $CO_2$ bottle that is manually tripped.
C.      It is inflated by blowing through an inflation tube.
D.      It inflates by sea water bleeding into the flotation bladder and reacting with a chemical therein.

5 - USCG 433
If passengers are on board when an abandon ship drill is carried out, they should _____.
A.      take part
B.      watch
C.      go to their quarters
D.      stay out of the way and do what they want

6 - USCG 503
Your vessel has lifeboats on both sides. Lifeboat No. 2 is located _____.
A.      forward of lifeboat No. 4 on the starboard side
B.      forward of lifeboat No. 4 on the port side
C.      aft of lifeboat No. 1 on the starboard side
D.      All of the above

7 - USCG 533
What is the purpose of limber holes?
A.      To allow for air circulation
B.      To allow for stress and strain in rough waters
C.      To allow water in the boat to drain overboard
D.      To allow water in the bilge to get to the boat drain

8 - USCG 713
Preventer bars are fitted on lifeboat releasing gear to prevent _____.
A.      the falls from unhooking if the releasing gear is operated accidentally
B.      operation of the release lever until the boat is waterborne
C.      the falls from rehooking after they have been released
D.      accidental unhooking when the falls become slack

9 - USCG 743
In order for the automatic lifeboat drain to operate properly _____.
A.      the cap should be removed to drain the boat when it is waterborne
B.      the cage must be free of rubbish or the ball may not seat properly
C.      there is an automatic ball check located in a siphon tube
D.      the small lever to release the rubber ball float must be turned counterclockwise

10 - USCG 1200
What is TRUE concerning frapping lines?
A.      They are used to steady a lifeboat when lowered.
B.      They are normally attached to the davit span.
C.      They are needed only on radial davits.
D.      They are used to clear the puddings.

11 - USCG 1270
The most common type of davit found on merchant vessels today is the _____.
A.      radial
B.      sheath-screw
C.      gravity
D.      quadrantal

12 - USCG 1280
On which type davit does the davit head stay at the same height?
A.      Radial
B.      Sheath-screw
C.      Quadrantal
D.      Gravity

13 - USCG 1290
Which davit type may be operated by one man?
A.      Quadrantal
B.      Gravity
C.      Sheath-screw
D.      Radial

14 - USCG 1513
Limit switches, winches, falls, etc. must be thoroughly inspected at least every _____.
A.      2 months
B.      4 months
C.      6 months
D.      year

15 - USCG 1085
When lowering lifeboats in heavy seas, a good practice is to rig frapping lines _____.
A.      on only the forward falls
B.      on only the after falls
C.      with a lead of about 45 degrees to the boat
D.      from the falls to the main deck of the vessel

16 - USCG 1095
When launching a lifeboat, frapping lines should be rigged _____.
A.      before the gripes are released
B.      before the boat is moved from the davits
C.      at the embarkation deck
D.      after the boat is in the water

17 - USCG 1125
What is the best procedure for picking up a lifeboat at sea while utilizing the lifeboat's sea painter?
A.      Place the lifeboat ahead and to windward of your vessel with the wind about broad on the bow of your ship.
B.      Place the lifeboat ahead and to leeward of your ship with the wind about broad on the bow of your ship.
C.      Place your ship to windward of the lifeboat with the wind on the quarter to allow your ship to drift down to the lifeboat.
D.      Place the lifeboat ahead and to windward of your ship with the wind about broad on the quarter of your ship.

18 - USCG 1155
When picking up a lifeboat at sea with way on the ship, the sea painter should be secured _____.
A.      well forward in the lifeboat
B.      about amidships in the lifeboat
C.      well aft in the lifeboat
D.      only after the falls have been attached

19 - USCG 1195
The command "Oars" means to _____.
A.      lift the oars to a vertical position
B.      complete the stroke and bring the oars horizontal, blades feathered
C.      place the oars in the boat with blades forward
D.      place the oars in the rowlocks directly from the boated position

20 - USCG 603
The painter which is to be attached to the thwart of a lifeboat should _____.
A.      be fitted at the end with an approved safety shackle
B.      have a long eye splice at the end, and a shackle and pin should be attached to the painter with a lanyard
C.      have a long eye splice at the end, and a hardwood toggle should be attached to the thwart with a lanyard
D.      be fitted with a swivel and quick-releasing pelican hook

21 - USCG 733
Lifeboat hatchets should be _____.
A.      kept in a locker
B.      secured at each end of the boat with a lanyard
C.      kept next to the boat coxswain
D.      kept in the emergency locker on the ship and brought to the lifeboat when needed

22 - USCG 1910
Which visual distress signal is acceptable for daylight use only?
A.      Hand-held red flare
B.      Self-contained rocket-propelled parachute red flare
C.      Hand-held orange smoke distress flare
D.      Red aerial pyrotechnic flare

23 - USCG 1385
An inflatable liferaft is hand-launched by _____.
A.　　pulling a cord
B.　　cutting the wire restraining bands
C.　　removing the rubber packing strip
D.　　throwing the entire container overboard

24 - USCG 1242
The bosun has thrown the liferaft into the water before abandoning the vessel. The operating cord
_____.
A.　　serves as a sea painter
B.　　detaches from the liferaft automatically
C.　　is used to rig the boarding ladder
D.　　is cut immediately as it is of no further use

25 - USCG 1346
The canopy of an inflatable liferaft should _____.
A.　　go into place as the raft is inflated
B.　　be put up after everyone is aboard
C.　　be put up only in severe weather
D.　　be used as a sail if the wind is blowing

26 - USCG 5154
The sea anchor shown as item number 18 will NOT _____.
See Diagram: D014SA
A.　　check the liferaft's way
B.　　keep the liferaft end on to the sea
C.　　reduce the possibility of capsizing or broaching
D.　　right the raft if it inflates inverted

27 - USCG 833
While reading the muster list you see that "3 short blasts on the whistle and 3 short rings on the general alarm bells" is the signal for _____.
A.　　abandon ship
B.　　dismissal from fire and emergency stations
C.　　fire and emergency
D.　　man overboard

28 - USCG 1555
Seawater may be used for drinking _____.
A.　　at a maximum rate of two ounces per day
B.　　after mixing with an equal quantity of fresh water
C.　　if gathered during or immediately after a hard rain
D.　　under no conditions

29 - USCG 676
Your vessel has 3 lifeboats on each side. The middle boat on the starboard side is designated as boat number _____.
A.　　2
B.　　2 STARBOARD
C.　　3
D.　　4

30 - USCG 636
What is required by regulations concerning the stowage of lifeboats on cargo vessels?
A.      Each lifeboat must have a launching appliance.
B.      Launching appliances must be of the gravity type.
C.      There may not be more than two launching appliances on the same deck.
D.      All of the above

31 - USCG 1585
Up to two thirds of a survival crafts required drinking water may be produced by a manually-powered reverse osmosis desalinator if it can be done in _____.
A.      12 hours
B.      1 day
C.      2 days
D.      4 days

32 - USCG 287
The Master shall insure that the Emergency Position Indicating Radio beacon (EPIRB) is _____.
A.      secured inside the wheelhouse
B.      tested annually
C.      tested monthly
D.      secured in the emergency locker

33 - USCG 1064
By day, the horizontal motion of a white flag, or arms extended horizontally, by a person on the beach indicates _____.
A.      "Haul away"
B.      "Tail block is made fast"
C.      "Negative"
D.      "Affirmative"

34 - USCG 10075
Provided every effort is made to preserve body moisture content by avoiding perspiration, how long is it normally possible to survive without water?
A.      Up to 3 days
B.      8 to 12 days
C.      15 to 20 days
D.      25 to 30 days

35 - USCG 0
Frapping lines _____.
A.      secure the lifeboat in the davits when in the stowed position
B.      bring the lifeboat close alongside the rail in the embarkation position
C.      give the occupants a safety line when the boat is being lowered from the embarkation level
D.      reduce the swinging of the lifeboat at the embarkation level

36 - USCG 1310
Frapping lines are fitted to lifeboat davits to _____.
A.      reduce the swinging of the lifeboat as it is being lowered from the embarkation level
B.      secure the lifeboat in the davits when in the stowed position
C.      hold the lifeboat to the ship's side until the tricing lines are passed
D.      be used as a safety line in an emergency

37 - USCG 573
The sea painter of a lifeboat should be led _____.
A.      forward and outside of all obstructions
B.      forward and inside of all obstructions
C.      up and down from the main deck
D.      to the foremost point on the ship

38 - USCG 1105
In launching a lifeboat, when should the tricing pendants be released?
A.      Before the boat is lowered from the stowage position
B.      As soon as the boat-fall blocks clear the davit head
C.      After the limit switch is activated
D.      After all people have been embarked

39 - USCG 1295
If you must land on a beach with an oar-propelled lifeboat through a heavy surf, the recommended method is
to _____.
A.      keep the bow directly in toward the beach, and tow the sea anchor off the stern
B.      ride in on the back of a large breaker
C.      keep the bow into the seas with the sea anchor out over the bow, and row to meet the breaking
        waves
D.      head directly into the beach by staying between the crests of the waves

40 - USCG 1353
In heavy seas the helmsman should steer the motor lifeboat _____.
A.      into the seas
B.      broadside to the seas
C.      in the same direction as the seas
D.      in a series of figure-eights

41 - USCG 1286
The inside light in an inflatable liferaft is turned on _____.
A.      automatically as the liferaft inflates
B.      with a switch near the boarding handle
C.      at night because the light has a photosensitive switch
D.      by screwing the bulb in after the raft is inflated

42 - USCG 1324
A hydrostatic release mechanism for a liferaft _____.
A.      must be wet before it will release
B.      should be kept in a watertight cover except in an emergency
C.      will inflate the raft in its cradle if operated manually
D.      must be submerged to a certain depth to release automatically

43 - USCG 1404
Signaling devices which are required on inflatable liferafts include _____.
A.      a rocket shoulder rifle
B.      an oil lantern
C.      red flares
D.      an air horn

44 - USCG 823
Traditionally, the signal for fire aboard ship is _____.
A.      more than 6 short blasts and 1 long blast on the whistle, and the same signal on the general alarm
B.      continuous sounding of the ship's whistle and the general alarm for at least 10 seconds
C.      1 short blast on the whistle
D.      alternating short and long blasts on the ship's whistle

45 - USCG 1491
You are in a lifeboat when you sight the stars shown. You will be heading almost due north when you head for Polaris which is marked by what letter?
See Diagram: D006SA
A.      C
B.      D
C.      E
D.      G

46 - USCG 5408
One of the first actions to be taken by survivors when they have boarded an inflatable liferaft is to _____.
A.      stream the sea anchor
B.      take an anti-seasickness pill
C.      open the pressure relief valve
D.      drink at least one can of water

47 - USCG 3789
The signal for a fire emergency on an OSV is _____.
A.      a 30 second on 30 second off alternating signal
B.      the continuous blast of the ships whistle for not less than 10 seconds supplemented by the continuous ringing of the general alarm bells for not less than 10 seconds
C.      an intermittent ringing of the general alarm for not less than ten seconds
D.      announced over the PA system
E.
48 - USCG 3418
Your 600 GT vessel must carry a line-throwing appliance if it is certificated for what type of service?
A.      river service
B.      Great Lakes service
C.      coastwise service
D.      None of the above

49 - USCG 1326
All inflatable liferafts have _____.
A.      safety straps from the overhead
B.      built in seats
C.      releasing hooks at each end
D.      water stabilizing pockets

50 - USCG 7578
When a helicopter is lifting personnel from an enclosed lifeboat, the other individuals in the boat should _____.
A.      enter the water in case the person being lifted slips from the sling
B.      stand on the outside of the boat to assist the person being lifted
C.      remove their life preservers to prepare for their transfer to the helicopter
D.      remain seated inside to provide body weight for stability

51 - USCG 3186
Using a sea anchor will _____.
A.      reduce the drift rate of the liferaft
B.      keep the liferaft from turning over
C.      aid in recovering the liferaft
D.      increase your visibility

52 - USCG 3767
When whistle signals are used for launching lifeboats, one short blast means _____.
A.      "use the float-free method only"
B.      "lower all boats"
C.      "raise all boats"
D.      "drill is over, secure all boats"

53 - USCG 3770
The abandon ship signal is _____.
A.      a continuous ringing of general alarm bells for at least 10 seconds
B.      a continuous ringing of the general alarm, and sounding of the ship's whistle
C.      more than 6 short blasts and 1 long blast of the ship's whistle and the same signal on the general alarm bells
D.      a continuous sounding of the ship's whistle

54 - USCG 944
The lifesaving signal indicating "You are seen - assistance will be given as soon as possible" is the
_____.
A.      vertical motion of white flags
B.      vertical motion of a white light or flare
C.      firing of a green star signal
D.      None of the above

55 - USCG 1054
By day, the signal meaning, "This is the best place to land" is a _____.
A.      vertical motion of a red flag
B.      vertical motion of a white flag or the arms
C.      white smoke signal
D.      white star rocket

56 - USCG 10025
The air spaces in the floor of an inflatable liferaft will provide protection against _____.
A.      asphyxiation from $CO_2$
B.      loss of air in the sides of the raft
C.      rough seas
D.      cold water temperatures

57 - USCG 643
The steering oar in a lifeboat is usually referred to as the _____.
A.      bumpkin oar
B.      stroke oar
C.      sweep oar
D.      becket oar

**58 - USCG 1506**
Before hydraulic starting of an engine on a covered lifeboat, what need NOT be checked?
A.     Fuel supply line valve
B.     Pressure registered on the accumulator gauge
C.     Cold-spark voltage readings test lamp
D.     Engine stop control

**59 - USCG 9197**
In the first 24 hours after abandoning a vessel, water should be given only to personnel who are _____.
A.     thirsty
B.     sick or injured
C.     wet
D.     awake

**60 - USCG 2794**
Which would influence a magnetic compass?
A.     Electrical wiring
B.     Iron pipe
C.     Radio
D.     All of the above

**61 - USCG 1074**
Which one of the following signals is made at night by a lifesaving station to indicate "Landing here highly dangerous"?
A.     Horizontal motion of a white light or flare
B.     Vertical motion of a white light or flare
C.     White star rocket
D.     Vertical motion of a red light or flare

**62 - USCG 5312**
As shown, the line indicated by number 4 is connected to the _____.
See Diagram: D016SA
A.     releasing gear
B.     sea painter
C.     McCluny hook
D.     Fleming gear

**63 - USCG 2219**
Each buoyant work vest must be _____.
A.     U.S. Coast Guard approved
B.     marked with the name of the vessel
C.     equipped with a water light
D.     All of the above

**64 - USCG 10046**
Which precaution should be taken when testing a line throwing gun?
A.     Never remove the line from the rocket.
B.     Fire it at an angle of approximately 90 degrees to the horizon.
C.     Wear asbestos gloves.
D.     All of the above

65 - USCG 293
Which statement is TRUE concerning life jackets which are severely damaged?
A.      They should be replaced.
B.      They must be tested for buoyancy before being continued in use.
C.      They can be repaired by a reliable seamstress.
D.      They can be used for children.

66 - USCG 2063
If there are a number of survivors in the water after abandoning ship, they should _____.
A.      tie themselves to the unit so they won't drift with the current
B.      form a small circular group to create a warmer pocket of water in the center of the circle
C.      send the strongest swimmer to shore for assistance
D.      form a raft by lashing their life preservers together

67 - USCG 2694
The heading of a vessel is indicated by what part of the compass?
A.      Card
B.      Needle
C.      Lubber's line
D.      Gimbals

68 - USCG 4125
BOTH INTERNATIONAL & INLAND If you saw flames aboard a vessel but could see the vessel was not on fire, you would know that the _____.
A.      crew was trying to get warm
B.      vessel required immediate assistance
C.      vessel was attempting to attract the attention of a pilot boat
D.      vessel was being illuminated for identification by aircraft

69 - USCG 4262
Which statement about immersion suits is TRUE?
A.      Prior to abandonment, the suit allows body movement such as walking, climbing a ladder and picking up small objects.
B.      The immersion suit seals in body heat and provides protection against hypothermia for weeks.
C.      The suit is flameproof and provides protection to the wearer while swimming through burning oil.
D.      The wearer of the suit is severely restricted and requires twice the time to climb a ladder than without the suit

70 - USCG 2811
A vessel heading SW is on a course of _____.
A.      202.5°
B.      225.0°
C.      247.5°
D.      270.0°

**LIFEBOATMAN**
**481XX-Deck Safety and Rules of the Road**
**Test No. 330701 - Answers**

| | | | |
|---|---|---|---|
| 1 | 102 | C | Rule 37; Annex IV |
| 2 | 313 | D | CHAPMAN; *46 CFR 160.47 |
| 3 | 1940 | C | *46 CFR 199.70 (b) (2) (i) |
| 4 | 781 | C | NVIC 5-86; *46 CFR 160.171-9 |
| 5 | 433 | A | *46 CFR 199.80 (b) (7) |
| 6 | 503 | B | AMSM; *46 CFR 199.176 |
| 7 | 533 | D | WSM; *46 CFR 160.35 |
| 8 | 713 | D | LBMAN; *46 CFR 160.33 |
| 9 | 743 | B | AMSM; *46 CFR 160.35 |
| 10 | 1200 | A | AMSM |
| 11 | 1270 | C | AMSM |
| 12 | 1280 | A | AMSM |
| 13 | 1290 | B | AMSM |
| 14 | 1513 | D | *46 CFR 199.190 (f) (2) |
| 15 | 1085 | C | LBMAN |
| 16 | 1095 | C | AMSM |
| 17 | 1125 | B | AMSM |
| 18 | 1155 | A | LBMAN; *46 CFR 199.175 (b) (21) |
| 19 | 1195 | B | WSM |
| 20 | 603 | C | WSM; *46 CFR 199.175 (b) (21) |
| 21 | 733 | B | LBMAN; *46 CFR 199.175 (b) (13) |
| 22 | 1910 | C | AMSM |
| 23 | 1385 | D | AMSM |
| 24 | 1242 | A | LBMAN |
| 25 | 1346 | A | LBMAN; *46 CFR 160.51 |
| 26 | 5154 | D | AMSM  D014SA |
| 27 | 833 | B | *46 CFR 35.10-5 (a) |
| 28 | 1555 | D | WSM |
| 29 | 676 | C | *46 CFR 97.37-37 (b) |
| 30 | 636 | A | *46 CFR 199.155 (a) |
| 31 | 1585 | C | *46 CFR 199.175 (b) (40) (ii); *46 CFR 160.58 |
| 32 | 287 | C | *46 CFR 97.15-65 |
| 33 | 1064 | C | AMSM |
| 34 | 10075 | B | WSM |
| 35 | 0 | D | AMSM |
| 36 | 1310 | A | AMSM |
| 37 | 573 | A | AMSM; *46 CFR 199.175 (b) (21) |
| 38 | 1105 | D | AMSM |
| 39 | 1295 | C | WSM |
| 40 | 1353 | A | USCGA BOATING SKILLS and SEAMANSHIP |
| 41 | 1286 | A | LBMAN; *46 CFR 160.51 |
| 42 | 1324 | D | AMSM |
| 43 | 1404 | C | *46 CFR 94.20-25, 160 |
| 44 | 823 | B | AMSM; *46 CFR 35.10-5 (a) |
| 45 | 1491 | A | BOWD  D006SA |
| 46 | 5408 | B | WSM |
| 47 | 3789 | B | *46 CFR 131.535 |
| 48 | 3418 | C | *46 CFR 199.170; *46 CFR 199.01 |
| 49 | 1326 | D | MIL; *46 CFR 160.51-4 (b) |
| 50 | 7578 | D | MSRS |

| 51 | 3186  | A | WHITTAKER |
| 52 | 3767  | B | *46 CFR 35.10-5 |
| 53 | 3770  | C | *46 CFR 35.10-5 |
| 54 | 944   | D | *H.O. 102 |
| 55 | 1054  | B | AMSM; *H.O. 102 |
| 56 | 10025 | D | WSM |
| 57 | 643   | C | AMSM; *46 CFR 199.175 (b) (20) |
| 58 | 1506  | C | WSM |
| 59 | 9197  | B | SAFETY AT SEA |
| 60 | 2794  | D | *BOWD 2 |
| 61 | 1074  | A | AMSM; *H.O. 102 |
| 62 | 5312  | C | AMSM  D016SA |
| 63 | 2219  | A | *46 CFR 108.697; *46 CFR 160.53 |
| 64 | 10046 | A | MSRS Page 246 |
| 65 | 293   | A | *46 CFR 160.006-2 (b) |
| 66 | 2063  | B | MSRS |
| 67 | 2694  | C | *BOWD 2 |
| 68 | 4125  | B | Rule 37; Annex IV |
| 69 | 4262  | A | *46 CFR 160.171-9 (m) |
| 70 | 2811  | B | *BOWD 2, TABLE 2 |

**LIFEBOATMAN**
**481XX-Deck Safety and Rules of the Road**
**Test No. 330705**

1 - USCG 4102
BOTH INTERNATIONAL & INLAND A distress signal _____.
A.      consists of 5 or more short blasts of the fog signal apparatus
B.      consists of the raising and lowering of a large white flag
C.      may be used separately or with other distress signals
D.      is used to indicate doubt about another vessel's intentions

2 - USCG 283
Spreading oil on the open sea has the effect of _____.
A.      diminishing the height of the seas
B.      lengthening the distance between successive crests
C.      increasing the height of the seas
D.      preventing the wave crests from breaking

3 - USCG 1920
Which statement is TRUE concerning life preservers?
A.      Buoyant vests may be substituted for life preservers.
B.      Kapok life preservers must have vinyl-covered pad inserts.
C.      Life preservers must always be worn with the same side facing outwards.
D.      Life preservers are not designed to turn a person's face clear of the water when unconscious.

4 - USCG 383
The purpose of the tripping line on a sea anchor is to _____.
A.      aid in casting off
B.      direct the drift of the vessel
C.      aid in its recovery
D.      maintain maximum resistance to broaching

5 - USCG 393
A sea anchor is _____.
A.      a heavy anchor with an extra long line used to anchor in deep water
B.      a cone shaped bag used to slow down the wind drift effect
C.      a pad eye to which the sea painter is made fast
D.      made of wood if it is of an approved type

6 - USCG 403
Due to the shape of the sea anchor, the best way to haul it back aboard is by _____.
A.      hauling in on the anchor line as you would any anchor
B.      getting all hands to assist
C.      its trip line
D.      cutting the line, as you cannot haul it back in

7 - USCG 1642
The Master or person in charge on a MODU shall insure that line throwing equipment is not operated

_____.
A.      during a rain storm
B.      in an explosive atmosphere
C.      near a lifeboat station
D.      by other than senior rig personnel

8 - USCG 673
The grab rail of a metal lifeboat is normally located _____.
A.      along the turn of the bilge
B.      along each side of the keel
C.      near the top of the gunwale
D.      at the bow and at the stern

9 - USCG 1121
As shown, number 1 operates the _____.
See Diagram: D011SA
A.      releasing gear
B.      McCluny hook
C.      sea painter
D.      Fleming gear

10 - USCG 1690
The tops of the thwarts, side benches, and the footings of a lifeboat are painted which color?
A.      International orange
B.      Yellow
C.      White
D.      Red

11 - USCG 1100
The maximum speed of lowering for a lifeboat on gravity davits is controlled by the _____.
A.      limit switches
B.      emergency disconnect switch
C.      governor brake
D.      position of the counterweight on the brake handle

12 - USCG 1170
When operating gravity davits, the _____.
A.      gripes should be released after the boat is moving
B.      davits should always be hand cranked the last 12 inches into the final stowed position
C.      boats are generally lowered by surging the falls around cruciform bitts
D.      tricing pendant should be tripped prior to releasing the gripes

13 - USCG 1190
What could be a result of insufficient lubrication of lifeboat winches and davits?
A.      Moisture accumulation in winch motor damaging the electrical wiring
B.      Freezing of gears in cold weather
C.      Corroding of sheaves on the davits so they will not rotate
D.      All of the above

14 - USCG 1270
The most common type of davit found on merchant vessels today is the _____.
A.      radial
B.      sheath-screw
C.      gravity
D.      quadrantal

15 - USCG 1290
Which davit type may be operated by one man?
A.      Quadrantal
B.      Gravity
C.      Sheath-screw
D.      Radial

16 - USCG 1300
Blocks and falls used as lifeboat gear must be designed with a minimum safety factor of _____.
A.      4, based on the breaking strength
B.      5, based on the maximum allowable stress
C.      6, based on the maximum working load
D.      8, based on the normal working load

17 - USCG 553
Which statement is TRUE concerning lifeboat gripes?
A.      They must be released by freeing a safety shackle.
B.      They should not be released until the boat is in lowering position.
C.      They may be adjusted by a turnbuckle.
D.      They are normally used only with radial davits.

18 - USCG 1075
Prior to lowering the lifeboat, the most important item to check is the _____.
A.      oars
B.      sail
C.      boat plug
D.      life preservers

19 - USCG 1095
When launching a lifeboat, frapping lines should be rigged _____.
A.      before the gripes are released
B.      before the boat is moved from the davits
C.      at the embarkation deck
D.      after the boat is in the water

20 - USCG 1125
What is the best procedure for picking up a lifeboat at sea while utilizing the lifeboat's sea painter?
A.      Place the lifeboat ahead and to windward of your vessel with the wind about broad on the bow of your ship.
B.      Place the lifeboat ahead and to leeward of your ship with the wind about broad on the bow of your ship.
C.      Place your ship to windward of the lifeboat with the wind on the quarter to allow your ship to drift down to the lifeboat.
D.      Place the lifeboat ahead and to windward of your ship with the wind about broad on the quarter of your ship.

21 - USCG 1225
If the coxswain of your lifeboat gives the command "HOLD WATER" you should _____.
A.      complete the stroke, raise your oar slightly, swinging the oar slightly forward, and place it in the boat
B.      lift the oar in a vertical position
C.      complete the stroke and hold the oar out of the water
D.      dip the blade of your oar into the water vertically and hold it perpendicular to the keel line

22 - USCG 1234
When landing a lifeboat through heavy surf with a strong current running parallel to the beach (from right to left when facing from seaward) the recommended procedure is to _____.
A.      approach while coming to the left to take advantage of the current
B.      drop an anchor outside the surf line, then pay out anchor line over the bow while the seas carry the boat toward the beach
C.      approach slow enough so that the boat can be brought around to meet breaking seas on the bow
D.      rig a drogue with tripping line over the bow, back ashore with drogue tripped between breakers

23 - USCG 763
Which item of lifeboat equipment would be most suitable for night signaling to a ship on the horizon?
A.      A red parachute flare
B.      A red hand-held flare
C.      A flashlight
D.      A lantern

24 - USCG 9167
To release the davit cable of a davit launched liferaft, you must _____.
A.      pull the release lanyard
B.      pull the hydraulic release
C.      push the release button
D.      pull on the ratchet handle

25 - USCG 1242
The bosun has thrown the liferaft into the water before abandoning the vessel. The operating cord _____.
A.      serves as a sea painter
B.      detaches from the liferaft automatically
C.      is used to rig the boarding ladder
D.      is cut immediately as it is of no further use

26 - USCG 1256
The water pockets located on the underside of inflatable liferafts _____.
A.      stow rainwater; these 4 spaces do not take up valuable space
B.      act as stabilizers by filling with sea water as soon as the raft is inflated and upright
C.      hold the freshwater required by regulation to be provided in the raft when packed
D.      None of the above

27 - USCG 1266
A life line must be connected to the liferaft _____.
A.      at the bow
B.      at the stern
C.      in the middle
D.      all around

28 - USCG 1314
Under normal conditions a liferaft is released from its cradle by _____.
A.      cutting the restraining strap
B.      unscrewing the turnbuckle on the back of the cradle
C.      lifting one end of the raft
D.      pushing the plunger on the center of the hydrostatic release

29 - USCG 833
While reading the muster list you see that "3 short blasts on the whistle and 3 short rings on the general alarm bells" is the signal for _____.
A.      abandon ship
B.      dismissal from fire and emergency stations
C.      fire and emergency
D.      man overboard

30 - USCG 1540
Which statement concerning the sources of drinking water is FALSE?
A.      Fresh water may be obtained from fish.
B.      Lifeboat covers or canopies should be washed with rain before drinking water is collected.
C.      Fresh water may be collected from condensation inside the liferaft.
D.      Seawater should never be consumed.

31 - USCG 8848
Enclosed lifeboats which have been afloat over a long period of time require _____.
A.      frequent opening of hatches to permit entry of fresh air
B.      regular checks of bilge levels
C.      use of ear plugs to dampen engine noise
D.      frequent flushing of the water spray system with fresh water

32 - USCG 9385
When personnel are lifted by a helicopter from an inflatable liferaft, the personnel on the raft should _____.
A.      deflate the floor of the raft to reduce the danger of the raft overturning
B.      inflate the floor of the raft to provide for additional stability
C.      remove their life preservers to prepare for the transfer
D.      take in the sea anchor to prevent fouling of the rescue sling

33 - USCG 3450
According to the regulations for lifeboat falls, which action must be taken at 30-month intervals?
A.      End-for-ended
B.      Renewed
C.      Inspected
D.      Weight tested

34 - USCG 866
The number of rowing oars that must be carried in a motor-propelled open lifeboat on a cargo vessel is _____.
A.      determined by the Master
B.      specified by the Coast Guard
C.      specified by the manufacturer
D.      None

35 - USCG 914
What is the lifesaving signal for "You are seen - assistance will be given as soon as possible"?
A.      Red star rocket
B.      Orange smoke signal
C.      Green star rocket
D.      Vertical motion of a flag

36 - USCG 1024
The firing of a red star signal may mean _____.
A.      "This is the best place to land"
B.      "You are seen - assistance will be given as soon as possible"
C.      "Tail block is made fast"
D.      "Slack away"

37 - USCG 843
The signal given to commence lowering the lifeboats is _____.
A.      3 short blasts of the ship's whistle
B.      specified on the muster list (station bill)
C.      3 long blasts of the ship's whistle
D.      1 long blast of the ship's whistle

38 - USCG 1230
The purpose of the tricing pendants is to _____.
A.      control the fore and aft motion of a lifeboat during lowering
B.      control the outboard swing of a lifeboat during lowering
C.      provide suspensions for the manropes
D.      hold a lifeboat next to the embarkation deck while loading

39 - USCG 1105
In launching a lifeboat, when should the tricing pendants be released?
A.      Before the boat is lowered from the stowage position
B.      As soon as the boat-fall blocks clear the davit head
C.      After the limit switch is activated
D.      After all people have been embarked

40 - USCG 1353
In heavy seas the helmsman should steer the motor lifeboat _____.
A.      into the seas
B.      broadside to the seas
C.      in the same direction as the seas
D.      in a series of figure-eights

41 - USCG 1680
In an open lifeboat, the lifeboat compass is usually _____.
A.      placed in a fixed bracket when being used
B.      clamped to any position convenient for the coxswain to see it
C.      permanently mounted on the lifeboat's centerline
D.      mounted in the center of the boat to eliminate deviation

42 - USCG 1286
The inside light in an inflatable liferaft is turned on _____.
A.      automatically as the liferaft inflates
B.      with a switch near the boarding handle
C.      at night because the light has a photosensitive switch
D.      by screwing the bulb in after the raft is inflated

43 - USCG 103
You have just abandoned ship and boarded a raft. After the raft is completely inflated you hear a whistling noise coming from a safety valve. You should _____.
A.      not become alarmed unless it continues for a long period of time
B.      plug the safety valve
C.      unscrew the deflation plugs
D.      remove the safety valve and replace it with a soft patch

44 - USCG 5408
One of the first actions to be taken by survivors when they have boarded an inflatable liferaft is to _____.
A.      stream the sea anchor
B.      take an anti-seasickness pill
C.      open the pressure relief valve
D.      drink at least one can of water

45 - USCG 3788
When you hear three short blasts on the ship's whistle and the same signal on the general alarm bells, you _____.
A.      are required to be at your liferaft
B.      are dismissed from drills
C.      should point to the man overboard
D.      should start the fire pump

46 - USCG 3789
The signal for a fire emergency on an OSV is _____.
A.      a 30 second on 30 second off alternating signal
B.      the continuous blast of the ships whistle for not less than 10 seconds supplemented by the continuous ringing of the general alarm bells for not less than 10 seconds
C.      an intermittent ringing of the general alarm for not less than ten seconds
D.      announced over the PA system

47 - USCG 696
For each person it is certified to carry, a lifeboat on an oceangoing passenger vessel must be provided with all of the following EXCEPT _____.
A.      3 liters of water
B.      1 unit of provisions
C.      1 seasickness kit
D.      1 life preserver

48 - USCG 4174
Each EPIRB shall be tested using the integrated test circuit and output indicator every _____.
A.      week
B.      two weeks
C.      month
D.      quarter

49 - USCG 1014
Which signal would be used by a shore rescue unit to indicate "Landing here highly dangerous"?
A.      The firing of a white star signal
B.      Horizontal motion with a white flag
C.      Vertical motion of a white light
D.      Code letter "K" by blinker light

50 - USCG 10063
What does the lifesaving signal indicated by a horizontal motion of a white light or white flare mean?
A.　　　"Landing here highly dangerous"
B.　　　"Negative"
C.　　　"Avast hauling"
D.　　　All of the above

51 - USCG 1851
When using a hand held smoke signal from a lifeboat, you should activate the signal _____.
A.　　　on the downwind side
B.　　　on the upwind side
C.　　　inside the boat
D.　　　at the stern

52 - USCG 3186
Using a sea anchor will _____.
A.　　　reduce the drift rate of the liferaft
B.　　　keep the liferaft from turning over
C.　　　aid in recovering the liferaft
D.　　　increase your visibility

53 - USCG 3770
The abandon ship signal is _____.
A.　　　a continuous ringing of general alarm bells for at least 10 seconds
B.　　　a continuous ringing of the general alarm, and sounding of the ship's whistle
C.　　　more than 6 short blasts and 1 long blast of the ship's whistle and the same signal on the general alarm bells
D.　　　a continuous sounding of the ship's whistle

54 - USCG 2779
Error may be introduced into a magnetic compass by _____.
A.　　　making a structural change to the vessel
B.　　　a short circuit near the compass
C.　　　belt buckles
D.　　　All of the above

55 - USCG 1720
Your vessel has 3 lifeboats on each side. The aftermost boat on the starboard side is designated as boat number _____.
A.　　　6
B.　　　5
C.　　　3
D.　　　3 STARBOARD

56 - USCG 1520
When operating the air supply system in a covered lifeboat the _____.
A.　　　fuel supply valve should be closed
B.　　　hatches, doors, and oar ports should be closed
C.　　　air cylinder shut-off valve should be closed
D.　　　engine should be shut off

57 - USCG 1206
Inflatable liferafts are provided with a _____.
A.      knife
B.      towing connection
C.      lifeline
D.      All of the above

58 - USCG 93
If, for any reason, it is necessary to abandon ship while far out at sea, it is important that the crew members should _____.
A.      separate from each other as this will increase the chances of being rescued
B.      get away from the area because sharks will be attracted to the vessel
C.      immediately head for the nearest land
D.      remain together in the area because rescuers will start searching at the vessel's last known position

59 - USCG 8662
When may a work vest be substituted for a required life preserver?
A.      To replace a damaged life preserver
B.      For use during fire drills
C.      For use during boat drills
D.      At no time

60 - USCG 4446
BOTH INTERNATIONAL & INLAND Which is NOT a distress signal?
A.      Flames on a vessel
B.      Vertical motion of a white lantern at night
C.      Code flags "November" and "Charlie"
D.      Dye marker on the water

61 - USCG 1414
What should be used to steer an open lifeboat if the rudder becomes lost or damaged?
A.      Sea anchor
B.      Steering oar
C.      Spare rudder
D.      Daggerboard

62 - USCG 1120
You will find a limit switch on a _____.
A.      liferaft cradle
B.      radial davit
C.      sheath-screw davit
D.      gravity davit

63 - USCG 5486
This illustration shows the correct method of securing a _____.
See Diagram: D009SA
A.      man-rope
B.      frapping line
C.      sea painter
D.      lifeline

64 - USCG 936
If your vessel is equipped with inflatable liferafts, how should they be maintained?
A.      Have your crew check them annually.
B.      They do not need any maintenance.
C.      Have them sent ashore to an approved maintenance facility annually.
D.      Have them serviced by the shipyard annually.

65 - USCG 1454
You are in a lifeboat when you sight the stars indicated in illustration D005SA. You will be heading due north when you head for Polaris which is indicated by what letter? See Diagram: D005SA
A.      A
B.      C
C.      E
D.      I

66 - USCG 10024
Signaling devices required on inflatable liferafts include a(n) _____.
A.      Very pistol
B.      orange smoke signal
C.      air horn
D.      lantern

67 - USCG 233
Most enclosed lifeboats will right themselves after capsizing IF the _____.
A.      lower ballast tanks are filled with water
B.      fuel tanks are not less than half full
C.      passengers are strapped to their seats
D.      sea anchor is deployed to windward

68 - USCG 2658
As a vessel changes course to starboard, the compass card in a magnetic compass _____.
A.      first turns to starboard then counterclockwise to port
B.      also turns to starboard
C.      turns counterclockwise to port
D.      remains aligned with compass north

69 - USCG 10023
Puncture leaks in the lower tubes or bottom of an inflatable liferaft should FIRST be stopped by using

_____.
A.      sealing clamps
B.      repair tape
C.      a tube patch
D.      sail twine and vulcanizing kit

70 - USCG 2835
A vessel heading NNE is on a course of _____.
A.      022.5°
B.      045.0°
C.      067.5°
D.      090.0°

**LIFEBOATMAN**
**481XX-Deck Safety and Rules of the Road**
**Test No. 330705 - Answers**

| | | | |
|---|---|---|---|
| 1 | 4102 | C | Rule 37; Annex IV |
| 2 | 283 | D | AMSM; *46 CFR 199.175 (b) (27) |
| 3 | 1920 | B | *46 CFR 180.25-1; *46 CFR 160.47 |
| 4 | 383 | C | AMSM; *46 CFR 199.175 (b) (27); *46 CFR 160.19 |
| 5 | 393 | B | AMSM; *46 CFR 199.175 (b) (27); *46 CFR 160.19 |
| 6 | 403 | C | AMSM; *46 CFR 199.175 (b) (27); *46 CFR 160.19 |
| 7 | 1642 | B | MSRS |
| 8 | 673 | A | AMSM; *46 CFR 160.35 |
| 9 | 1121 | D | AMSM  D011SA |
| 10 | 1690 | A | *46 CFR 160.35 (c) (1) |
| 11 | 1100 | C | *46 CFR 160.15-3 (g) |
| 12 | 1170 | B | AMSM |
| 13 | 1190 | D | WSM |
| 14 | 1270 | C | AMSM |
| 15 | 1290 | B | AMSM |
| 16 | 1300 | C | *46 CFR 160.32-3 (a) |
| 17 | 553 | C | AMSM |
| 18 | 1075 | C | AMSM; *46 CFR 160.35 |
| 19 | 1095 | C | AMSM |
| 20 | 1125 | B | AMSM |
| 21 | 1225 | D | AMSM |
| 22 | 1234 | D | AMSM |
| 23 | 763 | A | AMSM; *46 CFR 199.175 (b) (32); *46 CFR 160.36 |
| 24 | 9167 | A | SAFETY AT SEA |
| 25 | 1242 | A | LBMAN |
| 26 | 1256 | B | WSM; *46 CFR 160.51-4 (b) |
| 27 | 1266 | D | WSM; *46 CFR 160.51 |
| 28 | 1314 | D | AMSM; LBMAN |
| 29 | 833 | B | *46 CFR 35.10-5 (a) |
| 30 | 1540 | A | WSM |
| 31 | 8848 | B | MSRS |
| 32 | 9385 | A | MSRS |
| 33 | 3450 | A | SOLAS REG, CHAP III; *46 CFR 199.190 (j) (ii) |
| 34 | 866 | C | *46 CFR 199.175 |
| 35 | 914 | B | *H.O. 102 |
| 36 | 1024 | D | *H.O. 102 |
| 37 | 843 | B | *46 CFR 199.80 (b) (2) |
| 38 | 1230 | D | AMSM 39    1105    D    AMSM |
| 40 | 1353 | A | USCGA BOATING SKILLS and SEAMANSHIP |
| 41 | 1680 | A | WSM; *46 CFR 199.175 (b) (6) |
| 42 | 1286 | A | LBMAN; *46 CFR 160.51 |
| 43 | 103 | A | MIL |
| 44 | 5408 | B | WSM |
| 45 | 3788 | B | *46 CFR 35.10-5; *46 CFR 97.13-15 |
| 46 | 3789 | B | *46 CFR 131.535 |
| 47 | 696 | D | *46 CFR 199.175 (b) (40), (22), (29) |
| 48 | 4174 | C | *46 CFR 109.208 |
| 49 | 1014 | B | *H.O. 102 |
| 50 | 10063 | D | *H.O. 102 |

| 51 | 1851 | A | FVSM; *46 CFR 199.175 (b) (30) |
| 52 | 3186 | A | WHITTAKER |
| 53 | 3770 | C | *46 CFR 35.10-5 |
| 54 | 2779 | D | *BOWD 2 |
| 55 | 1720 | B | WSM Page 8 |
| 56 | 1520 | B | WSM |
| 57 | 1206 | D | AMSM; *46 CFR 199.175 |
| 58 | 93 | D | LBMAN |
| 59 | 8662 | D | *46 CFR 108.699; *46 CFR 160.53 |
| 60 | 4446 | B | Rule 37; Annex IV; Lifesaving Signals |
| 61 | 1414 | B | AMSM; SAFETY AT SEA; SURVIVAL GUIDE |
| 62 | 1120 | D | AMSM; *46 CFR 160.15-3 |
| 63 | 5486 | C | AMSM; *46 CFR 199.175 (b) (21)        D009SA |
| 64 | 936 | C | LBMAN; *46 CFR 199.190 (g) (3); *46 CFR 160.51-6 |
| 65 | 1454 | C | BOWD  D005SA |
| 66 | 10024 | B | *46 CFR 199.175 (b) (30) |
| 67 | 233 | C | WSM; MSRS |
| 68 | 2658 | D | *BOWD 2 |
| 69 | 10023 | A | MIL |
| 70 | 2835 | A | *BOWD 2, TABLE 2 |

**LIFEBOATMAN**
**481XX-Deck Safety and Rules of the Road**
**Test No. 330707**

1.    USCG 4733
BOTH INTERNATIONAL & INLAND A distress signal _____.
A.    consists of 5 or more short blasts of the fog signal apparatus
B.    consists of the raising and lowering of a large white flag
C.    may be used separately or with other distress signals
D.    is used to indicate doubt about another vessel's intentions

2.    USCG 353
When a sea anchor is used in landing stern first in a heavy surf, sternway is checked by _____.
A.    slacking the tripping line and towing the sea anchor from the stern
B.    slacking the tripping line and towing the sea anchor by the holding line
C.    towing with the tripping line and leaving the holding line slack
D.    towing the apex end forward with the tripping line

3.    USCG 383
The purpose of the tripping line on a sea anchor is to _____.
A.    aid in casting off
B.    direct the drift of the vessel
C.    aid in its recovery
D.    maintain maximum resistance to broaching

4.    USCG 856
Which statement about immersion suits is TRUE?
A.    Immersion suits should be worn during routine work on deck to provide maximum protection.
B.    After purchasing, the suit should be removed from its storage bag and hung on a hanger where readily accessible.
C.    Immersion suits must have a PFD light attached to the front shoulder area.
D.    Small leaks or tears may be repaired using the repair kit packed with the suit.

5.    USCG 1006
An immersion suit must be equipped with a(n) _____.
A.    air bottle for breathing
B.    orange smoke canister
C.    whistle, light and retroreflective material
D.    sea dye marker

6.    USCG 433
If passengers are on board when an abandon ship drill is carried out, they should _____.
A.    take part
B.    watch
C.    go to their quarters
D.    stay out of the way and do what they want

7.    USCG 1642
The Master or person in charge on a MODU shall insure that line throwing equipment is not operated _____.
A.    during a rain storm
B.    in an explosive atmosphere
C.    near a lifeboat station
D.    by other than senior rig personnel

8.        USCG 201
Your vessel is equipped with totally enclosed lifeboats. Which statement is TRUE when the boat is enveloped in flames?
A.        The ventilators will automatically close by the action of fusible links.
B.        The motor takes its air supply from outside the lifeboat to prevent asphyxiation of the crew.
C.        A water spray system to cool the outside of the boat is operated by a high-volume manual pump.
D.        An air tank will provide about ten minutes of air for the survivors and the engine.

9.        USCG 493
Why are lifeboats usually double-enders?
A.        They are more seaworthy and less likely to be swamped or broach to.
B.        They can go forward and backward more easily.
C.        They require less space for stowing aboard ship.
D.        There is no particular reason for this.

10.        USCG 3144
On a lifeboat equipped with Rottmer-type releasing gear, turning the releasing lever releases _____.
A.        the painter
B.        the after boat fall only if the boat is waterborne
C.        both falls at the same time only if the boat is waterborne
D.        both falls at the same time even if the boat has not reached the water

11.        USCG 1170
When operating gravity davits, the _____.
A.        gripes should be released after the boat is moving
B.        davits should always be hand cranked the last 12 inches into the final stowed position
C.        boats are generally lowered by surging the falls around cruciform bitts
D.        tricing pendant should be tripped prior to releasing the gripes

12.        USCG 1200
What is TRUE concerning frapping lines?
A.        They are used to steady a lifeboat when lowered.
B.        They are normally attached to the davit span.
C.        They are needed only on radial davits.
D.        They are used to clear the puddings.

13.        USCG 1270
The most common type of davit found on merchant vessels today is the _____.
A.        radial
B.        sheath-screw
C.        gravity
D.        quadrantal

14.        USCG 1300
Blocks and falls used as lifeboat gear must be designed with a minimum safety factor of _____.
A.        4, based on the breaking strength
B.        5, based on the maximum allowable stress
C.        6, based on the maximum working load
D.        8, based on the normal working load

15. USCG 1360

When lowering a boat with gravity davits, it will be pulled into the embarkation deck by the _____.

A. falls

B. tricing pendants

C. frapping lines

D. boat hooks

16. USCG 1390

Which sequence is correct when launching a lifeboat stowed in gravity davits?

A. Release gripes, turn on emergency disconnect switch, release frapping lines

B. Release tricing pennants, turn on emergency disconnect switch, release frapping lines

C. Operate limit switches, release gripes, lift brake

D. Release gripes, lift brake, release tricing pennants

17. USCG 1400

In rough weather, when a ship is able to maneuver, it is best to launch a lifeboat _____.

A. on the lee side

B. on the windward side

C. with the wind dead ahead

D. with the wind from astern

18. USCG 1234

When landing a lifeboat through heavy surf with a strong current running parallel to the beach (from right to left when facing from
seaward) the recommended procedure is to _____.

A. approach while coming to the left to take advantage of the current

B. drop an anchor outside the surf line, then pay out anchor line over the bow while the seas carry the boat toward the beach

C. approach slow enough so that the boat can be brought around to meet breaking seas on the bow

D. rig a drogue with tripping line over the bow, back ashore with drogue tripped between breakers

19. USCG 1305

When backing a motor propelled lifeboat (right-hand propeller) with the rudder amidships, the stern will back _____.

A. straight

B. to port

C. to starboard

D. None of the above

20. USCG 733

Lifeboat hatchets should be _____.

A. kept in a locker

B. secured at each end of the boat with a lanyard

C. kept next to the boat coxswain

D. kept in the emergency locker on the ship and brought to the lifeboat when needed

21. USCG 763

Which item of lifeboat equipment would be most suitable for night signaling to a ship on the horizon?

A. A red parachute flare

B. A red hand-held flare

C. A flashlight

D. A lantern

22.    USCG 1514
"Thermal protective aids" are required for what percentage of the persons a survival craft is equipped to carry?
A.    10%
B.    50%
C.    75%
D.    100%

23.    USCG 1345
An inflatable liferaft can be launched by _____.
A.    the float-free method ONLY
B.    breaking the weak link on the painter
C.    throwing the entire container overboard and then pulling on the operating cord to inflate the raft
D.    removing the securing straps

24.    USCG 1355
As a vessel sinks to a depth of 15 feet, the hydrostatic trip releases the liferaft container from its cradle by _____.
A.    breaking the weak link
B.    releasing the tie-down strap
C.    pulling the operating cord
D.    releasing the $CO_2$ canister

25.    USCG 1276
The lights on the outside of the canopy on an inflatable liferaft operate _____.
A.    by turning the globe clockwise
B.    by a switch at each light
C.    by a light sensor
D.    automatically when the raft is inflated

26.    USCG 1296
Hand holds or straps on the underside of an inflatable liferaft are provided _____.
A.    to right the raft if it capsizes
B.    to carry the raft around on deck
C.    for crewmen to hang on to
D.    to hang the raft for drying

27.    USCG 1493
A new liferaft has been installed on your vessel. The operating cord should be _____.
A.    attached to the raft stowage cradle or to a secure object nearby with a weak link
B.    checked to see that it's unattached
C.    coiled neatly on the raft container
D.    faked on deck and lead through a chock

28.    USCG 1059
Provided every effort is made to preserve body moisture content by avoiding perspiration, how long is it normally possible to survive without water?
A.    Up to 3 days
B.    8 to 14 days
C.    15 to 20 days
D.    25 to 30 days

29.     USCG 536
A fully loaded motor-propelled lifeboat must be capable of attaining a speed of at least _____.
A.      3 knots in smooth water
B.      6 knots in smooth water
C.      3 knots in rough water
D.      6 knots in rough water

30.     USCG 4242
A certificated lifeboatman assigned to command the lifeboat should _____.
A.      be the first individual to board the craft
B.      drain the hydraulic pressure before lowering the craft
C.      have a list of the persons assigned to the lifeboat
D.      All of the above

31.     USCG 1596
By regulation, orange smoke distress signals will expire not more than how many months from the date of manufacture?
A.      24 months
B.      36 months
C.      42 months
D.      54 months

32.     USCG 287
The Master shall insure that the Emergency Position Indicating Radio beacon (EPIRB) is _____.
A.      secured inside the wheelhouse
B.      tested annually
C.      tested monthly
D.      secured in the emergency locker

33.     USCG 964
Which signal is used by a rescue unit to indicate, "Avast hauling"?
A.      Firing of a green star signal
B.      Firing of a red star signal
C.      An orange smoke signal
D.      Three white star rockets fired at one-minute intervals

34.     USCG 112
Your small vessel is broken down and rolling in heavy seas. You can reduce the possibility of capsizing by _____.
A.      rigging a sea anchor
B.      constantly shifting the rudder
C.      moving all personnel forward and low
D.      moving all personnel aft

35.     USCG 8734
All personnel should be familiar with the lifeboats _____.
A.      boarding and operating procedures
B.      maintenance schedule
C.      navigational systems
D.      fuel consumption rates

36.    USCG 0
Frapping lines _____.
A.    secure the lifeboat in the davits when in the stowed position
B.    bring the lifeboat close alongside the rail in the embarkation position
C.    give the occupants a safety line when the boat is being lowered from the embarkation level
D.    reduce the swinging of the lifeboat at the embarkation level

37.    USCG 1230
The purpose of the tricing pendants is to _____.
A.    control the fore and aft motion of a lifeboat during lowering
B.    control the outboard swing of a lifeboat during lowering
C.    provide suspensions for the manropes
D.    hold a lifeboat next to the embarkation deck while loading

38.    USCG 5274
The type davits shown are _____.
See Diagram: D008SA
A.    round-bar davits
B.    radial davits
C.    gravity davits
D.    quadrantal davits

39.    USCG 1489
The boat command that means complete the stroke and level the oars horizontally with the blades trimmed fore and aft is

_____.
A.    "Oars"
B.    "Up oars"
C.    "Way enough"
D.    "Hold water"

40.    USCG 1680
In an open lifeboat, the lifeboat compass is usually _____.
A.    placed in a fixed bracket when being used
B.    clamped to any position convenient for the coxswain to see it
C.    permanently mounted on the lifeboat's centerline
D.    mounted in the center of the boat to eliminate deviation

41.    USCG 1214
An inflatable liferaft should be lifted back aboard the ship by using _____.
A.    the single hook at the top of the raft
B.    two lines passed under the raft
C.    the towing bridle
D.    All of the above

42.    USCG 1274
On inflatable liferafts, the operating cord should be renewed by _____.
A.    cutting the old line off and renewing same
B.    an approved servicing facility ashore
C.    opening the case and replacing the entire line
D.    one of the ship's officers

43.     USCG 1306
Water pockets on the underside of an inflatable liferaft are for _____.
A.      catching rain water
B.      stability
C.      easy drainage
D.      maneuverability

44.     USCG 1394
In each inflatable liferaft, what equipment is provided to make quick, emergency, temporary repairs to large holes in the raft?
A.      No equipment is provided.
B.      Glue and rubber patches
C.      Several various-sized sealing clamps
D.      Self-adhesive rubberized canvas patches

45.     USCG 1404
Signaling devices which are required on inflatable liferafts include _____.
A.      a rocket shoulder rifle
B.      an oil lantern
C.      red flares
D.      an air horn

46.     USCG 3234
The abandon ship signal is _____.
A.      a continuous ringing of general alarm bells for at least 10 seconds
B.      a continuous ringing of the general alarm, and sounding of the ship's whistle
C.      more than 6 short blasts and 1 long blast of the ship's whistle and the same signal on the general alarm bells
D.      a continuous sounding of the ship's whistle

47.     USCG 1491
You are in a lifeboat when you sight the stars shown. You will be heading almost due north when you head for Polaris which is marked by what letter? See Diagram: D006SA
A.      C
B.      D
C.      E
D.      G

48.     USCG 9195
When using the rain water collection tubes on a liferaft, the first collection should be _____.
A.      passed around so all can drink
B.      poured overboard because of salt washed off the canopy
C.      saved to be used at a later time
D.      used to boil food

49.     USCG 9205
When you are firing a pyrotechnic distress signal, it should be aimed _____.
A.      horizontally and directly abeam of your vessel
B.      at the vessel whose attention you want to attract
C.      into the wind
D.      at greater than 60 degrees above the horizon

50.    USCG 3788
When you hear three short blasts on the ship's whistle and the same signal on the general alarm bells, you

_____.
A.    are required to be at your liferaft
B.    are dismissed from drills
C.    should point to the man overboard
D.    should start the fire pump

51.    USCG 3789
The signal for a fire emergency on an OSV is _____.
A.    a 30 second on 30 second off alternating signal
B.    the continuous blast of the ships whistle for not less than 10 seconds supplemented by the
continuous ringing of the general alarm bells for not less than 10 seconds
C.    an intermittent ringing of the general alarm for not less than ten seconds
D.    announced over the PA system

52.    USCG 3470
According to the regulations for lifeboat falls, which action must be taken with the falls no later than 5-year
intervals?
A.    Proof tested
B.    End-for-ended
C.    Renewed
D.    Weight tested

53.    USCG 994
The signal to guide vessels in distress, which indicates, "This is the best place to land" is the _____.
A.    horizontal motion of a white flag
B.    letter K in Morse code given by light
C.    code flag S as a hoist
D.    firing of a white star signal

54.    USCG 1014
Which signal would be used by a shore rescue unit to indicate "Landing here highly dangerous"?
A.    The firing of a white star signal
B.    Horizontal motion with a white flag
C.    Vertical motion of a white light
D.    Code letter "K" by blinker light

55.    USCG 1713
Line throwing equipment should NOT be operated _____.
A.    during a rain storm
B.    in an explosive atmosphere
C.    near a liferaft canister
D.    by other than licensed officers

56.    USCG 2387
A magnetic compass card is marked in how many degrees?
A.    90
B.    180
C.    360
D.    400

57.     USCG 2779
Error may be introduced into a magnetic compass by _____.
A.      making a structural change to the vessel
B.      a short circuit near the compass
C.      belt buckles
D.      All of the above

58.     USCG 209
The number 2 lifeboat on a tanker would be found _____.
A.      on the port side
B.      on the starboard side
C.      abaft 1 lifeboat on the port side
D.      abaft 1 lifeboat on the starboard side

59.     USCG 3426
In illustration D011SA, number 1 operates the _____. See Diagram: D011SA
A.      releasing gear
B.      sea painter
C.      Fleming gear
D.      McCluny hook

60.     USCG 93
If, for any reason, it is necessary to abandon ship while far out at sea, it is important that the crew members
should _____.
A.      separate from each other as this will increase the chances of being rescued
B.      get away from the area because sharks will be attracted to the vessel
C.      immediately head for the nearest land
D.      remain together in the area because rescuers will start searching at the vessel's last known position

61.     USCG 9197
In the first 24 hours after abandoning a vessel, water should be given only to personnel who are _____.
A.      thirsty
B.      sick or injured
C.      wet
D.      awake

62.     USCG 924
What is the lifesaving signal for "You are seen and assistance will be given as soon as possible"?
A.      3 white star signals
B.      Horizontal motion with a white flag
C.      Vertical motion of a white light
D.      Code letter "K" by blinker light

63.     USCG 1120
You will find a limit switch on a _____.
A.      liferaft cradle
B.      radial davit
C.      sheath-screw davit
D.      gravity davit

64.     USCG 1875
After abandoning ship which action should be taken IMMEDIATELY upon entering a liferaft?
A.      Open equipment pack.
B.      Issue anti-seasickness medicine.
C.      Get clear of the ship.
D.      Dry the liferaft floor and inflate.

65.     USCG 3879
The signal given to commence lowering the lifeboats is _____.
A.      1 short blast on the ship's whistle
B.      3 short blasts on the ship's whistle
C.      3 long blasts on the ship's whistle
D.      1 long blast on the ship's whistle

66.     USCG 936
If your vessel is equipped with inflatable liferafts, how should they be maintained?
A.      Have your crew check them annually.
B.      They do not need any maintenance.
C.      Have them sent ashore to an approved maintenance facility annually.
D.      Have them serviced by the shipyard annually.

67.     USCG 1613
Steering a motor lifeboat broadside to the sea could cause it to _____.
A.      capsize
B.      run smoother
C.      run faster
D.      sink

68.     USCG 4786
Which number indicates the hydrostatic release? See Diagram: D015SA
A.      3
B.      6
C.      7
D.      10

69.     USCG 4269
BOTH INTERNATIONAL & INLAND All of the following are distress signals under the Rules EXCEPT
_____.
A.      International Code Signal "AA"
B.      orange-colored smoke
C.      red flares
D.      the repeated raising and lowering of outstretched arms

70.     USCG 2835
A vessel heading NNE is on a course of _____.
A.      022.5°
B.      045.0°
C.      067.5°
D.      090.0°

**LIFEBOATMAN**
**481XX-Deck Safety and Rules of the Road**
**Test No. 330707.      Answers**

| | | |
|---|---|---|
| 1. | 4733 | ANS: C RULE 37; ANNEX IV |
| 2. | 353 | ANS: B LBMAN |
| 3. | 383 | ANS: C AMSM; *46 CFR 199.175 (b) (27); *46 CFR 160.19 |
| 4. | 856 | ANS: C NVIC 1/92; *46 CFR 160.171 |
| 5. | 1006 | ANS: C *46 CFR 160.171-9 (h) |
| 6. | 433 | ANS: A *46 CFR 199.80 (b) (7) |
| 7. | 1642 | ANS: B MSRS |
| 8. | 201 | ANS: D WSM |
| 9. | 493 | ANS: A LBMAN; *46 CFR 160.35 |
| 10. | 3144 | ANS: D LBMAN; *46 CFR 160.33 |
| 11. | 1170 | ANS: B AMSM |
| 12. | 1200 | ANS: A AMSM |
| 13. | 1270 | ANS: C AMSM |
| 14. | 1300 | ANS: C *46 CFR 160.32-3 (a) |
| 15. | 1360 | ANS: B AMSM |
| 16. | 1390 | ANS: D LBMAN |
| 17. | 1400 | ANS: A AMSM |
| 18. | 1234 | ANS: D AMSM |
| 19. | 1305 | ANS: B AMSM |
| 20. | 733 | ANS: B LBMAN; *46 CFR 199.175 (b) (13) |
| 21. | 763 | ANS: A AMSM; *46 CFR 199.175 (b) (32); *46 CFR 160.36 |
| 22. | 1514 | ANS: A *46 CFR 199.175 |
| 23. | 1345 | ANS: C AMSM |
| 24. | 1355 | ANS: B AMSM; *46 CFR 160.62 |
| 25. | 1276 | ANS: D WSM; *46 CFR 160.51-7 (b) (5) |
| 26. | 1296 | ANS: A LBMAN; *46 CFR 160.51 |
| 27. | 1493 | ANS: A AMSM; *46 CFR 160.73 |
| 28. | 1059 | ANS: B WSM |
| 29. | 536 | ANS: B *46 CFR 160.35-5 (a) (5) (i) |
| 30. | 4242 | ANS: C *46 CFR 199.100 (c) (2) |
| 31. | 1596 | ANS: C *46 CFR 160.57-5 (c) |
| 32. | 287 | ANS: C *46 CFR 97.15-65 |
| 33. | 964 | ANS: B *H.O. 102 |
| 34. | 112 | ANS: A AMSM; *46 CFR 199.175 (b) (27); *46 CFR 160.19 |
| 35. | 8734 | ANS: A WHITTAKER |
| 36. | 0 | ANS: D AMSM |
| 37. | 1230 | ANS: D AMSM |
| 38. | 5274 | ANS: C AMSM D008SA |
| 39. | 1489 | ANS: A AMSM |
| 40. | 1680 | ANS: A WSM; *46 CFR 199.175 (b) (6) |
| 41. | 1214 | ANS: C LBMAN |
| 42. | 1274 | ANS: B LBMAN; *46 CFR 199.190 (g) (3); *46 CFR 160.51-6 |
| 43. | 1306 | ANS: B MIL; *46 CFR 160.51-4 (b) |
| 44. | 1394 | ANS: C WSM |
| 45. | 1404 | ANS: C SAFETY; *46 CFR 94.20-25, 160 |
| 46. | 3234 | ANS: C *46 CFR 35.10-5 |
| 47. | 1491 | ANS: A BOWDITCH D006SA |
| 48. | 9195 | ANS: B SAFETY AT SEA |
| 49. | 9205 | ANS: D FVSM |
| 50. | 3788 | ANS: B *46 CFR 35.10-5; *46 CFR 97.13-15 |

**LIFEBOATMAN**
**481XX-Deck Safety and Rules of the Road**
**Test No. 330707**       **Answers**

| | | |
|---|---|---|
| 51. | 3789 | ANS: B *46 CFR 131.535 |
| 52. | 3470 | ANS: C SOLAS REG, CHAP III; *46 CFR 199.190 (j) (ii) |
| 53. | 994 | ANS: B *H.O. 102 |
| 54. | 1014 | ANS: B *H.O. 102 |
| 55. | 1713 | ANS: B MSRS |
| 56. | 2387 | ANS: C *BOWDITCH 2, TABLE 2 |
| 57. | 2779 | ANS: D *BOWDITCH 2 |
| 58. | 209 | ANS: A AMSM; *46 CFR 199.176 |
| 59. | 3426 | ANS: C AMSM D011SA |
| 60. | 93 | ANS: D LBMAN |
| 61. | 9197 | ANS: B SAFETY AT SEA |
| 62. | 924 | ANS: A *H.O. 102 |
| 63. | 1120 | ANS: D AMSM; *46 CFR 160.15-3 |
| 64. | 1875 | ANS: C NVIC 2/92; LIFERAFT SURVIVAL; SURVIVAL GUIDE Pages 14, 84-86 |
| 65 | 3879 | ANS: A *46 CFR 35.10-5; *46 CFR 97.13-15 |
| 66. | 936 | ANS: C LBMAN; *46 CFR 199.190 (g) (3); *46 CFR 160.51-6 |
| 67. | 1613 | ANS: A WHITTAKER |
| 68. | 4786 | ANS: B AMSM; *46 CFR 160.62 D015SA |
| 69. | 4269 | ANS: A RULE 37; ANNEX IV; LIFESAVING SIGNALS |
| 70. | 2835 | ANS: A *BOWDITCH 2, TABLE 2 |

**LIFEBOATMAN LIMITED**
**441XX-Survival Craft For Vessels Without Lifeboats**
**Test No. 330724**

1 - USCG 3414
A rigid lifesaving device designed to support survivors in the water is a _____.
A.      rigid liferaft
B.      life float
C.      inflatable liferaft
D.      survival capsule

2 - USCG 2935
Which statement is TRUE concerning life jackets which are severely damaged?
A.      They should be replaced.
B.      They must be tested for buoyancy before being continued in use.
C.      They can be repaired by a reliable seamstress.
D.      They can be used for children.

3 - USCG 2965
Which is TRUE concerning immersion suits and their use?
A.      Only a light layer of clothing may be worn underneath.
B.      They provide sufficient flotation to do away with the necessity of wearing a life jacket.
C.      They should be tight fitting.
D.      A puncture in the suit will not appreciably reduce its value.

4 - USCG 3003
How is the external flotation bladder of an immersion suit inflated?
A.      It is inflated by a small $CO_2$ bottle that is automatically tripped when the front zipper is at the top of the zipper track.
B.      It is inflated by a small $CO_2$ bottle that is manually tripped.
C.      It is inflated by blowing through an inflation tube.
D.      It inflates by seawater bleeding into the inflation bladder and reacting with a chemical.
E.

5 - USCG 3976
In the illustration, which item number correctly identifies the ballast bags?
See Diagram: D014SA
A.      2
B.      12
C.      13
D.      22

6 - USCG 3558
Limit switches are located on the survival craft winch systems for OSVs to _____.
A.      stop the winch just before the survival craft reaches final stowage position
B.      limit the amount of cable on the drum
C.      limit the ascent rate
D.      stop the winch in case the craft's weight exceeds the load lift limit

7 - USCG 3569
If help has not arrived in 10-12 hours after abandoning a vessel in a rescue boat, you should _____.
A.      go in one direction until the fuel runs out
B.      steer a course for the nearest land
C.      steer a course for the nearest sea lane
D.      shut down the engines if installed and put out the sea anchor

8 - USCG 3588
For the purpose of training and drills, if reasonable and practicable, rescue boats on an OSV must be launched with their assigned crew _____.
A.      once a week
B.      once a month
C.      once a year
D.      twice a year

9 - USCG 3810
If help has not arrived in 10-12 hours after having abandoned an OSV in a survival craft, you should _____.
A.      go in one direction until the fuel runs out
B.      plot course for the nearest land
C.      take a vote on the direction in which to go
D.      shutdown the engines and put out the sea anchor

10 - USCG 3782
You have abandoned ship in tropical waters. Which procedure should be used during a prolonged period in a liferaft?
A.      Wet clothes during the day to decrease perspiration.
B.      Get plenty of rest.
C.      Keep the entrance curtains open.
D.      All of the above

11 - USCG 3639
Which condition represents the appropriate time for setting off distress flares and rockets?
A.      Only when there is a chance of their being seen by rescue vessels
B.      At half hour intervals
C.      At one hour intervals
D.      Immediately upon abandoning the vessel

12 - USCG 3672
Which item of the listed survival craft equipment would be the most suitable for night signaling to a ship on the horizon?
A.      A red parachute flare
B.      A red handheld flare
C.      An orange smoke flare
D.      A flashlight

13 - USCG 2803
When a magnetic compass is not in use for a prolonged period of time it should _____.
A.      be shielded from direct sunlight
B.      be locked into a constant heading
C.      have any air bubbles replaced with nitrogen
D.      have the compensating magnets removed

14 - USCG 3865
What is the minimum required number of ring life buoys on an OSV certified for ocean service?
A.      4
B.      8
C.      12
D.      16

15 - USCG 3684

The rescuer can best provide an airtight seal during mouth-to-mouth resuscitation by pinching the victim's nostrils and

_____.

A.      cupping a hand around the patient's mouth
B.      keeping the head elevated
C.      applying his mouth tightly over the victim's mouth
D.      holding the jaw down firmly

16 - USCG 3715

The necessity for administering artificial respiration may be recognized by the victim's _____.
A.      vomiting
B.      blue color and lack of breathing
C.      irregular breathing
D.      unconscious condition

17 - USCG 3053

On an OSV, when may a work vest be substituted for a required life jacket?
A.      To replace a damaged life jacket
B.      For use during fire drills
C.      For use during boat drills
D.      At no time

18 - USCG 3894

A liferaft with a capacity of 8 people used in ocean service is required by regulations to carry _____.
A.      8 liters of fresh water
B.      12 units of provisions
C.      12 liters of fresh water
D.      24 units of provisions

19 - USCG 3556

The normal equipment of every rescue boat shall include _____.
A.      compass
B.      one 50 meter line
C.      one can opener
D.      All of the above

20 - USCG 3950

You are picking up a conscious person that has fallen overboard. Recovery is easier if you approach with the

_____.

A.      victim to leeward
B.      victim to windward
C.      wind on your port side
D.      wind on your starboard side

21 - USCG 3951

All personnel on board a vessel should be familiar with the rescue boat's _____.
A.      boarding and operating procedure
B.      maintenance schedules
C.      navigational systems
D.      fuel consumption rates

22 - USCG 3769

You hear the general alarm and ship's whistle sound for over 10 seconds. Traditionally, this is the signal for _____.

A.      abandon ship
B.      dismissal from fire and emergency stations
C.      fire and emergency
D.      man overboard

23 - USCG 3800

If you have to jump in the water when abandoning ship, your legs should be _____.
A.      spread apart as far as possible
B.      held as tightly against your chest as possible
C.      in a kneeling position
D.      extended straight down and crossed at the ankles

24 - USCG 3912

If you must enter water on which there is an oil fire, you should _____.
A.      protect your life preserver by holding it above your head
B.      enter the water on the windward side of the vessel
C.      keep both hands in front of your face to break the water surface when diving head first
D.      wear very light clothing

25 - USCG 3748

A victim is coughing and wheezing from a partial obstruction of the airway. An observer should _____.
A.      perform the Heimlich maneuver
B.      immediately start CPR
C.      give back blows and something to drink
D.      allow the person to continue coughing and dislodge the obstruction on his own

26 - USCG 3081

A person who observes an individual fall overboard from an OSV should _____.
A.      immediately jump into the water to assist the individual
B.      call for help and keep the individual in sight
C.      run to the radio room to send an emergency message
D.      go to the control room for the distress flares

27 - USCG 4316

In the illustration shown, the righting strap is shown as item number _____.
See Diagram: D014SA
A.      8
B.      9
C.      12
D.      16

28 - USCG 3842

You must ensure that lifesaving equipment is _____.
A.      locked up
B.      readily accessible for use
C.      inaccessible to passengers
D.      on the topmost deck of the vessel at all times

29 - USCG 3335
Inflatable liferafts are provided with a _____.
A.      jackknife
B.      towing connection
C.      lifeline
D.      All of the above

30 - USCG 3914
If you must jump from a vessel, the correct posture includes _____.
A.      holding down the life preserver against the chest with one arm crossing the other, covering the mouth
and nose with a hand, and feet together
B.      knees bent and held close to the body with both arms around legs
C.      body straight and arms held tightly at the sides for feet first entry into the water
D.      both hands holding the life preserver below the chin with knees bent and legs crossed

31 - USCG 3918
If your liferaft is to leeward of a fire on the water, you should FIRST _____.
A.      cut the line to the sea anchor
B.      paddle away from the fire
C.      splash water over the liferaft to cool it
D.      get out of the raft and swim to safety

32 - USCG 2421
How many degrees are there on a compass card?
A.      360°
B.      380°
C.      390°
D.      420°

33 - USCG 2794
Which would influence a magnetic compass?
A.      Electrical wiring
B.      Iron pipe
C.      Radio
D.      All of the above

34 - USCG 3849
The capacity of any liferaft on board a vessel can be determined by _____.
A.      examining the Certificate of Inspection
B.      examining the plate on the outside of the raft container
C.      referring to the Muster List ("Station Bill")
D.      referring to the shipping articles

35 - USCG 3043
Which statement concerning immersion suits is TRUE?
A.      Immersion suits should be worn while performing routine work on deck.
B.      After purchasing, the suit should be stowed in the storage bag in which it was received.
C.      During the annual maintenance, the front zipper should be lubricated using light machine oil or
        mineral oil.
D.      Any tear or leak will render the suit unserviceable and it must be replaced.

36 - USCG 3207
The lights on the outside of the canopy of an inflatable liferaft operate _____.
A.      by turning the globe clockwise
B.      by a switch at the light
C.      by a light sensor
D.      automatically when the raft is inflated

37 - USCG 3879
The signal given to commence lowering the lifeboats is _____.
A.      1 short blast on the ship's whistle
B.      3 short blasts on the ship's whistle
C.      3 long blasts on the ship's whistle
D.      1 long blast on the ship's whistle

38 - USCG 3876
What is NOT a requirement for testing the line throwing appliance on a vessel?
A.      A drill should be conducted every three months.
B.      A regular service line must be used when it's fired.
C.      A regular projectile must be used when it's fired.
D.      The actual firing is at the discretion of the Master.

39 - USCG 3692
Before CPR is started, you should _____.
A.      establish an open airway
B.      treat any bleeding wounds
C.      insure the victim is conscious
D.      make the victim comfortable

40 - USCG 3407
The most important thing to remember when launching an inflatable liferaft by hand is to _____.
A.      open the $CO_2$ inflation valve
B.      open the raft container
C.      ensure that the operating cord is secured to the vessel
D.      inflate the raft on the vessel, then lower it over the side

41 - USCG 3645
Signaling devices which are required on inflatable liferafts include _____.
A.      a rocket shoulder rifle
B.      an oil lantern
C.      red flares
D.      an air horn

42 - USCG 3469
The knife on an inflatable liferaft will always be located _____.
A.      in one of the equipment bags
B.      in a special pocket on the exterior of the canopy
C.      on a cord hanging from the canopy
D.      in a pocket on the first aid kit

43 - USCG 3830
Inflatable liferafts must be overhauled and inspected at a U. S. Coast Guard approved service facility every _____.
A.      six months
B.      twelve months
C.      eighteen months
D.      twenty-four months

44 - USCG 3736
The most effective treatment for warming a crew member suffering from hypothermia is _____.
A.      running or jumping to increase circulation
B.      raising body temperature rapidly by placing hands and feet in hot water
C.      bundling the body in blankets to rewarm gradually
D.      laying prone under heat lamps to rewarm rapidly

45 - USCG 3213
A safety feature provided on all inflatable liferafts is _____.
A.      overhead safety straps
B.      built in seats
C.      internal releasing hooks
D.      water stabilizing pockets

46 - USCG 3457
Using a sea anchor will _____.
A.      reduce your drift rate
B.      keep the liferaft from turning over
C.      aid in recovering the liferaft
D.      increase your visibility

47 - USCG 3936
After abandoning ship which action should be taken IMMEDIATELY upon entering a liferaft?
A.      Open equipment pack.
B.      Issue anti-seasickness medicine.
C.      Get clear of the ship.
D.      Dry the liferaft floor and inflate.

48 - USCG 4270
Which statement about immersion suits is TRUE?
A.      The primary color of the suit's exterior may be red, orange or yellow.
B.      The suit must, without assistance, turn an unconscious person's mouth clear of the water within 5 seconds.
C.      The suit is flameproof and provides protection to a wearer swimming in burning oil.
D.      The suit may be stored in a machinery space where the ambient temperature is 160° F.

49 - USCG 2833
A vessel heading NE is on a course of _____.
A.      022.5°
B.      045.0°
C.      067.5°
D.      090.0°

50 - USCG 3653

When a vessel signals her distress by means of a gun or other explosive signal, the firing should be at intervals of approximately

_____.

A.     10 minutes
B.     1 minute
C.     1 hour
D.     3 minutes

**LIFEBOATMAN LIMITED**
**441XX-Survival Craft For Vessels Without Lifeboats**
**Test No. 330724 - Answers**

| | | | |
|---|---|---|---|
| 1 | 3414 | B | *46 CFR 160.027-2 |
| 2 | 2935 | A | *46 CFR 160.006-2 (b) |
| 3 | 2965 | B | *46 CFR 160.171-9; *46 CFR 160.171-11 (a) (4) |
| 4 | 3003 | C | NVIC 5-86; WSM |
| 5 | 3976 | C | WATER SURVIVAL MANUAL    D014SA |
| 6 | 3558 | A | AMSM; LBMN; *46 CFR 131.530 |
| 7 | 3569 | D | WHITTAKER |
| 8 | 3588 | B | *46 CFR 131.530 |
| 9 | 3810 | D | WHITTAKER |
| 10 | 3782 | D | WSM |
| 11 | 3639 | A | AMSM |
| 12 | 3672 | A | *46 CFR 133.175 |
| 13 | 2803 | A | *BOWD 2 |
| 14 | 3865 | B | *46 CFR 133.70 |
| 15 | 3684 | C | SHIP'S MEDICINE CHEST |
| 16 | 3715 | B | SHIP'S MEDICINE CHEST |
| 17 | 3053 | D | *46 CFR 131.720 (c) |
| 18 | 3894 | C | *46 CFR 199.175 |
| 19 | 3556 | A | *46 CFR 199.175 (b) (6) |
| 20 | 3950 | A | SAFETY AT SEA; SURVIVAL GUIDE |
| 21 | 3951 | A | AMSM |
| 22 | 3769 | C | AMSM |
| 23 | 3800 | D | MSRS; AMSM; LBMN |
| 24 | 3912 | B | WSM |
| 25 | 3748 | D | SHIP'S MEDICINE CHEST |
| 26 | 3081 | B | CHAPMAN |
| 27 | 4316 | B | WATER SURVIVAL MANUAL    D014SA |
| 28 | 3842 | B | *46 CFR 180.25-10 |
| 29 | 3335 | D | AMSM; *46 CFR 160.51-7 |
| 30 | 3914 | A | MSRS; AMSM; LBMN |
| 31 | 3918 | A | MIL |
| 32 | 2421 | A | *BOWD 2, TABLE 2 |
| 33 | 2794 | D | *BOWD 2 |
| 34 | 3849 | B | *46 CFR 199.178 (d) |
| 35 | 3043 | B | NVIC 5-86; WSM |
| 36 | 3207 | D | WSM |
| 37 | 3879 | A | *46 CFR 35.10-5; *46 CFR 97.13-15 |
| 38 | 3876 | B | *46 CFR 97.15-25; *46 CFR 160.31; *46 CFR 160.40; *46 CFR 199.180 (e) |
| 39 | 3692 | A | SHIP'S MEDICINE CHEST |
| 40 | 3407 | C | AMSM |
| 41 | 3645 | C | *46 CFR 94.20-25, 160 |
| 42 | 3469 | B | MIL; *46 CFR 199.175 (b) (16), (17); *46 CFR 160.51-7 (b) (8) |
| 43 | 3830 | B | LBMAN; *46 CFR 199.190 (g) (3); *46 CFR 160.51-6 |
| 44 | 3736 | C | RED CROSS Page 222 |
| 45 | 3213 | D | MIL; *46 CFR 160.51-4 (b) |
| 46 | 3457 | A | WHITTAKER |
| 47 | 3936 | C | NVIC 2-92; LIFERAFT SURVIVAL; SURVIVAL GUIDE Page 14, 84-86 |
| 48 | 4270 | B | *46 CFR 160.171-11 (b) |
| 49 | 2833 | B | *BOWD 2, TABLE 2 |
| 50 | 3653 | B | *H.O. 102 |

**LIFEBOATMAN LIMITED**
**441XX-Survival Craft For Vessels Without Lifeboats**
**Test No. 330714**

1 - USCG 3057
Each buoyant work vest on an OSV must be _____.
A.      Coast Guard Approved
B.      marked with the name of the unit
C.      equipped with a waterlight
D.      All of the above

2 - USCG 2970
An immersion suit must be equipped with a/an _____.
A.      air bottle for breathing
B.      orange smoke canister
C.      whistle, light and retroreflective material
D.      sea dye marker

3 - USCG 3143
The instructions for rescue boats and liferafts on an OSV must be approved by the _____.
A.      lease operator
B.      Minerals Management Service
C.      Coast Guard
D.      person-in-charge of the unit

4 - USCG 3972
The external recognition light can be seem up to two miles and is shown as item number _____.
See Diagram: D014SA
A.      3
B.      5
C.      8
D.      23

5 - USCG 3353
An inflatable liferaft can be launched by _____.
A.      the float free method only
B.      kicking the hydrostatic release
C.      throwing the entire container overboard, then pulling on the operating cord to inflate the raft
D.      removing the securing straps

6 - USCG 3559
The rescue boat on an OSV is not required to carry a _____.
A.      fishing kit
B.      searchlight
C.      sea anchor
D.      radar reflector

7 - USCG 3564
The sea painter of a rescue boat should be led _____.
A.      forward and outboard of all obstructions
B.      forward and inboard of all obstructions
C.      up and down from the main deck
D.      to the foremost point on the vessel

**8 - USCG 3585**

When a man who has fallen overboard is being picked up by a rescue boat, the boat should normally approach with the wind _____.

A.     astern and the victim just off the bow
B.     ahead and the victim just off the bow
C.     just off the bow and the victim to windward
D.     just off the bow and the victim to leeward

**9 - USCG 3586**

A person has fallen overboard and is being picked up with a rescue boat. If the person appears in danger of drowning, the rescue boat should be maneuvered to make _____.

A.     an approach from leeward
B.     an approach from windward
C.     the most direct approach
D.     an approach across the wind

**10 - USCG 3788**

When you hear three short blasts on the ship's whistle and the same signal on the general alarm bells, you _____.

A.     are required to be at your liferaft
B.     are dismissed from drills
C.     should point to the man overboard
D.     should start the fire pump

**11 - USCG 3778**

When a ship is abandoned and there are several liferafts in the water, one of the FIRST things to be done is _____.

A.     separate the rafts as much as possible to increase chances of detection
B.     transfer all supplies to one raft
C.     transfer all the injured to one raft
D.     secure the rafts together to keep them from drifting apart

**12 - USCG 3796**

Which of the following steps should normally be taken first by those who have boarded a liferaft in an emergency situation?
A.     Ration food and water supplies
B.     Search for survivors
C.     Determine position and closest point of land
D.     Check pyrotechnic supplies

**13 - USCG 3061**

When transferring survivors from a survival craft to a rescue vessel, personnel on board the craft should _____.

A.     remove their lifejackets to make it easier to climb on board the rescue vessel
B.     climb on top of the survival craft while waiting their turn to transfer to the rescue vessel
C.     remain seated inside the survival craft and make the transfer one person at a time
D.     enter the water and swim over to the rescue vessel

14 - USCG 3782
You have abandoned ship in tropical waters. Which procedure should be used during a prolonged period in a liferaft?
A.      Wet clothes during the day to decrease perspiration.
B.      Get plenty of rest.
C.      Keep the entrance curtains open.
D.      All of the above

15 - USCG 3594
After having activated the emergency position indicating radio beacon, you should _____.
A.      turn it off for 5 minutes every half-hour
B.      turn it off and on at 5 minute intervals
C.      turn it off during daylight hours
D.      leave it on continuously

16 - USCG 3639
Which condition represents the appropriate time for setting off distress flares and rockets?
A.      Only when there is a chance of their being seen by rescue vessels
B.      At half hour intervals
C.      At one hour intervals
D.      Immediately upon abandoning the vessel

17 - USCG 3870
Each EPIRB required on an OSV shall be tested using the integrated test circuit and output indicator every _____.
A.      week
B.      two weeks
C.      month
D.      two months

18 - USCG 3853
Coast Guard Regulations (46 CFR) require inflatable liferafts to be equipped with _____.
A.      a first aid kit
B.      an instruction manual
C.      a sea anchor
D.      All of the above

19 - USCG 3864
Of the required ring life buoys for an OSV, how many must be equipped with a waterlight?
A.      8
B.      4
C.      2
D.      1

20 - USCG 3865
What is the minimum required number of ring life buoys on an OSV certified for ocean service?
A.      4
B.      8
C.      12
D.      16

21 - USCG 3704
After a person has been revived by artificial respiration, he should be _____.
A.       walked around until he is back to normal
B.       given several shots of whiskey
C.       kept lying down and warm
D.       allowed to do as he wishes

22 - USCG 43
If an inflatable liferaft is overturned, it may be righted by _____.
A.       filling the stabilizers on one side with water
B.       releasing the $CO_2$ cylinder
C.       pushing up from under one end
D.       standing on the inflating cylinder and pulling on the straps on the underside of the raft

23 - USCG 3053
On an OSV, when may a work vest be substituted for a required life jacket?
A.       To replace a damaged life jacket
B.       For use during fire drills
C.       For use during boat drills
D.       At no time

24 - USCG 4068
On board an OSV, the key to the most rapid and effective response to a man overboard situation is
_____.
A.       switching to hydraulic steering
B.       a dedicated crew
C.       good equipment
D.       good communication

25 - USCG 3203
The inside light in an inflatable liferaft is turned on _____.
A.       automatically as the liferaft inflates
B.       with a switch near the boarding handle
C.       at night because the light has a photosensitive switch
D.       by screwing the bulb in after the raft inflates

26 - USCG 3217
Which of the devices listed will prevent an inflated liferaft from being pulled under by a vessel which sinks in water over 100 feet deep?
A.       The hydrostatic release
B.       A shear pin
C.       A Rottmer release
D.       A weak link in the painter

27 - USCG 4069
In the illustration, the sea anchor is number _____.
See Diagram: D014SA
A.       1
B.       12
C.       14
D.       18

28 - USCG 3416
The instructions for the launching of lifeboats and liferafts must be approved by the _____.
A.      lease operator
B.      Minerals Management Service
C.      Coast Guard
D.      person-in-charge of the unit

29 - USCG 3951
All personnel on board a vessel should be familiar with the rescue boat's _____.
A.      boarding and operating procedure
B.      maintenance schedules
C.      navigational systems
D.      fuel consumption rates

30 - USCG 3647
A distress signal _____.
A.      consists of 5 or more short blasts of the fog signal apparatus
B.      consists of the raising and lowering of a large white flag
C.      may be used individually or in conjunction with other distress signals
D.      is used to indicate doubt about another vessel's intentions

31 - USCG 2387
A magnetic compass card is marked in how many degrees?
A.      90
B.      180
C.      360
D.      400

32 - USCG 3748
A victim is coughing and wheezing from a partial obstruction of the airway. An observer should _____.
A.      perform the Heimlich maneuver
B.      immediately start CPR
C.      give back blows and something to drink
D.      allow the person to continue coughing and dislodge the obstruction on his own

33 - USCG 4316
In the illustration shown, the righting strap is shown as item number _____.
See Diagram: D014SA
A.      8
B.      9
C.      12
D.      16

34 - USCG 3960
A rigid lifesaving device designed to support survivors in the water is a _____.
A.      rigid liferaft
B.      life float
C.      inflatable liferaft
D.      survival capsule

35 - USCG 3842
You must ensure that lifesaving equipment is _____.
A.      locked up
B.      readily accessible for use
C.      inaccessible to passengers
D.      on the topmost deck of the vessel at all times

36 - USCG 3566
The normal equipment of every rescue boat shall include _____.
A.      buoyant oars
B.      one 50 meter line
C.      one first aid kit
D.      All of the above

37 - USCG 3918
If your liferaft is to leeward of a fire on the water, you should FIRST _____.
A.      cut the line to the sea anchor
B.      paddle away from the fire
C.      splash water over the liferaft to cool it
D.      get out of the raft and swim to safety

38 - USCG 2794
Which would influence a magnetic compass?
A.      Electrical wiring
B.      Iron pipe
C.      Radio
D.      All of the above

39 - USCG 3051
The external flotation bladder on an immersion suit should be inflated _____.
A.      only after two hours in the water
B.      only after four hours in the water
C.      before entry into the water
D.      upon entry into the water

40 - USCG 3341
Inflatable liferafts are provided with a _____.
A.      Very pistol
B.      towing connection
C.      portable radio
D.      canned milk

41 - USCG 3641
Signaling devices required on inflatable liferafts include a(n) _____.
A.      Very pistol
B.      orange smoke signal
C.      air horn
D.      lantern

42 - USCG 3729
A crew member suffering from hypothermia should be given _____.
A.      a small dose of alcohol
B.      treatment for shock
C.      a large meal
D.      a brisk rub down

43 - USCG 3744
Which should NOT be a treatment for a person who has received a head injury and is groggy or unconscious?
A.      Give a stimulant.
B.      Elevate his head.
C.      Stop severe bleeding.
D.      Treat for shock.

44 - USCG 3409
To launch a liferaft by hand, you should _____.
A.      cut the casing bands, throw the raft over the side and it will inflate by itself
B.      detach the operating cord, throw the liferaft over the side and it will then inflate
C.      cut the casing bands, throw the raft over the side and pull the operating cord
D.      throw the liferaft over the side and pull the operating cord

45 - USCG 2777
The lubber's line on a magnetic compass indicates _____.
A.      compass north
B.      the direction of the vessel's head
C.      magnetic north
D.      a relative bearing taken with azimuth circle

46 - USCG 3756
Treatment of sunstroke consists principally of _____.
A.      cooling, removing to shaded area, and lying down
B.      bathing with rubbing alcohol
C.      drinking ice water
D.      All of the above

47 - USCG 3932
You have hand launched an inflatable liferaft. What should be one of your FIRST actions after all persons have boarded the liferaft?
A.      Open the equipment pack.
B.      Inflate the liferaft floor.
C.      Decide on food and water rations.
D.      Cut the sea painter and clear the vessel.

48 - USCG 3926
To keep injured survivors warm in the water after abandoning ship, they should _____.
A.      be placed in the middle of a small circle formed by the other survivors in the water
B.      float on their backs with their arms extended for maximum exposure to the air
C.      remove their life preservers and hold on to the uninjured survivors
D.      sip water at intervals of fifteen minutes

49 - USCG 2815
A vessel heading WNW is on a course of _____.
A.      270.0°
B.      292.5°
C.      315.0°
D.      337.5°

50 - USCG 4269

Which statement about immersion suits is TRUE?

A.    Prior to abandonment, the suit allows body movement such as walking, climbing a ladder and picking up small objects.

B.    The immersion suit seals in body heat and provides protection against hypoglycemia for weeks.

C.    The suit is flameproof and provides protection to the wearer while swimming through burning oil.

D.    The wearer of the suit is severely restricted and requires 1.5 times more time to climb a ladder than without the suit.

**LIFEBOATMAN LIMITED**
**441XX-Survival Craft For Vessels Without Lifeboats**
Test No. 330714          Answers

| | | | |
|---|---|---|---|
| 1 | 3057 | A | *46 CFR 131.710 |
| 2 | 2970 | C | *46 CFR 160.171-9 |
| 3 | 3143 | C | *46 CFR 133.40 |
| 4 | 3972 | A | WATER SURVIVAL MANUAL    D014SA |
| 5 | 3353 | C | LBMAN |
| 6 | 3559 | A | *46 CFR 133.175; SOLAS Regulation 47 |
| 7 | 3564 | A | SEATECH; *46 CFR 199.175 (b) (21) |
| 8 | 3585 | D | SAFETY AT SEA; SURVIVAL GUIDE |
| 9 | 3586 | C | SAFETY AT SEA; SURVIVAL GUIDE |
| 10 | 3788 | B | *46 CFR 35.10-5; *46 CFR 97.13-15 |
| 11 | 3778 | D | WSM |
| 12 | 3796 | B | WSM |
| 13 | 3061 | C | CHAPMAN |
| 14 | 3782 | D | WSM |
| 15 | 3594 | D | NPFVOA; *PUB 117 |
| 16 | 3639 | A | AMSM |
| 17 | 3870 | C | *46 CFR 131.565; *46 CFR 199.190 (e) (2) |
| 18 | 3853 | D | MIL; *46 CFR 199.175 (b) (10), (15), (27); *46 CFR 160.51-7 (b) |
| 19 | 3864 | C | *46 CFR 133.70 |
| 20 | 3865 | B | *46 CFR 133.70 |
| 21 | 3704 | C | SHIP'S MEDICINE CHEST |
| 22 | 43 | D | SAFETY AND SURVIVAL AT SEA |
| 23 | 3053 | D | *46 CFR 131.720 (c) |
| 24 | 4068 | D | SURVIVAL GUIDE |
| 25 | 3203 | A | SURVIVAL AT SEA |
| 26 | 3217 | D | AMSM; *46 CFR 160.73 |
| 27 | 4069 | D | WATER SURVIVAL MANUAL    D014SA |
| 28 | 3416 | C | *46 CFR 199.180 |
| 29 | 3951 | A | AMSM |
| 30 | 3647 | C | *H.O. 102 |
| 31 | 2387 | C | *BOWD 2, TABLE 2 |
| 32 | 3748 | D | SHIP'S MEDICINE CHEST |
| 33 | 4316 | B | WATER SURVIVAL MANUAL    D014SA |
| 34 | 3960 | B | *46 CFR 160.027-2 |
| 35 | 3842 | B | *46 CFR 180.25-10 |
| 36 | 3566 | D | *46 CFR 199.175 (b) (20); *46 CFR 199.175 (b) (14); *46 CFR 199.175 (b) (11) |
| 37 | 3918 | A | MIL |
| 38 | 2794 | D | *BOWD 2 |
| 39 | 3051 | D | NVIC 5-86; FISHING VESSEL SAFETY MANUAL |
| 40 | 3341 | B | AMSM |
| 41 | 3641 | B | *46 CFR 199.175 (b) (30) |
| 42 | 3729 | B | SHIP'S MEDICINE CHEST |
| 43 | 3744 | A | SHIP'S MEDICINE CHEST |
| 44 | 3409 | D | AMSM |
| 45 | 2777 | B | *BOWD 2 |
| 46 | 3756 | A | SHIP'S MEDICINE CHEST |
| 47 | 3932 | D | NVIC 2-92; WSM; SURVIVAL GUIDE Page 59-68, 85 |
| 48 | 3926 | A | MSRS |
| 49 | 2815 | B | *BOWD 2, TABLE 2 |
| 50 | 4269 | A | *46 CFR 160.171-9 (m) |

**LIFEBOATMAN LIMITED**
**441XX-Survival Craft For Vessels Without Lifeboats**
**Test No. 330734**

1 - USCG 3414
A rigid lifesaving device designed to support survivors in the water is a _____.
A.      rigid liferaft
B.      life float
C.      inflatable liferaft
D.      survival capsule

2 - USCG 2903
Life jackets should be marked with the _____.
A.      maximum weight allowed
B.      stowage space assigned
C.      vessel's home port
D.      vessel's name

3 - USCG 2965
Which is TRUE concerning immersion suits and their use?
A.      Only a light layer of clothing may be worn underneath.
B.      They provide sufficient flotation to do away with the necessity of wearing a life jacket.
C.      They should be tight fitting.
D.      A puncture in the suit will not appreciably reduce its value.

4 - USCG 2970
An immersion suit must be equipped with a/an _____.
A.      air bottle for breathing
B.      orange smoke canister
C.      whistle, light and retroreflective material
D.      sea dye marker

5 - USCG 3003
How is the external flotation bladder of an immersion suit inflated?
A.      It is inflated by a small $CO_2$ bottle that is automatically tripped when the front zipper is at the top of the zipper track.
B.      It is inflated by a small $CO_2$ bottle that is manually tripped.
C.      It is inflated by blowing through an inflation tube.
D.      It inflates by seawater bleeding into the inflation bladder and reacting with a chemical.
E.

6 - USCG 3037
An immersion suit should be equipped with a/an _____.
A.      air bottle for breathing
B.      whistle and hand held flare
C.      whistle, strobe light and reflective tape
D.      whistle, hand held flare and sea dye marker

7 - USCG 3188
The air spaces in the floor of an inflatable liferaft will provide protection against _____.
A.      asphyxiation from $CO_2$
B.      loss of air in the sides of the raft
C.      rough seas
D.      cold water temperatures

8 - USCG 3479
A feature of an inflatable raft which helps keep people stationary in rough weather is _____.
A.      lashings on the floor of the raft for the passenger's feet
B.      straps from the overhead
C.      lifelines on the inside of the raft
D.      ridges in the floor of the raft

9 - USCG 3972
The external recognition light can be seem up to two miles and is shown as item number _____.
See Diagram: D014SA
A.      3
B.      5
C.      8
D.      23

10 - USCG 3979
In the illustration shown, where would you find the knife?
See Diagram: D014SA
A.      23
B.      21
C.      8
D.      4

11 - USCG 3984
As shown in the illustration, item 8 would be a(n) _____.
See Diagram: D014SA
A.      recognition light
B.      rain water catchment tube assembly
C.      pressure relief valve
D.      floating sheath knife

12 - USCG 3988
In the illustration shown, the weak link is item number _____.
See Diagram: D015SA
A.      8
B.      6
C.      4
D.      1

13 - USCG 3095
While retrieving the survival craft, the engine should be stopped _____.
A.      when the craft clears the water
B.      when the cable has been attached
C.      on approach to the platform
D.      at the embarkation

14 - USCG 3097
When retrieving the survival craft, the winch operator should stop the winch and check _____.
A.      that all personnel are seated in the craft
B.      that the cable has not jumped any grooves on the drum
C.      which way the wind is blowing
D.      the hydraulic fuel level before lifting

15 - USCG 3558
Limit switches are located on the survival craft winch systems for OSVs to _____.
A.       stop the winch just before the survival craft reaches final stowage position
B.       limit the amount of cable on the drum
C.       limit the ascent rate
D.       stop the winch in case the craft's weight exceeds the load lift limit

16 - USCG 3564
The sea painter of a rescue boat should be led _____.
A.       forward and outboard of all obstructions
B.       forward and inboard of all obstructions
C.       up and down from the main deck
D.       to the foremost point on the vessel

17 - USCG 3569
If help has not arrived in 10-12 hours after abandoning a vessel in a rescue boat, you should _____.
A.       go in one direction until the fuel runs out
B.       steer a course for the nearest land
C.       steer a course for the nearest sea lane
D.       shut down the engines if installed and put out the sea anchor

18 - USCG 3586
A person has fallen overboard and is being picked up with a rescue boat. If the person appears in danger of drowning, the rescue boat should be maneuvered to make _____.
A.       an approach from leeward
B.       an approach from windward
C.       the most direct approach
D.       an approach across the wind

19 - USCG 3810
If help has not arrived in 10-12 hours after having abandoned an OSV in a survival craft, you should

_____.
A.       go in one direction until the fuel runs out
B.       plot course for the nearest land
C.       take a vote on the direction in which to go
D.       shutdown the engines and put out the sea anchor

20 - USCG 3129
If water is rising in the bilge of a survival craft, you should first _____.
A.       abandon the survival craft
B.       check for cracks in the hull
C.       shift all personnel to the stern
D.       check the bilge drain plug

21 - USCG 3782
You have abandoned ship in tropical waters. Which procedure should be used during a prolonged period in a liferaft?
A.       Wet clothes during the day to decrease perspiration.
B.       Get plenty of rest.
C.       Keep the entrance curtains open.
D.       All of the above

22 - USCG 3820
Once the daily ration of drinking water in a survival situation has been established, the drinking routine should include

_____.
A.      small sips at regular intervals during the day
B.      a complete daily ration at one time during the day
C.      one-third the daily ration three times during the day
D.      small sips only after sunset

23 - USCG 3628
Each vessel in ocean and coastwise service must have an approved EPIRB. An EPIRB _____.
A.      must be stowed in a manner so that it will float free if the vessel sinks
B.      must be stowed where it is readily accessible for testing and use
C.      is a devise that transmits a radio signal
D.      All of the above

24 - USCG 3666
When you are firing a pyrotechnic distress signal, it should be aimed at _____.
A.      straight overhead
B.      at the vessel whose attention you are trying to get
C.      into the wind
D.      about 60 degrees above the horizon

25 - USCG 3672
Which item of the listed survival craft equipment would be the most suitable for night signaling to a ship on the horizon?
A.      A red parachute flare
B.      A red handheld flare
C.      An orange smoke flare
D.      A flashlight

26 - USCG 2127
On vessels on an international voyage, each inflatable liferaft shall have a carrying capacity of not less than

_____.
A.      50 percent of all persons on board
B.      75 percent of all persons on board
C.      6 persons
D.      10 persons

27 - USCG 3861
Coast Guard Regulations (46 CFR) require that life jackets shall be _____.
A.      provided for each person onboard
B.      provided for all personnel of watch
C.      readily accessible to persons in the engine room
D.      All of the above

28 - USCG 3715
The necessity for administering artificial respiration may be recognized by the victim's _____.
A.      vomiting
B.      blue color and lack of breathing
C.      irregular breathing
D.      unconscious condition

29 - USCG 3716

In order to initiate CPR on a drowning victim, _____.
A.      start chest compressions before the victim is removed from the water
B.      drain water from the lungs before ventilating
C.      begin mouth-to-mouth ventilations
D.      do not tilt the head back since it may cause vomiting

30 - USCG 3970

In the illustration, the sea painter is number _____.
See Diagram: D014SA
A.      1
B.      12
C.      16
D.      18

31 - USCG 3053

On an OSV, when may a work vest be substituted for a required life jacket?
A.      To replace a damaged life jacket
B.      For use during fire drills
C.      For use during boat drills
D.      At no time

32 - USCG 3055

Which statement is TRUE concerning life jackets?
A.      Buoyant vests may be substituted for life jackets.
B.      Life jackets are designed to turn an unconscious person's face clear of the water.
C.      Life jackets must always be worn with the same side facing outwards to float properly.
D.      Lightly stained or faded life jackets will fail in the water and should not be used.

33 - USCG 3203

The inside light in an inflatable liferaft is turned on _____.
A.      automatically as the liferaft inflates
B.      with a switch near the boarding handle
C.      at night because the light has a photosensitive switch
D.      by screwing the bulb in after the raft inflates

34 - USCG 3456

When a sea anchor for a survival craft is properly rigged, it will _____.
A.      completely stop the survival craft from drifting
B.      help to prevent broaching
C.      prevent the survival craft from pitching
D.      prevent the survival craft from rolling

35 - USCG 3790

While reading the muster list you see that "3 short blasts on the whistle and three short rings on the general alarm bell bells" is the signal for _____.
A.      abandon ship
B.      dismissal from fire and emergency stations
C.      fire and emergency
D.      man overboard

36 - USCG 3800

If you have to jump in the water when abandoning ship, your legs should be _____.

A.　　spread apart as far as possible

B.　　held as tightly against your chest as possible

C.　　in a kneeling position

D.　　extended straight down and crossed at the ankles

37 - USCG 3748

A victim is coughing and wheezing from a partial obstruction of the airway. An observer should _____.

A.　　perform the Heimlich maneuver

B.　　immediately start CPR

C.　　give back blows and something to drink

D.　　allow the person to continue coughing and dislodge the obstruction on his own

38 - USCG 3774

The signal given to commence lowering the lifeboats is _____.

A.　　3 short blasts of the ship's whistle

B.　　1 short blast of the ship's whistle

C.　　3 long blasts of the ship's whistle

D.　　1 long blast of the ship's whistle

39 - USCG 3914

If you must jump from a vessel, the correct posture includes _____.

A.　　holding down the life preserver against the chest with one arm crossing the other, covering the mouth and nose with a hand, and feet together

B.　　knees bent and held close to the body with both arms around legs

C.　　body straight and arms held tightly at the sides for feet first entry into the water

D.　　both hands holding the life preserver below the chin with knees bent and legs crossed

40 - USCG 3816

When abandoning an OSV, following the launching of the survival craft you should _____.

A.　　plot a course for the nearest land

B.　　take a vote on the direction in which to go

C.　　stay in the immediate area

D.　　go in one direction until fuel runs out

41 - USCG 2421

How many degrees are there on a compass card?

A.　　360°

B.　　380°

C.　　390°

D.　　420°

42 - USCG 2794

Which would influence a magnetic compass?

A.　　Electrical wiring

B.　　Iron pipe

C.　　Radio

D.　　All of the above

43 - USCG 3955

The person-in-charge shall insure that each rescue boat on an OSV is lowered to the water, launched and operated at least once every _____.

A. week
B. two months
C. three months
D. six months

44 - USCG 2125

Who should inspect and test an inflatable liferaft?

A. The Chief Mate
B. An approved servicing facility
C. Shipyard personnel
D. A certificated lifeboatman

45 - USCG 3745

In reviving a person who has been overcome by gas fumes, what would you AVOID doing?

A. Giving stimulants
B. Prompt removal of the patient from the suffocating atmosphere
C. Applying artificial respiration and massage
D. Keeping the patient warm and comfortable

46 - USCG 3719

Symptoms of heat stroke are _____.

A. cold and moist skin, high body temperature
B. cold and dry skin, low body temperature
C. hot and moist skin, high body temperature
D. hot and dry skin, high body temperature

47 - USCG 2777

The lubber's line on a magnetic compass indicates _____.

A. compass north
B. the direction of the vessel's head
C. magnetic north
D. a relative bearing taken with azimuth circle

48 - USCG 4266

Which statement about immersion suits is TRUE?

A. The suit must, without assistance, turn an unconscious person's mouth clear of the water within 5 seconds.
B. The immersion suit seals in body heat and provides protection against hypothermia for weeks.
C. The suit will still be serviceable after a brief (2-6 minutes) exposure to flame and burning.
D. The collar must be inflated before abandoning ship.

49 - USCG 2833

A vessel heading NE is on a course of _____.

A. 022.5°
B. 045.0°
C. 067.5°
D. 090.0°

50 - USCG 3651
Distress signals may be _____.
A.      red flares
B.      smoke signals
C.      sound signals
D.      Any of the above

**LIFEBOATMAN LIMITED**
**441XX-Survival Craft For Vessels Without Lifeboats**
Test No. 330734          Answers

| | | | |
|---|---|---|---|
| 1 | 3414 | B | *46 CFR 160.027-2 |
| 2 | 2903 | D | *46 CFR 185.604 (b); *46 CFR 199.70 (b) (3) |
| 3 | 2965 | B | *46 CFR 160.171-9; *46 CFR 160.171-11 (a) (4) |
| 4 | 2970 | C | *46 CFR 160.171-9 |
| 5 | 3003 | C | NVIC 5-86; WSM |
| 6 | 3037 | C | NPFVOA |
| 7 | 3188 | D | WSM |
| 8 | 3479 | C | MIL |
| 9 | 3972 | A | WATER SURVIVAL MANUAL    D014SA |
| 10 | 3979 | A | WATER SURVIVAL MANUAL    D014SA |
| 11 | 3984 | B | MIL; WSM; *46 CFR 160.51    D014SA |
| 12 | 3988 | A | MIL; WSM; *46 CFR 160.51    D015SA |
| 13 | 3095 | A | WSM |
| 14 | 3097 | B | WSM |
| 15 | 3558 | A | AMSM; LBMN; *46 CFR 131.530 |
| 16 | 3564 | A | SEATECH; *46 CFR 199.175 (b) (21) |
| 17 | 3569 | D | WHITTAKER |
| 18 | 3586 | C | SAFETY AT SEA; SURVIVAL GUIDE |
| 19 | 3810 | D | WHITTAKER |
| 20 | 3129 | D | WSM |
| 21 | 3782 | D | WSM |
| 22 | 3820 | C | SAFETY AT SEA; SURVIVAL GUIDE |
| 23 | 3628 | D | *46 CFR 199.510; *46 CFR 199.01; *46 CFR 160.11 |
| 24 | 3666 | D | FVSM |
| 25 | 3672 | A | *46 CFR 133.175 |
| 26 | 2127 | C | *46 CFR 160.51; *46 CFR 199.201; *46 CFR 199.261 |
| 27 | 3861 | D | *46 CFR 185.604 (b); *46 CFR 199.70 (b) (3) |
| 28 | 3715 | B | SHIP'S MEDICINE CHEST |
| 29 | 3716 | C | SHIP'S MEDICINE CHEST |
| 30 | 3970 | C | WATER SURVIVAL MANUAL    D014SA |
| 31 | 3053 | D | *46 CFR 131.720 (c) |
| 32 | 3055 | B | *46 CFR 160.06-2 (b) |
| 33 | 3203 | A | SURVIVAL AT SEA |
| 34 | 3456 | B | AMSM; *46 CFR 199.175 (b) (27); *46 CFR 160.19 |
| 35 | 3790 | B | *46 CFR 35.10-5 (a) |
| 36 | 3800 | D | MSRS; AMSM; LBMN |
| 37 | 3748 | D | SHIP'S MEDICINE CHEST |
| 38 | 3774 | B | *46 CFR 35.10-5; *46 CFR 97.13-15 |
| 39 | 3914 | A | MSRS; AMSM; LBMN |
| 40 | 3816 | C | LBMAN; AMSM |
| 41 | 2421 | A | *BOWD 2, TABLE 2 |
| 42 | 2794 | D | *BOWD 2 |
| 43 | 3955 | C | *46 CFR 131.530 (7) (ii) |
| 44 | 2125 | B | LBMAN; *46 CFR 199.190 (g) (3); *46 CFR 160.51-6; *46 CFR 160.151-57 |
| 45 | 3745 | A | SHIP'S MEDICINE CHEST |
| 46 | 3719 | D | SHIP'S MEDICINE CHEST |
| 47 | 2777 | B | *BOWD 2 |
| 48 | 4266 | A | *46 CFR 160.171-11 (b) |
| 49 | 2833 | B | *BOWD 2, TABLE 2 |
| 50 | 3651 | D | *H.O. 102 |

## International Maritime Organization (IMO) Safety Symbols

**International & Inland Distress Signals**
**Rule 37 (72 COLREGS) 33 CFR 87.1 - Need of assistance**

The following signals, used or exhibited either together or separately, indicate distress and need of assistance:

a. A gun or other explosive signal fired at intervals of about a minute;
b. A continuous sounding with any fog-signaling apparatus;
c. Rockets or shells, throwing red stars fired one at a time at short intervals;
d. A signal made by radiotelegraphy or by any other signaling method consisting of the group  . . .– – –. . .  (SOS) in the Morse Code;
e. A signal sent by radiotelephony consisting of the spoken word "Mayday";
f. The International Code Signal of distress indicated by N.C.;
g. A signal consisting of a square flag having above or below it a ball or anything resembling a ball;
h. Flames on the vessel (as from a burning tar barrel, oil barrel, etc.);
i. A rocket parachute flare or a hand flare showing a red light;
j. A smoke signal giving off orange-colored smoke;
k. Slowly and repeatedly raising and lowering arms outstretched to each side;
l. A distress alert by means of digital selective calling (DSC) transmitted on:
    a. VHF channel 70, or
    b. MF/HF on the frequencies 2187.5 kHz, 8414.5 kHz, 4207.5 kHz, 6312 kHz, 12577 kHz or 16804.5 kHz;
m. A ship-to-shore distress alert transmitted by the ship's Inmarsat or other mobile satellite service provider ship earth station;
n. signals transmitted by emergency position-indicating radio beacons;
o. Approved signals transmitted by radiocommunication systems, including survival craft radar transponders.
p. A high intensity white light flashing at regular intervals from 50 to 70 times per minute.

1. The use or exhibition of any of the foregoing signals except for the purpose of indicating distress and need of assistance and the use of other signals which may be confused with any of the above signals is prohibited.

2. Attention is drawn to the relevant sections of the International Code of Signals, the Merchant Ship Search and Rescue Manual, Volume III and the following signals:
    (i) a piece of orange-colored canvas with either a black square and circle or other appropriate symbol (for identification from the air)
    (ii) a dye marker.

# CHAPTER 4

## SECTION 2: TABLE OF LIFESAVING SIGNALS

### I LANDING SIGNALS FOR THE GUIDANCE OF SMALL BOATS WITH CREWS OR PERSONS IN DISTRESS

| | MANUAL SIGNALS | LIGHT SIGNALS | OTHER SIGNALS | SIGNIFICATION |
|---|---|---|---|---|
| Day Signals | Vertical motion of a white flag or of the arms | or firing of a **green** star signal | or code letter K given by light or sound-signal apparatus | This is the best place to land |
| Night Signals | Vertical motion of a white light or flare | or firing of a **green** star signal | or code letter K given by light or sound-signal apparatus | |

A range (indication of direction) may be given by placing a steady white light or flare at a lower level and in line with the observer

| | MANUAL SIGNALS | LIGHT SIGNALS | OTHER SIGNALS | SIGNIFICATION |
|---|---|---|---|---|
| Day Signals | Horizontal motion of a white flag or of the arms extended horizontally | or firing of a **red** star signal | or code letter S given by light or sound-signal apparatus | Landing here highly dangerous |
| Night Signals | Horizontal motion of a light or flare | or firing of a **red** star signal | or code letter S given by light or sound-signal apparatus | |
| Day Signals | 1 Horizontal motion of a white flag, followed by 2 the placing of the white flag in the ground and 3 by the carrying of another white flag in the direction to be indicated | 1 or firing of a **red** star signal vertically and 2 a **white** star signal in the direction towards the better landing place | 1 or signalling the code letter S (...) followed by the code letter R (. _ .) if a better landing place for the craft in distress is located more to the *right* in the direction of approach 2 or signaling the code letter S (...) followed by the code letter L (. _ ..) if a better landing place for the craft in distress is located more to the *left* in the direction of approach | Landing here highly dangerous. A more favorable location for landing is in the direction indicated |
| Night Signals | 1 Horizontal motion of a white light or flare 2 followed by the placing of the white light or flare on the ground and 3 the carrying of another white light or flare in the direction to be indicated | 1 or firing of a **red** star signal vertically and a 2 white star signal in the direction towards the better landing place | 1 or signalling the code letter S (...) followed by the code letter R (. _ .) if a better landing place for the craft in distress is located more to the *right* in the direction of approach 2 or signaling the code letter S (...) followed by the code letter L (. _ ..) if a better landing place for the craft in distress is located more to the *left* in the direction of approach | |

## II SIGNALS TO BE EMPLOYED IN CONNECTION WITH THE USE OF SHORE LIFESAVING APPARATUS

| | MANUAL SIGNALS | LIGHT SIGNALS | OTHER SIGNALS | SIGNIFICATION |
|---|---|---|---|---|
| Day Signals | Vertical motion of a white flag or of the arms | or firing of a **green** star signal | | In general: affirmative Specifically: rocket line is held — tail block is made fast — hawser is made fast — man is in the breeches buoy — haul away |
| Night Signals | Vertical motion of a white light or flare | or firing of a **green** star signal | | |
| Day Signals | Horizontal motion of a white flag or of the arms extended horizontally | or firing of a **red** star signal | | In general: negative Specifically: slack away - avast hauling |
| Night Signals | Horizontal motion of a white light or flare | or firing of a **red** star signal | | |

## III REPLIES FROM LIFESAVING STATIONS OR MARITIME RESCUE UNITS TO DISTRESS SIGNALS MADE BY A SHIP OR PERSON

| | | | | |
|---|---|---|---|---|
| Day Signals | | Orange smoke signal | or combined *light* and *sound* signal (thunder-light) consisting of 3 single signals which are fired at intervals of approximately one minute | You are seen - assistance will be given as soon as possible (Repetition of such signal shall have the same meaning) |
| Night Signals | | White star rocket consisting of 3 single signals which are fired at intervals of approximately one minute | | |

If necessary, the day signals may be given at night or the night signals by day

## *Points of the Compass*

*Examination Room Reference: Pub. No. 9, American Practical Navigator, Volume 2, Bowditch, Table 2*

| North to East | | | South to West | | |
|---|---|---|---|---|---|
| *DIRECTION* | *POINT* | *DEGREES* | *DIRECTION* | *POINT* | *DEGREES* |
| North | N | 000° | South | S | 180° |
| North by East | N x E | 011-1⁄4° | South by West | S x W | 191-1⁄4° |
| North North East | NNE | 022-1⁄2° | South South West | SSW | 202-1⁄2° |
| North East by North | NE x N | 033-3⁄4° | South West by South | SW x S | 213-3⁄4° |
| North East | NE | 045° | South West | SW | 225° |
| North East by East | NE x E | 056-1⁄4° | South West by West | SW x W | 236-1⁄4° |
| East North East | ENE | 067-1⁄2° | West South West | WSW | 247-1⁄2° |
| East by North | E x N | 078-3⁄4° | West by South | W x S | 258-3⁄4° |
| East | E | 090° | West | W | 270° |

| East to South | | | West to North | | |
|---|---|---|---|---|---|
| *DIRECTION* | *POINT* | *DEGREES* | *DIRECTION* | *POINT* | *DEGREES* |
| East | E | 090° | West | W | 270° |
| East by South | E x S | 101-1⁄4° | West by North | W x N | 281-1⁄4° |
| East South East | ESE | 112-1⁄2° | West North West | WNW | 292-1⁄2° |
| South East by East | SE x E | 123-3⁄4° | North West by West | NW x W | 303-3⁄4° |
| South East | SE | 135° | North West | NW | 315° |
| South East by South | SE x S | 146-1⁄4° | North West by North | NW x N | 326-1⁄4° |
| South South East | SSE | 157-1⁄2° | North North West | NNW | 337-1⁄2° |
| South by East | S x E | 168-3⁄4° | North by West | N x W | 348-3⁄4° |
| South | S | 180° | North | N | 360° |

**The Cardinal Points of the Compass are: North (N), East (E), South (S), and West (W)**
**The Intercardinal Points of the Compass are:     Northeast (NE), Southeast (SE), Southwest (SW), and Northwest (NW)**

*There are 32 points of the compass. One point is equal to 11-1⁄4°*

## LIFEBOATS
Sailing Lifeboat

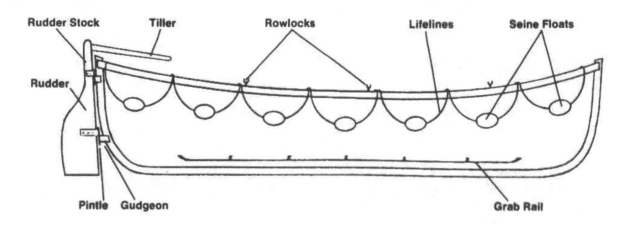

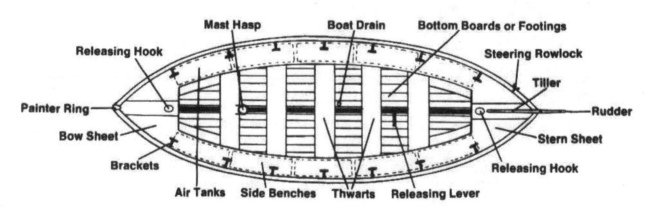

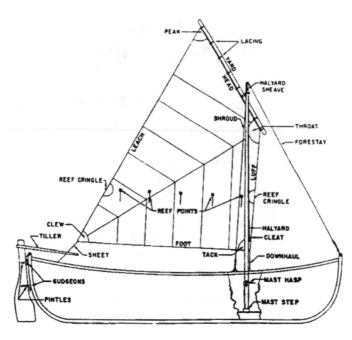

## Hand Propelled Lifeboat

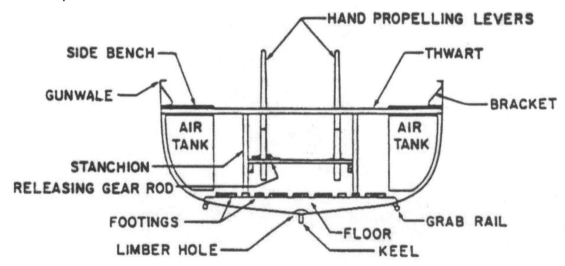

**Transverse cross section**

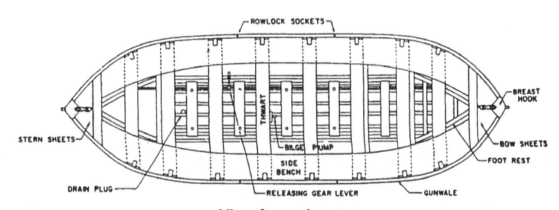

**View from above**

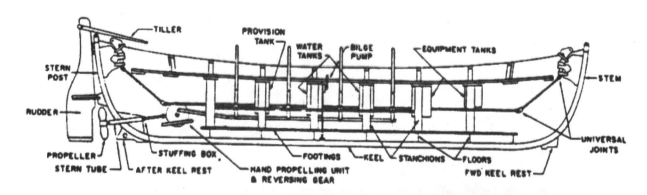

**Profile view**

## Enclosed Lifeboat

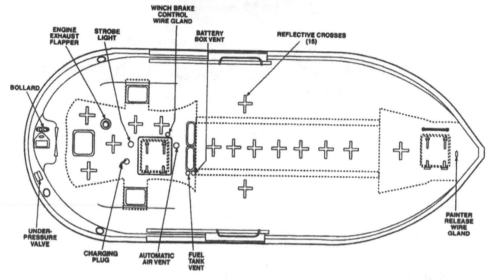

**View from above**

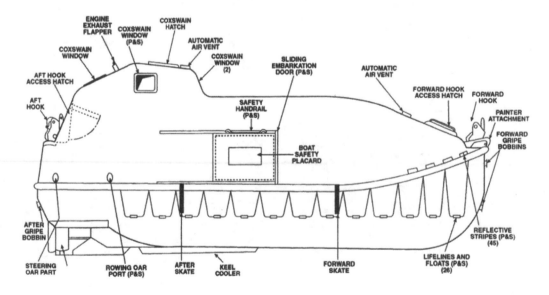

**Profile view**

## LIFEBOAT DAVIT SYSTEMS

The typical lifeboat davit system is made up of five major subsystems. The five subsystems are the:

1. lifeboat davit arms, trackway and sheaves system
2. electrical system
3. lifeboat winch and controls
4. lifeboat falls and fittings
5. the stowage cradle

**Definitions**

**Mechanical Davit** - A davit requiring the application of an external force (other than gravity) to move the lifeboat from the inboard position to the outboard position in preparation for launching.

**Pivoted Davit** - A davit consisting of an arm or arms which pivot around a single axis to move inboard and outboard.

**Gravity Davit** - A davit that requires only the force of gravity to move a lifeboat from the inboard launching position to the waterborne position.

**46 CFR 160.032–2 General requirements for davits.**

(a) The requirements of this section apply to all new construction. Davits approved and in use prior to the regulations in this subpart may be continued in service if in satisfactory condition.

(b) Davits may be either of the mechanical or gravity types.

(1) Mechanical davits shall be designed to be swung out by screws, gears, or other means, using manual power for operation. Radial type davits with mechanical means for operating are not acceptable under this category.

(2) Gravity davits shall be designed to be swung out without the use of manual, electric, steam, or other power supplied by the vessel.

(3) Other types of davits will be given special consideration.

(c) Davits shall be so designed that it will not be necessary to take up or slack the falls in order to crank out the davits.

(d) For the purpose of calculations and conducting tests, the weight of the persons shall be taken at 165 pounds each.

(e) The requirements of this subpart shall be complied with unless other arrangements in matters of construction details, design, strength, equivalent in safety and efficiency are approved by the Commandant.

**46 CFR 160.032–3 Construction of davits.**

(a)  *Strength required.* Davits shall be of such strength that the lifeboat may be lowered safely with its full complement of persons and equipment, it being assumed that the vessel is heeled 15 degrees in either direction and with a 10-degree trim. A minimum factor of safety of 6 on the ultimate strength of the materials shall be maintained at all times based on the approved working load.

(b)  *Turning out.* (1) Mechanical davits shall be designed so that they may be operated from the full inboard to the full outboard position when the lifeboat is fully equipped, but not loaded with persons, it being assumed that the vessel is heeled 15 degrees in either direction and with a 10-degree trim.

(2)    Gravity davits shall be designed so that they may be operated automatically from the full inboard to the full outboard position when the lifeboat is fully equipped, but not loaded with persons, it being assumed that the vessel is heeled 15 degrees in either direction and with a 10-degree trim. This operation shall be accomplished by merely releasing the brake of the lifeboat winch.

## LIFEBOAT DAVIT SYSTEMS
### Radial or Round Bar Davit

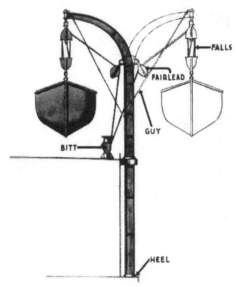

Radial davit systems consist of a pair of vertical arms each extending from a pedestal. The lifeboat is moved to the outboard position by partially rotating the arms. The lifeboat falls on this type of davit may be of manila or double braided nylon rope handled by a deck winch or block and tackle.

### Radial or Round Bar Davit Operation

1. Clear the boat gripes.
2. Remove the chocks.
3. Slack and tend the guys. Guys should be tended until secured with the boat ready to lower.
4. Swing boat aft.
5. Swing bow and forward davit outboard.
6. Swing both davits forward and the stern and after davit outboard.
7. Swing davits aft until boat is in position for lowering.
8. Haul the guys taut and secure them.
9. Lower away boat by slacking the falls evenly.

## MECHANICAL LIFEBOAT DAVIT SYSTEMS
### Sheath-Screw Boom Davit

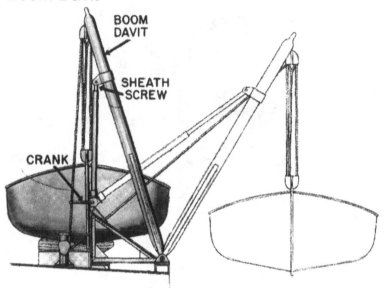

Pivoted Sheath-Screw Davit is a mechanical davit, the arms of which are generally in crescent form, which is mechanically operated in and out by means of a sheath screw.

The lifeboat is carried on chocks on deck under a pair of davits. The davits are pivoted near their foot and are cranked to the inboard or outboard position by a hand crank and sheath-screw gear.

### Sheath-Screw Crescent Davit

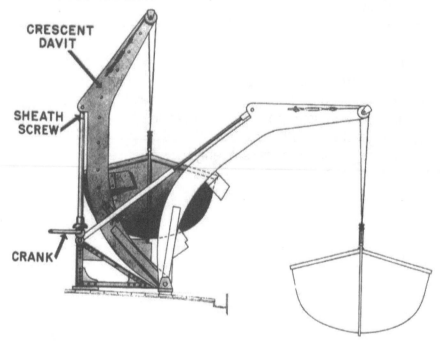

# MECHANICAL LIFEBOAT DAVIT SYSTEMS
## Sheath-Screw Crescent Davit Launching

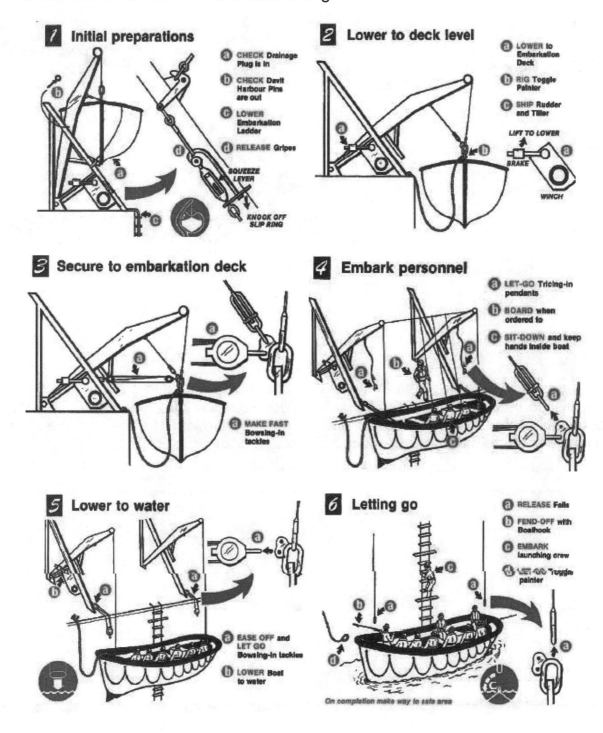

**1 Initial preparations**
- (a) CHECK Drainage Plug is in
- (b) CHECK Davit Harbour Pins are out
- (c) LOWER Embarkation Ladder
- (d) RELEASE Gripes

SQUEEZE LEVER

KNOCK OFF SLIP RING

**2 Lower to deck level**
- (a) LOWER to Embarkation Deck
- (b) RIG Toggle Painter
- (c) SHIP Rudder and Tiller

LIFT TO LOWER

BRAKE

WINCH

**3 Secure to embarkation deck**
- (a)
- (a) MAKE FAST Bowsing-in tackles

**4 Embark personnel**
- (a) LET-GO Tricing-in pendants
- (b) BOARD when ordered to
- (c) SIT-DOWN and keep hands inside boat

**5 Lower to water**
- (a) EASE OFF and LET GO Bowsing-in tackles
- (b) LOWER Boat to water

**6 Letting go**
- (a) RELEASE Falls
- (b) FEND-OFF with Boathook
- (c) EMBARK launching crew
- (d) LET-GO Toggle painter

On completion make way to safe area

# MECHANICAL LIFEBOAT DAVIT SYSTEMS
## Pivoted Quadrantal Davit

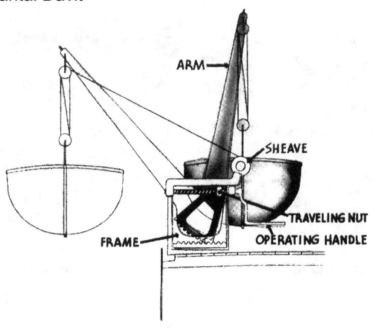

Pivoted Quadrantal Davit is a mechanical davit, which is mechanically operated inboard and outboard by means of a screw gear attached to a quadrantal toothed gear.

With quadrantal davit systems, lifeboats do not require lifting before being swung out. The lifeboat is carried in chocks on deck between the pair of davits. The davit arms, pivoted near their base, can be cranked outboard by turning cranks which operate a worm gear, thus swinging the boat out over the side to lowering position.

## MECHANICAL LIFEBOAT DAVIT SYSTEMS
### Gravity Davit (Open Lifeboat)

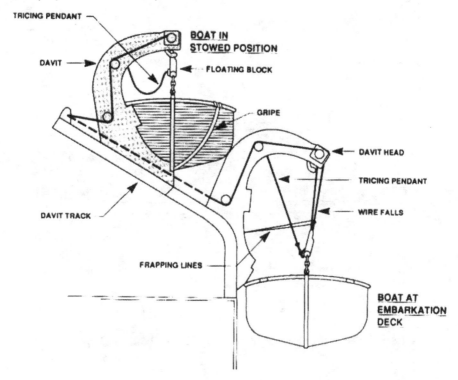

### Miranda Gravity Davit (Enclosed Lifeboat)

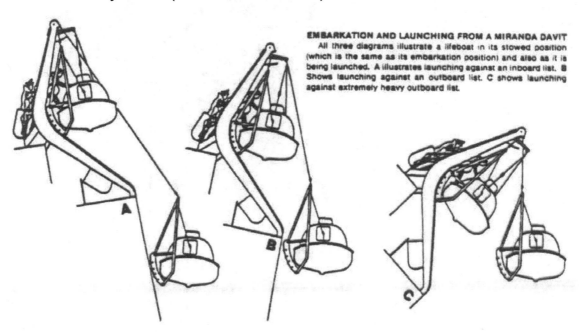

**EMBARKATION AND LAUNCHING FROM A MIRANDA DAVIT**
All three diagrams illustrate a lifeboat in its stowed position (which is the same as its embarkation position) and also as it is being launched. A illustrates launching against an inboard list. B shows launching against an outboard list. C shows launching against extremely heavy outboard list.

## Gravity Davit (Enclosed Lifeboat)

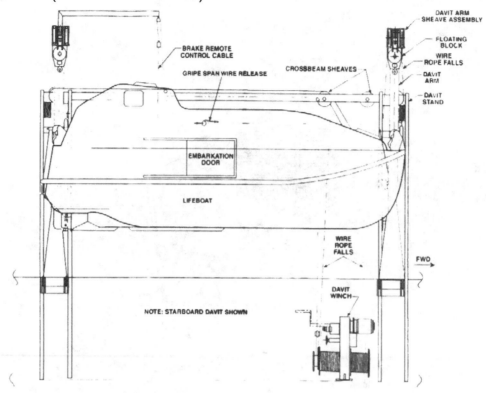

## Free Fall Davit (Enclosed Lifeboat)

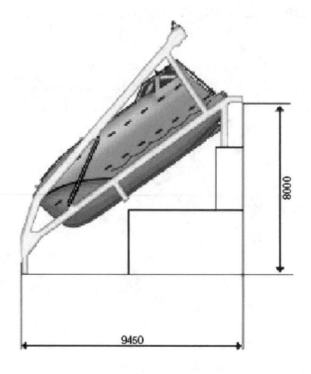

## Gravity Davit (Enclosed Lifeboat)

### 1 Initial preparations

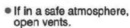

- Ensure harbour securing pins are removed.
- Disconnect electrical charge cable.
- Close drain plugs.
- Place E.P.I.R.B. and S.A.R.T. in boat.
- Board when instructed, sit and fasten seat belts.

### 2 Launch actions

- Release gripes/securing wires.
- Secure hatches.
- If in a safe atmosphere, open vents.
- If in a dangerous atmosphere, close vents.
- Suitable jackets (inflatable) are to be worn by the boats crew.

### 3 Lower to water

- Check clear below.
- Operate brake release.
- Boat may swing during launch.
- Keep lowering boat at a steady rate.

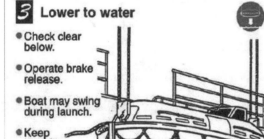

### 4 Entering water

- Allow boat to settle in the water.
- Keep brake off.
- Release falls.
- If falls do not disengage, operate emergency release as follows:-
    1) Break glass.
    2) Move lever to green zone.
    3) Release falls.

### 5 Letting go

- Start engine.
- If in a dangerous atmosphere, open air supply and water spray valves.
- Release painter when ready.
- Steer away from ship.

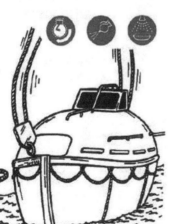

### 6 Final actions

- Rescue any swimming survivors if safe to do so.
- When clear of vessel, stream sea anchors.
- Operate E.P.I.R.B. and S.A.R.T.

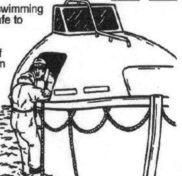

## Davit Equipment & Fittings

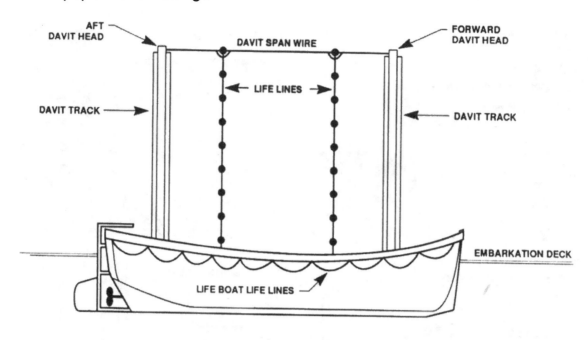

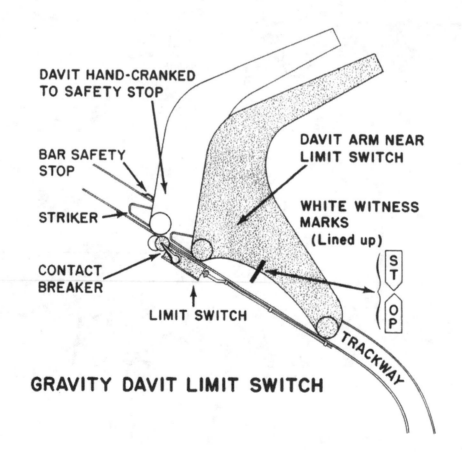

**GRAVITY DAVIT LIMIT SWITCH**

## Davit Equipment & Fittings

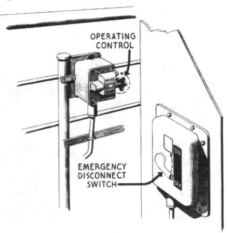

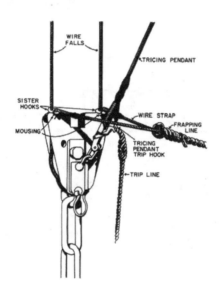

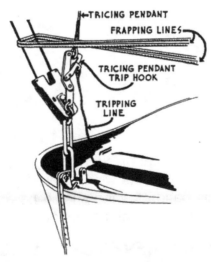

## Davit Equipment & Fittings

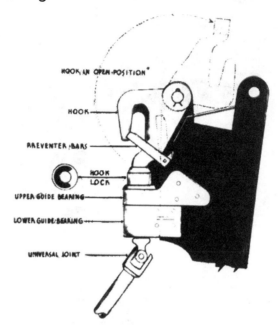

### ROTTMER
## LIFEBOAT RELEASING GEAR

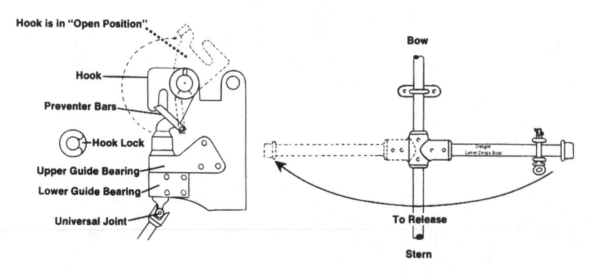

**Rottmer Releasing Hook**

**Rottmer Releasing Gear**

The area in way of the red mechanical disengaging gear control lever, from the keel to the side bench, shall be painted or otherwise colored white, to provide a contrasting background for the lever. This band of white should be approximately 12 inches wide depending on the internal arrangements of the lifeboat.

## "DANGER-LEVER DROPS BOAT"

# Lifeboat Equipment

**Exam room Reference: 46 CFR 199.175 Survival craft and rescue boat equipment.**

(a)     All lifeboat and rescue boat equipment—

(1)     Must be secured within the boat by lashings, by storage in lockers or compartments, by storage in brackets or similar mounting arrangements, or by other suitable means;

(2)     Must be secured in such a manner as not to interfere with any abandonment procedures or reduce seating capacity;

(3)     Must be as small and of as little mass as possible;

(4)     Must be packed in a suitable and compact form; and

(5)     Should be stowed so the items do not—

(i)Reduce the seating capacity;

(ii)     Adversely affect the seaworthiness of the survival craft or rescue boat; or

(iii)     Overload the launching appliance.

(b)     Each lifeboat, rigid liferaft, and rescue boat, unless otherwise stated in this paragraph, must carry the equipment listed in this paragraph and specified for it in table 199.175 of this section under the vessel's category of service. A lifeboat that is also a rescue boat must carry the equipment in the table column marked for a lifeboat.

(1)     *Bailer.* The bailer must be buoyant.

(2)     *Bilge pump.* The bilge pump must be approved under approval series 160.044 and must be installed in a ready-to-use condition as follows:

(i)The bilge pump for a lifeboat approved for less than 70 persons must be either size 2 or 3.

(ii)     The bilge pump for a lifeboat approved for 70 persons or more must be size 3.

(3)     *Boathook.* In the case of a boat launched by falls, the boathook must be kept free for fending-off purposes. For inflated rescue boats and for rigid-inflated rescue boats, each boathook must be designed to minimize the possibility of damage to the inflated portions of the hull.

(4)     *Bucket.* The bucket must be made of corrosion-resistant material and should either be buoyant or have an attached lanyard at least 1.8 meters (6 feet) long.

(5)     *Can opener.* A can opener may be in a jackknife approved under approval series 160.043.

(6)     *Compass.* The compass and its mounting arrangement must be approved under approval series 160.014. In a totally enclosed lifeboat, the compass must be permanently fitted at the steering position; in any other boat it must be provided with a binnacle, if necessary to protect it from the weather, and with suitable mounting arrangements.

(7)     *Dipper.* The dipper must be rustproof and attached to a lanyard that should be at least 0.9 meters (3 feet) long.

(8)     *Drinking cup.* The drinking cup must be graduated and rustproof. The cup should also be of a breakage-resistant material.

(9)    *Fire extinguisher.* The fire extinguisher must be approved under approval series 162.028. The fire extinguisher must be type B-C, size II, or larger. Two type B-C, size I fire extinguishers may be carried in place of a type B-C, size II fire extinguisher.

(10)    *First aid kit.* The first aid kit in a lifeboat and in a rescue boat must be approved under approval series 160.041. The first aid kit in a rigid liferaft must be approved under approval series 160.054.

(11)    *Fishing kit.* The fishing kit must be approved under approval series 160.061.

(12)    *Flashlight.* The flashlight must be a type I or type III that is constructed and marked in accordance with the American Society of Testing and Materials (ASTM) F 1014 (incorporated by reference, see §199.05). One spare set of batteries and one spare bulb, stored in a watertight container, must be provided for each flashlight.

(13)    *Hatchet.* The hatchet must be approved under approval series 160.013. The hatchet should be stowed in brackets near the release mechanism and, if more than one hatchet is carried, the hatchets should be stowed at opposite ends of the boat.

(14)    *Heaving line.* The heaving line must be buoyant, must be at least 30 meters (99 feet) long, must have a buoyant rescue quoit attached to one end, and should be at least 8 millimeters (5/16 inches) in diameter.

(15)    *Instruction card.* The instruction card must be waterproof and contain the information required by IMO Resolution A.657(16). The instruction card should be located so that it can be easily seen upon entering the liferaft.

(16)    *Jackknife.* The jackknife must be approved under approval series 160.043 and must be attached to the boat by its lanyard.

(17)    *Knife.* The knife must be of the non-folding type with a buoyant handle as follows:
   (i) The knife for a rigid liferaft must be secured to the raft by a lanyard and stowed in a pocket on the exterior of the canopy near the point where the painter is attached to the liferaft. If an approved jackknife is substituted for the second knife required on a liferaft equipped for 13 or more persons, the jackknife must also be secured to the liferaft by a lanyard.
   (ii)    The knife in an inflated or rigid-inflated rescue boat must be of a type designed to minimize the possibility of damage to the fabric portions of the hull.

(18)    *Ladder.* The boarding ladder must be capable of being used at each entrance on either side or at the stern of the boat to enable persons in the water to board the boat. The lowest step of the ladder must be not less than 0.4 meters (15.75 inches)    below the boat's light waterline.

(19)    *Mirror.* The signaling mirror must be approved under approval series 160.020.

(20)    *Oars and paddles.* Each lifeboat and rescue boat must have buoyant oars or paddles of the number, size, and type specified by the manufacturer of the boat. An oarlock or equivalent device, either permanently installed or attached to the boat by a lanyard or chain, must be provided for each oar. Each oar should have the vessel's name marked on it in block letters.

(21)   *Painter.* (i) One painter on a lifeboat and the painter on a rescue boat must be attached by a painter release device at the forward end of the lifeboat. The second painter on a lifeboat must be secured at or near the bow of the lifeboat, ready for use. On lifeboats to be launched by free-fall launching, both painters must be stowed near the bow ready for use.

(A)   If the painter is of synthetic material, the painter must be of a dark color or certified by the manufacturer to be resistant to deterioration from ultraviolet light.

(B)   The painter for a lifeboat and each painter for a rescue boat must be of a length that is at least twice the distance from the stowage position of the boat to the waterline with the vessel in its lightest seagoing condition, or must be 15 meters (50 feet) long, whichever is the greater.

(C)   The painter must have a breaking strength of at least 34 kilo-Newtons (7,700 pounds-force).

(ii)   The painter for a rigid liferaft must be of a length that is at least 20 meters (66 feet) plus the distance from the liferaft's stowed position to the waterline with the vessel in its lightest seagoing condition, or must be 15 meters (50 feet) long, whichever is the greater.

(A)   If the painter is of synthetic material, the painter must be of a dark color or certified by the manufacturer to be resistant to deterioration from ultraviolet light.

(B)   The painter must have a breaking strength of at least 15 kilo-Newtons (3,370 pounds-force) for liferafts approved for more than 25 persons, of at least 20 kilo-Newtons (2,250 pounds-force) for liferafts approved for 9 to 25 persons, and of at least 7.5 kilo-Newtons (1,687 pounds-force) for any other liferaft.

(C)   The painter must have a float-free link meeting the requirements of part 160, subpart 160.073 of this chapter secured to the end of the painter that is attached to the vessel. The float-free link arrangement must break under a load of 2.2±0.4 kilo-Newtons (400 to 536 pounds-force).

(22)   *Provisions.* Each unit of provisions must be approved under approval series 160.046 and must provide at least 10,000 kilo-Joules (2,390 calories). Individual provision packages may provide less than 10,000 kilo-Joules, as long as the total quantity of provisions on board provides for at least 10,000 kilo-Joules per person.

(23)   *Pump.* The pump or bellows must be manually operated and should be arranged so it is capable of inflating any part of the inflatable structure of the rescue boat.

(24)   *Radar reflector.* The radar reflector must be capable of detection at a distance of 4 nautical miles and must have a mounting arrangements to install it on the boat in its proper orientation. A 9-GigaHertz radar transponder may be substituted for the radar reflector if the transponder is accepted by the Federal Communications Commission as meeting the requirements of 47 CFR part 80 and is stowed in the boat or raft.

(25)   *Rainwater collection device.* The rainwater collection device must be arranged to collect falling rain and direct it into the water tanks in the lifeboat. If the lifeboat carries a manually-powered, reverse osmosis desalinator approved under approval series 160.058, a rainwater collection device is not required.

(26)   *Repair kit.* The repair kit for an inflated and a rigid-inflated rescue boat must be packed in a suitable container and include at least—

(i) Six sealing clamps;

(ii) Five 50-millimeter (2-inch) diameter tube patches;

(iii) A roughing tool; and

(iv) A container of cement compatible with the tube fabric. The cement must have an expiration date on its container that is not more than 24 months after the date of manufacture of the cement.

(27)   *Sea anchor.* (i) The sea anchor for a lifeboat must be approved under approval series 160.019.

(ii) Each sea anchor for a rigid liferaft must be of the type specified by the liferaft manufacturer and must be fitted with a shock resistant hawser. It may also be fitted with a tripping line. One sea anchor must be permanently attached to the liferaft in such a way that, when the liferaft is waterborne, it will cause the liferaft to lie oriented to the wind in the most stable manner. The second sea anchor must be stowed in the liferaft as a spare. A davit-launched liferaft and a liferaft on a passenger vessel must have the permanently attached sea anchor arranged to deploy automatically when the liferaft floats free.

(iii) The sea anchor for a rescue boat must be of the type specified by the rescue boat manufacturer, and must have a hawser of adequate strength that is at least 10 meters (33 feet) long.

(28)   *Searchlight.* (i) The searchlight must be of the type originally provided with the approved lifeboat or rescue boat, or must be certified by the searchlight manufacturer to meet ASTM F 1003 (incorporated by reference, see §199.05). The boat must carry two spare bulbs.

(ii) The searchlight must be permanently mounted on the canopy or must have a stanchion-type or collapsible-type, portable mounting on the canopy. The mounting must be located to enable operation of the searchlight by the boat operator.

(iii) The searchlights power source must be capable of operating the light without charging or recharging for not less than—

(A)      Three hours of continuous operation; or

(B)      Six hours total operation when it is operated in cycles of 15 minutes on and 5 minutes off.

(iv) If the searchlight's power source is an engine starting battery, there must be sufficient battery capacity to start the engine at the end of either operating period specified in paragraph (b)(28)(iii) of this section.

(v) The searchlight's power source must be connected to the searchlight using watertight electrical fittings.

(29)   *Seasickness kit.* The seasickness kit must be in a waterproof package and must include one waterproof seasickness bag, anti-seasickness medication sufficient for one person for 48 hours, and instructions for using the medication. Each seasickness kit should be stowed within reach of the seat for which it is intended.

(30)   *Signal, smoke.* The smoke signal must be approved under approval series 160.122.

(31)   *Signal, hand flare.* The hand flare must be approved under approval series 160.121.

(32)   *Signal, rocket parachute flare.* The rocket parachute flare must be approved under approval series 160.136.

(33)   *Skates and fenders.* The skates and fenders must be as specified by the lifeboat or rescue boat manufacturer to facilitate launching and prevent damage to a lifeboat intended for launching down the side of a vessel.

(34)   *Sponge.* The sponge must be suitable for soaking up water.

(35)   *Survival instructions.* The survival instructions must be as described in IMO Resolution A.657(16), Annex I for liferafts and Annex II for lifeboats.

(36)   *Table of lifesaving signals.* The table of lifesaving signals must be as described in Annex IV to the International Regulations for Preventing Collisions at Sea 1972, as amended, and must be printed on a waterproof card or stored in a waterproof container.

(37)   *Thermal protective aid.* The thermal protective aid must be approved under approval series 160.174.

(38)   *Tool kit.* The tool kit must contain sufficient tools for minor adjustments to the engine and its accessories.

(39)   *Towline.* The towline must be buoyant and at least 50 meters (164 feet) long. The towline must have a breaking strength of not less than 13.3 kilo-Newtons (3,000 pounds-force) or be of sufficient strength to tow the largest liferaft carried on the vessel when loaded with its full complement of persons and equipment at a speed of at least 2 knots.

(40)   *Water.* The water must be emergency drinking water approved under approval series 160.026.

(i)   The requirement for up to one-third of the emergency drinking water may be met by a desalting apparatus approved under approval series 160.058 that is capable of producing the substituted amount of water in 2 days.

(ii)   The requirement for up to two-thirds of the emergency drinking water may be met by a manually-powered, reverse osmosis desalinator approved under approval series 160.058 and that is capable of producing the substituted amount of water in 2 days.

(41)   *Whistle.* The whistle must be corrosion-resistant, and should be a ball-type or multi-tone whistle that is attached to a lanyard.

Lifeboat Equipment

# JACKKNIFE
## (WITH CAN OPENER)

### INSTRUCTIONS

CAN OPENER: PLACE HOOK "A" UNDER TOP RIM ON OUTSIDE OF CAN. PRESS CUTTER "B" INTO TOP OF CAN AS NEAR RIM AS POSSIBLE. OPEN CAN WITH ROCKING MOTION, TAKING SHORT BITES AND TURNING CAN COUNTER CLOCKWISE. SEE ILLUSTRATION.

MADE IN U. S. A. BY
CAMILLUS
CUTLERY
COMPANY
CAMILLUS, N. Y.

TO USE SIGNALLING MIRROR:

1. Place lanyard around neck. Hold clean mirror between the tips of your fingers and thumbs to form a nearly complete cup with hands as sides and mirror as bottom. Bring cup against face and enclose eyes in it.

2. Face half-way between sun and rescuer and see reflected in rear of mirror an image on your hands or face of the spot of sunlight coming through sighting hole.

3. Using eye nearest sun, sight the rescuer through the center hole, and at the same time turn the mirror until the spot of light becomes a perfect bright ring around the sighting hole. Sunlight from mirror now strikes rescuer.

4. When sun and rescuer are separated by a great angle, the hand nearest sun may have to be removed to turn it to the required slant.

5. For best results when signalling use 2 mirrors (1 per person.) Practice sweeping horizon at all times even if no rescuer is visible. Signals can be clearly seen at 10 miles.

TYPE SMC SIGNALLING MIRROR
**Made by SAFETY MIRROR COMPANY, New York City**
Approved by United States Coast Guard

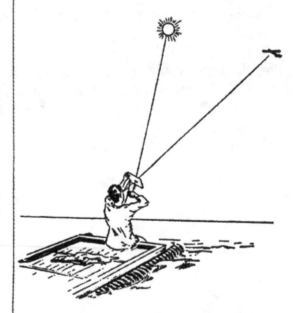

## Lifeboat Equipment

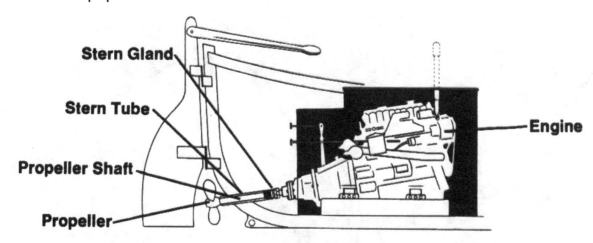

**Propeller System of an Engine-Powered Lifeboat**

All lifeboats certified to carry 60 or more but not over 100 persons shall be either motor lifeboats or shall be fitted with an approved type of hand propelling gear. All enclosed lifeboats must be motor lifeboats.

**46 CFR 160.035–8 Construction of fibrous glass reinforced plastic (F.R.P.), oar-, hand-, and motor-propelled lifeboats.**

1. The engine shall be a reliable, marine, compression-ignition type and shall be capable of propelling the fully equipped and loaded lifeboat at a sustained speed of not less than 6 knots through smooth water over a measured course.
2. Provision shall be made for going astern.
3. Sufficient fuel for 24 hours continuous operation at 6 knots shall be provided.
4. The engine used in approved lifeboats shall be capable of being started without the use of starting aids at a temperature of 20°F., by the use of an acceptable cranking system.
5. If water cooled, the engine shall be equipped with a closed fresh water cooling system. This system shall be cooled by a secondary medium, such as a water cooled heat exchanger.

*Oars are conspicuously marked (stenciled) with the ship's name.*

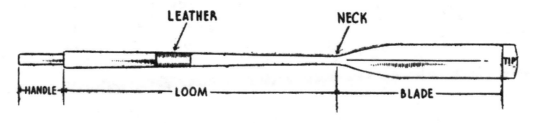

**Oar Nomenclature**

Lifeboat Equipment

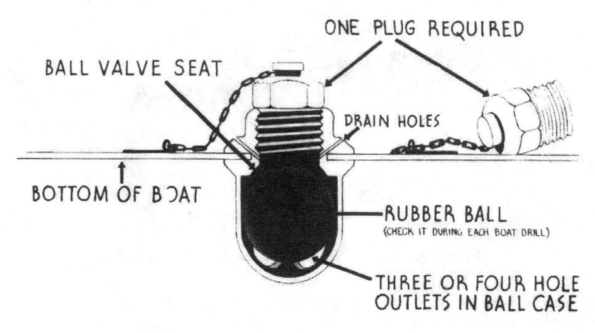

ONE PLUG REQUIRED

BALL VALVE SEAT

DRAIN HOLES

BOTTOM OF BOAT

RUBBER BALL
(CHECK IT DURING EACH BOAT DRILL)

THREE OR FOUR HOLE
OUTLETS IN BALL CASE

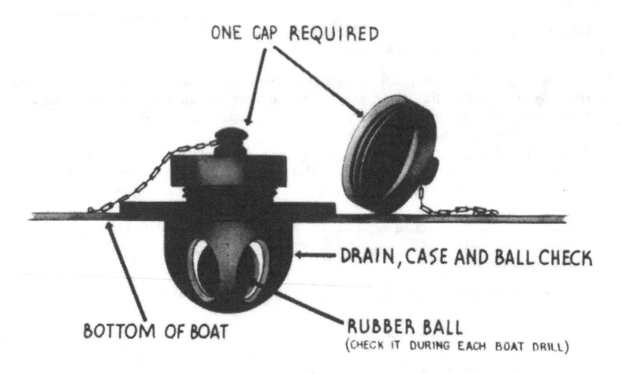

ONE CAP REQUIRED

DRAIN, CASE AND BALL CHECK

BOTTOM OF BOAT

RUBBER BALL
(CHECK IT DURING EACH BOAT DRILL)

## Lifeboat Equipment

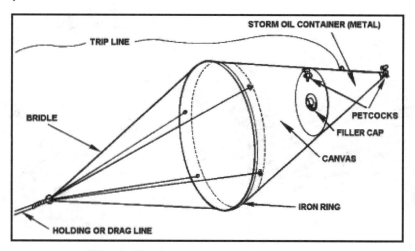

### Use of the Sea Anchor

Stream the sea anchor when the lifeboat is upwind and clear of the vessel. The sea anchor positions the lifeboat bow or stern into the wind easing the lifeboat's motion while hove to, helps reduce the risk of the lifeboat capsizing, and slows the rate of drift allowing you to stay closer to your last reported position. When hove to, the sea anchor is led-out over the bow with sufficient drag line to place the sea anchor at the far end of the sea trough with the lifeboat on the crest of the wave. Never pay-out the drag line to the bitter end. Make the bitter end fast to a secure object. Always keep enough slack to allow for a round turn on the object and a couple of fathoms to spare line. Then when the full force of the wave hits the boat, the strain on the drag line can be eased off to prevent the possibility of parting the drag line. After the wave passes, the line will slack as the lifeboat runs down the back side of the wave allowing an opportunity to recover the slack that was paid-out.

Avoid streaming the sea anchor from the stern whenever possible because it reduces steering effectiveness. Stern towing is appropriate for steadying the lifeboat when beach landing through heavy surf or running before the wind under sail. The sea anchor may be towed point first on the tripping line to reduce drag or spread storm oil. Drag can be quickly increased from the towing position by hauling back on the drag line when needed. The sea anchor should be inspected frequently. If the sea anchor is lost, it is important to improvise with other devices to take its place. Discarded clothing, oars tied to a life jacket and buckets can be used to jury rig drogues. If you have to increase your drift rate to clear an obstacle or make land fall, haul the sea anchor up to the lifeboat and remove it from the water.

## Lifeboat Equipment

Sea Painter Attachment: The sea painter should be rigged inboard of the falls and outboard of everything else.

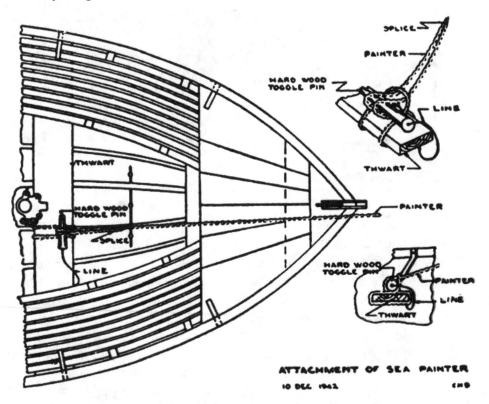

ATTACHMENT OF SEA PAINTER
10 DEC 1942

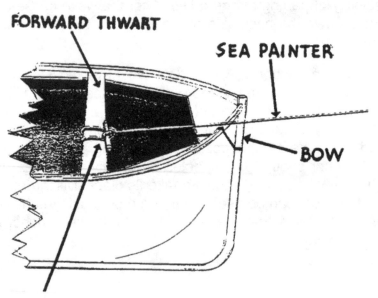

Lifeboat Markings

**Builder's Plate**

**Exam room Reference: 46 CFR 199.178 Marking of stowage locations.**

Survival craft should be numbered consecutively starting from the vessel's bow. Survival craft on the starboard side should be numbered with odd numerals and survival craft on the port side should be numbered with even numerals.

1. The ship's name, port of registry and the boat's number are stenciled on the bow of each boat in letters and numbers not less than 3 inches high.
2. The cubic capacity and number of persons allowed is marked on each bow in letters and numbers not less than 1 1/2 inches high.
3. The number of persons allowed also appears on at least two thwarts in letters and numbers at least 3 inches high.

**Where is this lifeboat located on board the S.S. Grand Canyon State?**

*(Answer: The first lifeboat on the port side.)*

## Emergency Training & Drills

Principles of survival at sea include:

1. Regular training and drills
2. Preparedness for any emergency
3. Knowledge of actions to be taken:
   a. duties when called to survival craft stations
   b. duties when required to abandon ship
   c. duties when in the water
   d. duties when aboard a survival craft
4. Knowledge of the main dangers to survivors

The choices you make in life ultimately determine your destiny. In a survival situation, the decisions you make will be far more important than the equipment you carry with you. You must train yourself to: Look, think, act and then monitor the results of your efforts. Caution and creativity are your best friends. Use them to survive!

## Emergency Training & Drills

The principle values of training and drills are:

1. The promotion of seaworthiness, safe navigation and operation as well as compliance with national and international laws and regulations.
2. The creation of uniform procedures aboard ships

Shipboard contingency plans provide procedures and guidance to the ship's emergency responders on the protecting life, property and the environment. The effectiveness of the emergency response depends in large part on the expertise of the ship's personnel.

## SOLAS Survival Instructions

### ANNEX 2
### LIST OF CONTENTS FOR THE
### LIFEBOAT SURVIVAL INSTRUCTIONS OR MANUAL

1. The person in charge of the lifeboat shall immediately. after clearing the ship. organize the following:
   a. look for and pick up other survivors from the water;
   b. marshal liferafts;
   c. secure survival craft together, distribute survivors and equipment between survival craft;
   d. stream sea-anchor; and
   e. if appropriate. rig exposure cover or foldable canopy.
2. Post a look-out.
3. Issue anti-seasickness medicine and seasickness bags.
4. Administer first aid, if appropriate.
5. Arrange watches and duties.
6. Prepare and use detection equipment including radio equipment.
7. Gather up any useful floating objects.
8. Protect against heat, cold and wet conditions.
9. Decide on food and water rations.
10. Take measures to maintain morale.
11. Make sanitary arrangements to keep lifeboat habitable.
12. Prepare for onset of adverse weather.
13. Make proper use of survival equipment.
14. Prepare action for:
    a. arrival of rescue units;
    b. being taken in tow;
    c. rescue by helicopter; and
    d. landing and beaching.

## LIFERAFTS -Liferaft Construction

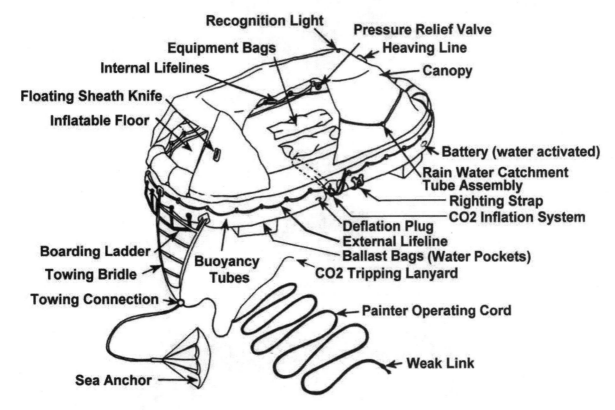

## Buoyant Apparatus - Life Float (Rigid Liferaft)

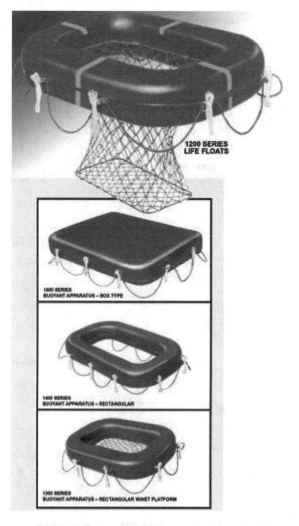

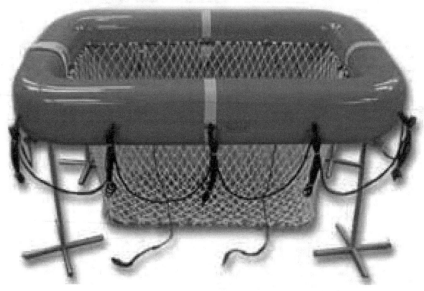

## Liferaft Equipment

To obtain Coast Guard approval, the equipment in each SOLAS A and SOLAS B inflatable liferaft must meet the following specific requirements when complying with the indicated regulations of SOLAS:

(a) Heaving line (Regulation III/38.5.1.1). The buoyant heaving line described by Regulation III/38.5.1.1 must have a breaking strength of not less than 1.1 kN (250 lb), and must be attached to the inflatable liferaft near the entrance furthest from the painter attachment.

(b) Jackknife (Regulation III/38.5.1.2). Each folding knife carried as permitted by Regulation III/38.5.1.2 must be a jackknife approved by the Commandant under approval series 160.043.

(c) Bailer (Regulation III/38.5.1.3). Each bailer described by Regulation III/38.5.1.3 must have a volume of at least 2 L (125 in\3\).

(d) Sponge (Regulation III/38.5.1.4). Each sponge described by Regulation III/38.5.1.4 must have a volume of at least 750 cm\3\ (48 in\3\) when saturated with water.

(e) Sea anchors (Regulation III/38.5.1.5). Sea anchors without the swivels described by Regulation III/38.5.1.5 may be used if, during the towing test, a sea anchor of their design does not rotate when streamed. The sea anchors need not have the tripping lines described by Regulation III/38.5.1.5 if, during the towing test, a sea anchor of their design can be hauled in by one person.

(f) Paddles (Regulation III/38.5.1.6).The paddles must be at least 1.2 m (4 ft) long and must be of the same size and type as used to pass the maneuverability test in paragraph 1/5.10 of IMO Resolution A.689(17).

(g) Tin-opener (Regulation III/38.5.1.7). Each sharp part of a tin-opener described by Regulation III/38.5.1.7 must have a guard.

(h) First-aid kit (Regulation III/38.5.1.8). Each first-aid kit described by Regulation III/38.5.1.8 must be approved by the Commandant under approval series 160.054.

(i) Whistle (Regulation III/38.5.1.9). The whistle described by Regulation III/38.5.1.9 must be a ball-type or multi-tone whistle of corrosion-resistant construction.

(j) Rocket parachute flare (Regulation III/38.5.1.10). Each rocket parachute flare described by Regulation III/38.5.1.10 must be approved by the Commandant under approval series 160.136.

(k) Hand flare (Regulation III/38.5.1.11). Each hand flare described by Regulation III/38.5.1.11 must be approved by the Commandant under approval series 160.121.

(l) Buoyant smoke signal (Regulation III/38.5.1.12). Each buoyant smoke signal described by Regulation III/38.5.1.12 must be of the floating type approved by the Commandant under approval series 160.122.

(m) Electric torch (Regulation III/38.5.1.13). The waterproof electric torch described by Regulation III/38.5.1.13 must be a Type I or Type III flashlight constructed and marked in accordance with ASTM F 1014 (incorporated by reference, see Sec. 160.151-5. Three-cell-size flashlights bearing Coast Guard approval numbers in the 161.008 series may continue to be used as long as they are serviceable.

(n) Radar reflector (Regulation III/38.5.1.14). The radar reflector may be omitted if the outside of the container of the inflatable liferaft includes a notice near the ``SOLAS A'' or ``SOLAS B'' marking indicating that no radar reflector is included.

(o) Signaling mirror (Regulation III/38.5.1.15). Each signaling mirror described by Regulation III/38.5.1.15 must be approved by the Commandant under approval series 160.020.

(p) Lifesaving signals (Regulation III/38.5.1.16). If not provided on a waterproof card or sealed in a transparent waterproof container as described in Regulation III/38.5.1.16, the table of lifesaving signals may be provided as part of the instruction manual.

(q) Fishing tackle (Regulation III/38.5.1.17). The fishing tackle must be in a kit approved by the Commandant under approval series 160.061.

(r) Food rations (Regulation III/38.5.1.18.) The food rations must be approved by the Commandant under approval series 160.046.

(s) Drinking water (Regulation III/38.5.1.19). The fresh water required by Regulation III/38.5.1.19 must be ``emergency drinking water'' approved by the Commandant under approval series 160.026. The desalting apparatus described in Regulation III/38.5.1.19 must be approved by the Commandant under approval series 160.058. 1.0 liter/person of the required water may be replaced by an approved manually powered reverse osmosis desalinator capable of producing an equal amount of water in two days.

(t) Drinking cup (Regulation III/38.5.1.20). The drinking cup described in Regulation III/38.5.1.20 must be graduated in ounces or milliliters or both.

(u) Anti-seasickness medicine (Regulation III/38.5.1.21). The anti-seasickness medicine required by Regulation III/38.5.1.21 must include instructions for use and be marked with an expiration date.

(v) Survival instructions (Regulation III/38.5.1.22). The instructions required by Regulation III/38.5.1.22 on how to survive in a liferaft must--
   (1) Be waterproof;
   (2) Whatever other language or languages they may be in, be in English;
   (3) Meet the guidelines in IMO Resolution A.657(16); and
   (4) Be suspended in a clear film envelope from one of the arch tubes of the canopy.

(w) Instructions for immediate action (Regulation III/38.5.1.23). The instructions for immediate action must--
   (1) Be waterproof;
   (2) Whatever other language or languages they may be in, be in English;
   (3) Meet the guidelines in IMO Resolution A.657(16);
   (4) Explain both the noise accompanying the operation of any provided pressure-relief valves, and the need to render them inoperable after they complete venting; and
   (5) Be suspended from the inside canopy, so they are immediately visible by survivors on entering the inflatable liferaft. They may be contained in the same envelope with the instructions on how to survive if the instructions for immediate action are visible through both faces of the envelope.

(x) Thermal protective aid (Regulation III/38.5.1.24). Each thermal protective aid described by Regulation III/38.5.1.24 must be approved by the Commandant under approval series 160.174.

(y) Repair outfit (Regulation III/39.10.1.1). The repair outfit required by Regulation III/39.10.1.1 must include--
   (1) Six or more sealing clamps or serrated conical plugs, or a combination of the two;
   (2) Five or more tube patches at least 50 mm (2 in) in diameter;
   (3) A roughing tool, if necessary to apply the patches; and
   (4) If the patches are not self-adhesive, a container of cement compatible with the liferaft fabric and the patches, marked with instructions for use and an expiration date.

(z) Pump or bellows (Regulation III/39.10.1.2). The pump or bellows required by Regulation III/39.10.1.2 must be manually operable and arranged to be capable of inflating any part of the inflatable structure of the liferaft.

(aa) Plugs for pressure-relief valves. Plugs for rendering pressure-relief valves inoperable must be provided in any liferaft fitted with such valves, unless the valves are of a type that can be rendered inoperable without separate plugs. If provided, plugs for pressure-relief valves must be usable with hands gloved in an immersion suit, and must either float or be secured to the liferaft by

## Liferaft Equipment

Sea anchor and 30 m line

Rescue quoit and 30 m line

Floating knife

Paddle

Bailer

Sponge

Repair kit

Hand flare

Smoke signal

Food

Drinking water

Tin opener

Drinking cup

First aid kit

Pump

Fishing kit

Signaling mirror

Whistle

Torch and spare batteries

Rocket parachute flare

Anti-seasickness tablet

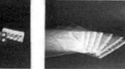
Seasickness bag

Thermal protective aid

Radar reflector

Relief valve cap

Leak stopper

(Pictures are indicative)

## Use of the Sea Anchor

Once the liferaft has been cut clear of the parent vessel, check that the liferaft's sea anchor has been properly streamed. The sea anchor, which is deployed automatically upon inflation, serves to position the entrances at right angles to the weather, helps stabilize the liferaft in the water, and reduces the rate of drift helping you to stay closer to your last reported position. The sea anchor should be inspected frequently and is so important that a spare one can be found packed aboard. By changing the drogue's point of attachment, you can position the openings of the liferaft to gain increased ventilation during hot weather or increased protection during heavy seas. If both anchors have been lost, it is important to improvise (jury rig) with other devices to take their place. Discarded clothing, paddles tied to a life jacket and buckets can be used as substitute drogues. If you have to increase your drift rate to clear an obstacle or make land fall, haul the sea anchor up to the liferaft and remove it from the water.

When properly streamed the sea anchor will maintain the raft's position in the water with regards to the crests and troughs of the waves and prevent the raft from speeding down the face of the swells or waves. In doing this, it also prevents rotation of the raft. Without a working sea anchor the raft will continually run up and down the wave faces, making for a very sickening experience, even in relatively calm waters. With nothing to stop it, the raft can carrousel wildly which can be a dizzying and sickening experience.

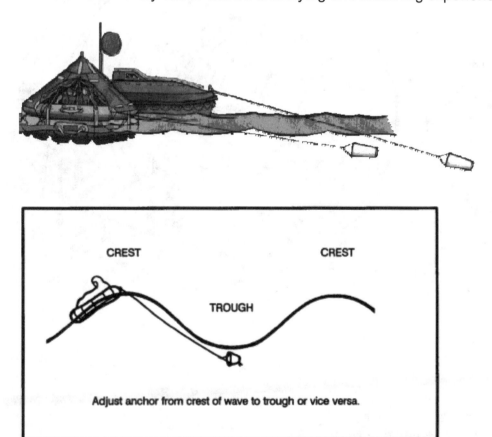

CREST                                          CREST

TROUGH

Adjust anchor from crest of wave to trough or vice versa.

## Liferaft Stowage

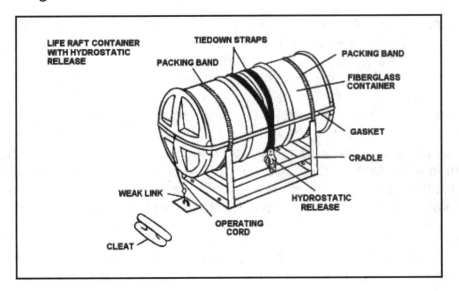

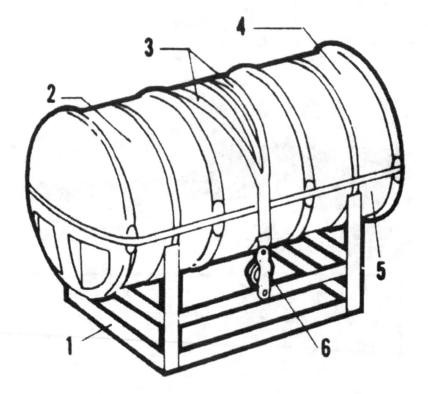

1.  Liferaft cradle
2.  Inflatable liferaft
3.  Liferaft tie down cable
4.  Stainless steel packing bands
5.  Fiberglass liferaft container
6.  Hydrostatic release mechanism

## Liferaft Stowage

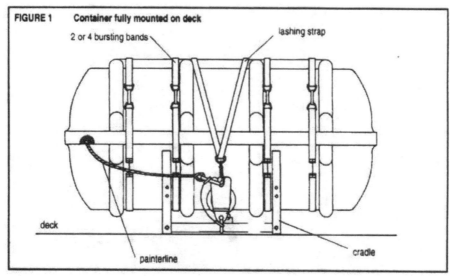

FIGURE 1    Container fully mounted on deck

2 or 4 bursting bands

lashing strap

deck

painterline

cradle

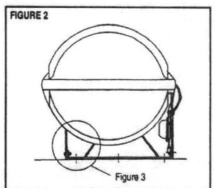

FIGURE 2

Figure 3

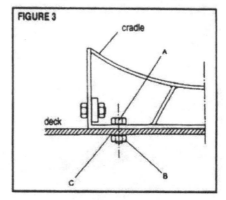

FIGURE 3

cradle

A

deck

C

B

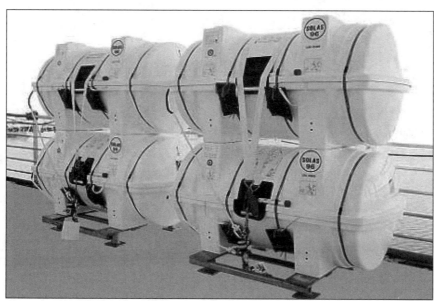

Hydrostatic Release & Weak Link

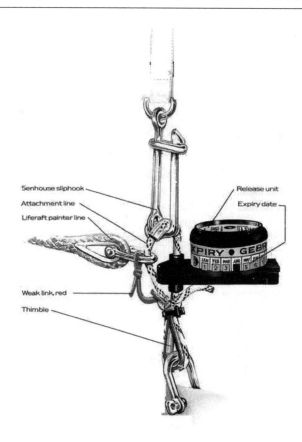

Senhouse sliphook
Attachment line
Liferaft painter line

Release unit
Expiry date

Weak link, red
Thimble

### Hydrostatic Release
1. U.S. Coast Guard approved 46 CFR 160.062/5/0; 46 CFR 160.162/3/2.
2. Meets SOLAS 74/83.
3. Disposable - Service life is two years. Visible expiration date.
4. Easy to install. No maintenance. No annual service required
5. Does not require positive buoyancy of the liferaft to activate. Releases at all angles with a required buoyancy force of between 10 kp to 1.700 kp. Designed to operate at a water depth of 1.5 to 4.0 meters.

### Weak Link 46 CFR 160.073-10 Construction and performance.
(a) The link must be constructed essentially as shown in figure 160.073-10. The link must be formed from a single salt water corrosion-resistant wire. A loop at least 50 mm (2 in.) in diameter must be provided at each end of the wire. Each loop must be permanently secured.
(b) The breaking strength of each link must be between:
    (1) 450 N (100 lb.) and 600 N (134 lb.) for links intended for life floats and buoyant apparatus of 10 persons and less capacity.
    (2) 900 N (200 lb.) and 1200 N (268 lb.) for links intended for life floats and buoyant apparatus of 11 to 20 persons capacity.
    (3) 1800 N (400 lb.) and 2400 N (536 lb.) for links intended for life floats and buoyant apparatus of 21 persons and more capacity.

## Automatic Liferaft Launching

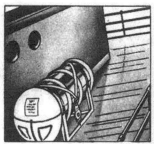   

## Automatic Liferaft Launching Instructions

1. The liferaft is secured to its cradle with a hydrostatic release which, if time permits, can be tripped for manual release and inflation off the raft. If time does not permit manual release and inflation, this will be accomplished automatically.

2. As the vessel sinks, the pressure of the water at a depth of not more than 13 feet actuates the hydrostatic release mechanism, freeing the liferaft container to float free from the stowage cradle. The liferaft is inherently buoyant and will float to the surface.

3. The sinking vessel pulls on the painter line triggering the automatic inflation of the raft. This step can be accomplished manually by survivors if the canister is floating on the surface. The $CO_2$ gas expands into the buoyancy chambers in a few seconds so the liferaft cannot be pulled down by the sinking vessel. The sea anchor is streamed automatically when the liferaft inflates, to reduce drift. Every raft is equipped with an additional sea anchor in the emergency equipment bags.

4. The U.S.C.G./SOLAS approved weak link attaches the painter to the ship; this device will part allowing the liferaft to float free from the sinking vessel. The water-activated light comes on to guide survivors to the liferaft. Once aboard, help others to board, and then read the raft manual to learn the details of liferaft operation and other data to insure survival.

Automatic Liferaft Launching

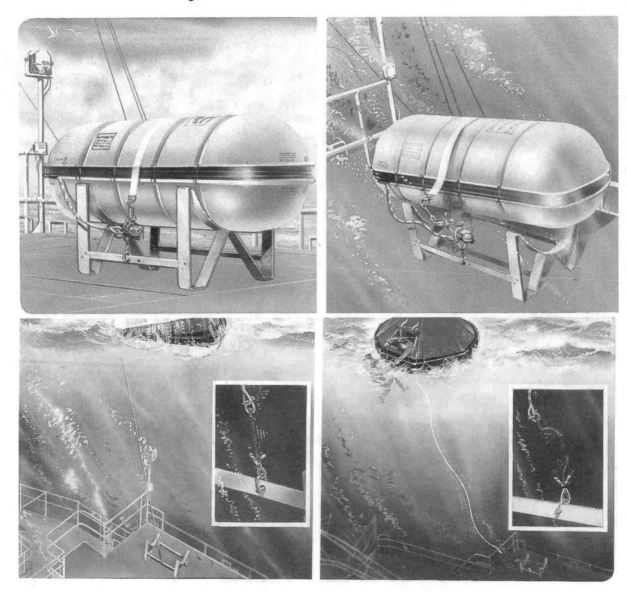

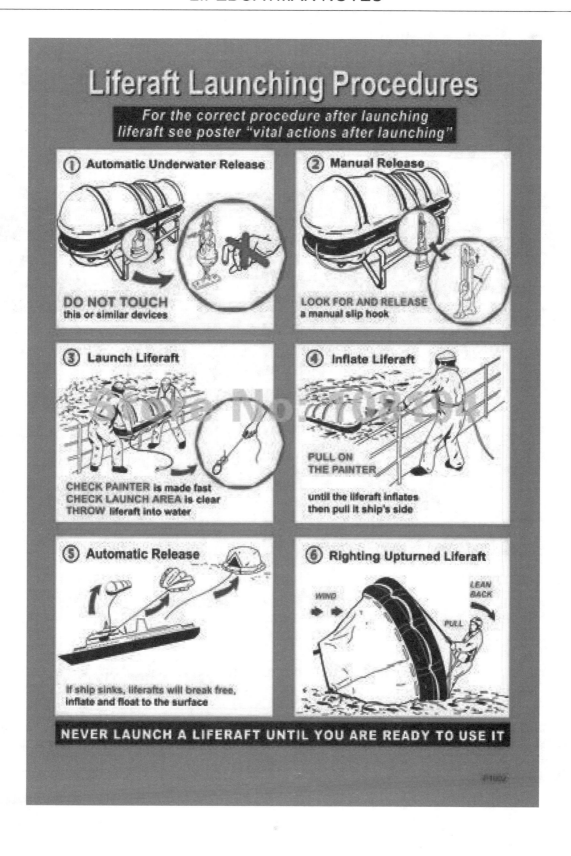

## Manual Liferaft Launching

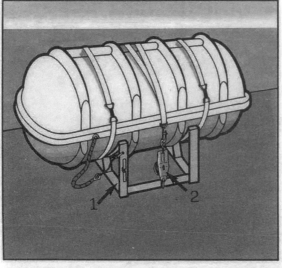

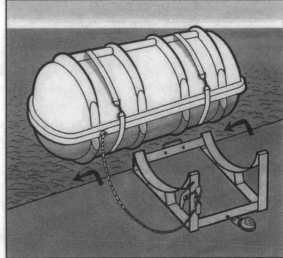

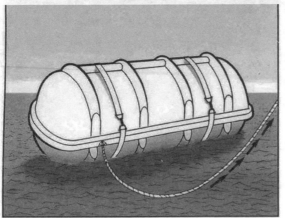

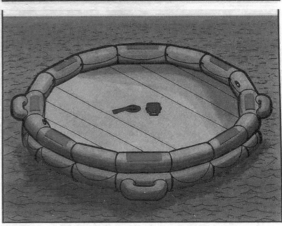

Manual

1. Pull out approximately 3 feet of the painter line from the liferaft container. Make the painter line fast to the cleat (1) on the container cradle. If you fail to make the liferaft painter fast properly the weak link may break and allow the liferaft to drift away
2. Release the liferaft container from the cradle by releasing the hydrostatic release (2). Throw the liferaft container overboard.
3. Haul out the remaining painter line from the liferaft container. Then give a sharp tug on the painter which initiates the liferaft inflation process. The liferaft will inflate in approximately 30 seconds.
4. Board the liferaft by best means. Once the survivors are aboard, cut the painter line that connects the liferaft to the vessel with the knife attached near the liferaft entrance. Persons in distress can be rescued using the heaving line and quoit.

## Manual Liferaft Launching

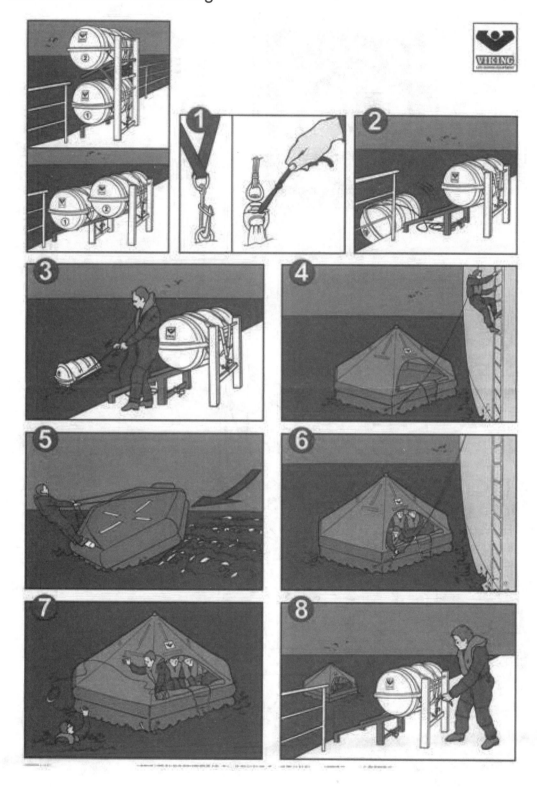

## Davit Launched Liferaft

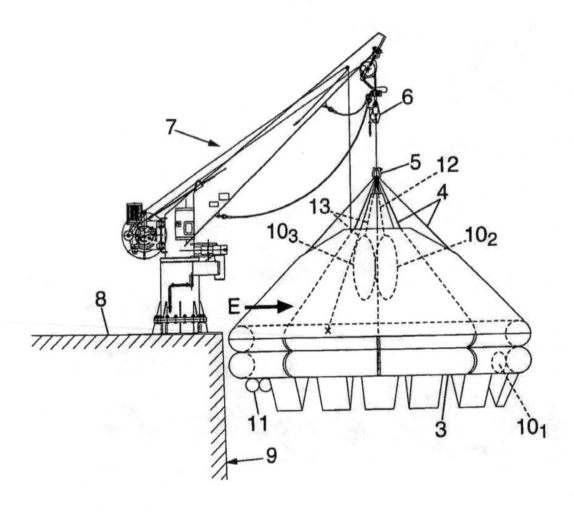

## Davit Launched Liferaft – Launching Instructions

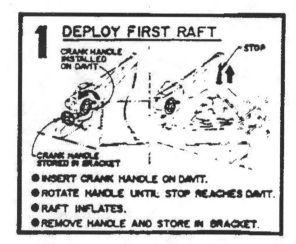

**1 DEPLOY FIRST RAFT**

CRANK HANDLE INSTALLED ON DAVIT

STOP

CRANK HANDLE STORED IN BRACKET

- INSERT CRANK HANDLE ON DAVIT.
- ROTATE HANDLE UNTIL STOP REACHES DAVIT.
- RAFT INFLATES.
- REMOVE HANDLE AND STORE IN BRACKET.

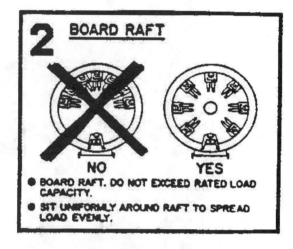

**2 BOARD RAFT**

NO          YES

- BOARD RAFT. DO NOT EXCEED RATED LOAD CAPACITY.
- SIT UNIFORMLY AROUND RAFT TO SPREAD LOAD EVENLY.

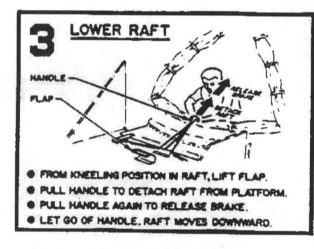

**3 LOWER RAFT**

HANDLE

FLAP

- FROM KNEELING POSITION IN RAFT, LIFT FLAP.
- PULL HANDLE TO DETACH RAFT FROM PLATFORM.
- PULL HANDLE AGAIN TO RELEASE BRAKE.
- LET GO OF HANDLE. RAFT MOVES DOWNWARD.

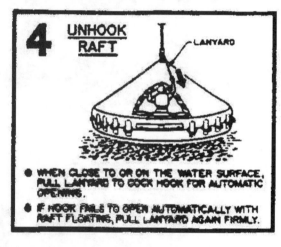

**4 UNHOOK RAFT**

LANYARD

- WHEN CLOSE TO OR ON THE WATER SURFACE, PULL LANYARD TO COCK HOOK FOR AUTOMATIC OPENING.
- IF HOOK FAILS TO OPEN AUTOMATICALLY WITH RAFT FLOATING, PULL LANYARD AGAIN FIRMLY.

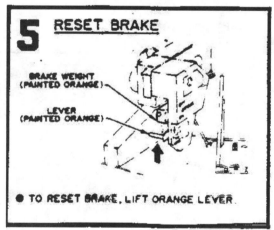

**5 RESET BRAKE**

BRAKE WEIGHT (PAINTED ORANGE)

LEVER (PAINTED ORANGE)

- TO RESET BRAKE, LIFT ORANGE LEVER.

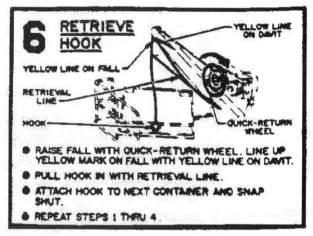

**6 RETRIEVE HOOK**

YELLOW LINE ON DAVIT

YELLOW LINE ON FALL

RETRIEVAL LINE

HOOK

QUICK-RETURN WHEEL

- RAISE FALL WITH QUICK-RETURN WHEEL. LINE UP YELLOW MARK ON FALL WITH YELLOW LINE ON DAVIT.
- PULL HOOK IN WITH RETRIEVAL LINE.
- ATTACH HOOK TO NEXT CONTAINER AND SNAP SHUT.
- REPEAT STEPS 1 THRU 4.

## Viking Davit Launched Liferaft – Launching Instructions

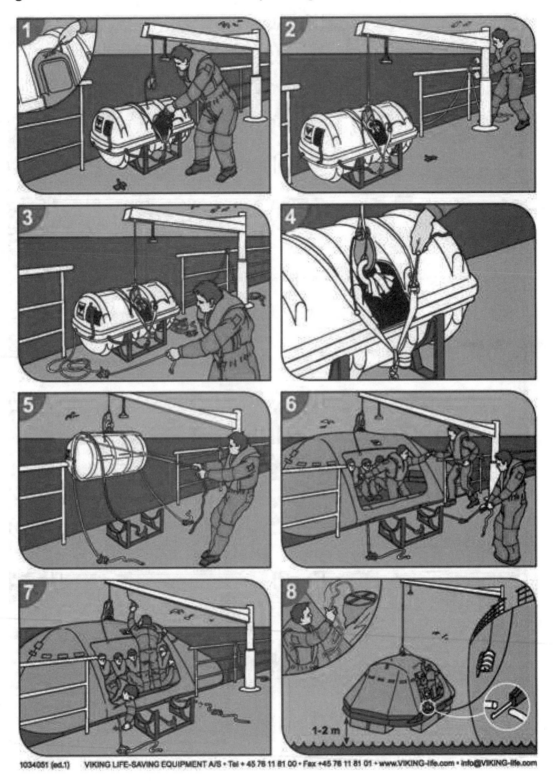

1034051 (ed.1)    VIKING LIFE-SAVING EQUIPMENT A/S · Tel + 45 76 11 81 00 · Fax +45 76 11 81 01 · www.VIKING-life.com · info@VIKING-life.com

## Righting A Capsized Liferaft

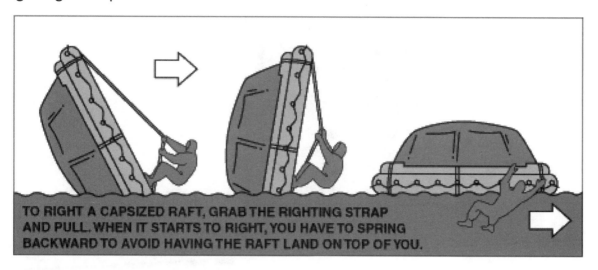

TO RIGHT A CAPSIZED RAFT, GRAB THE RIGHTING STRAP AND PULL. WHEN IT STARTS TO RIGHT, YOU HAVE TO SPRING BACKWARD TO AVOID HAVING THE RAFT LAND ON TOP OF YOU.

## Righting A Capsized Liferaft

1. Locate the area of the raft marked **"RIGHT HERE"**. *In darkness feel for the inflation piping connected to the $CO_2$ inflation bottle.*

2. Turn the liferaft into the wind so that the wind will help right the raft. Position yourself downwind so that the raft will blow over towards you. Grab the righting strap then pull yourself up on the bottom of the raft.

3. Place your feet on the $CO_2$ bottle(s), get a firm grip on the righting strap and then lean backwards pulling the raft toward you. In this position, the $CO_2$ bottle(s) can't strike you when the liferaft turns over.

4. Move away and clear of the liferaft when it turns over. *Never let go of the raft or it will drift away from you.*

5. If the liferaft lands on top of you, remain face-up to the surface of the water and move out from under the liferaft to safety. Remaining face-up to the bottom of the liferaft keeps your lifejacket from getting caught, trapping and then drowning you under the liferaft.

Evacuation Slide

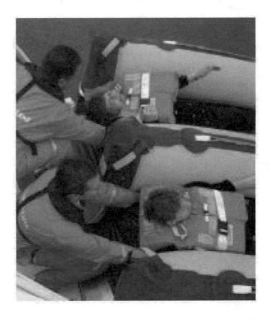

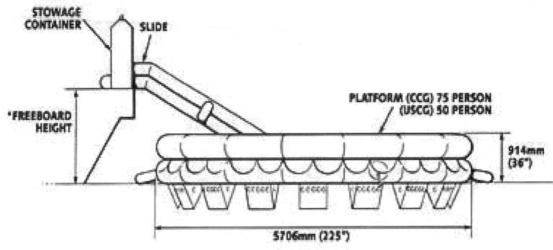

# System in action
# Deployment in 6 easy steps:

**It requires just one crew member pulling on the release handle to commence deployment of the VIKING evacuation slide.**

The first steps are entirely automatic, from the gas release of the covering front door to the descent and inflation of the slide and platform.

Just 2-3 minutes later, the slide and platform are inflated.

The platform itself can hold up to 100 people. Evacuation can commence before the liferafts are fully inflated and attached, saving valuable time.

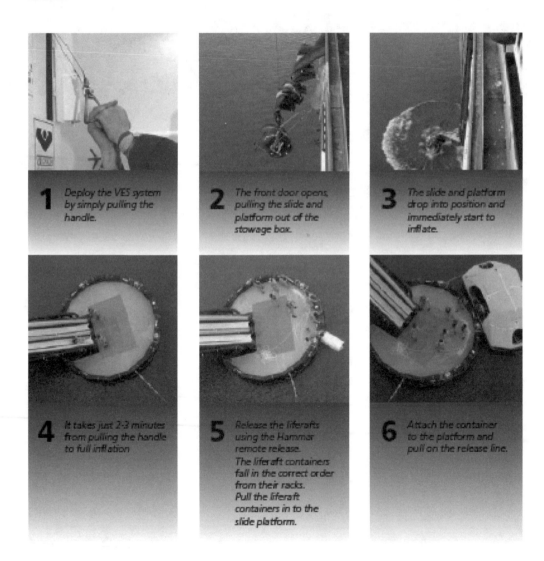

**1** Deploy the VES system by simply pulling the handle.

**2** The front door opens, pulling the slide and platform out of the stowage box.

**3** The slide and platform drop into position and immediately start to inflate.

**4** It takes just 2-3 minutes from pulling the handle to full inflation

**5** Release the liferafts using the Hammar remote release. The liferaft containers fall in the correct order from their racks. Pull the liferaft containers in to the slide platform.

**6** Attach the container to the platform and pull on the release line.

# Passenger instructions

*Clear and easy to understand instruction posters are affixed the system and/or on the nearby bulkhead.*

Evacuation Chute

# Fully deployed within two minutes

The system is activated by pulling on the handle.
The chute and liferaft sledge are automatically deployed and the descending sledge pulls
the chute box into the correct position for the following deployment steps.

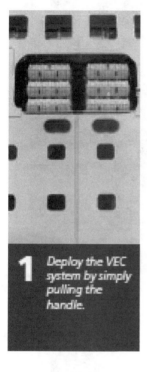

**1** Deploy the VEC system by simply pulling the handle.

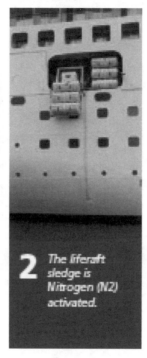

**2** The liferaft sledge is Nitrogen (N2) activated.

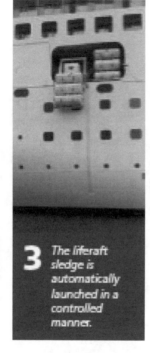

**3** The liferaft sledge is automatically launched in a controlled manner.

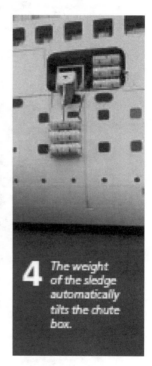

**4** The weight of the sledge automatically tilts the chute box.

The sledge continues to pull the chute out of the chute box and into position.
It sinks in the water, automatically inflating the liferafts. During the final stage, the chute is pulled automatically into the inflated liferaft ready for evacuation to begin. The entire process takes just two minutes.

**5** The weight of the sledge pulls the chute out of the box.

**6** The sledge and the liferafts reach the water.

**7** The sledge sinks away, automatically releasing the liferafts by pulling the lines.

**8** The chute is automatically pulled into the inflated liferaft.

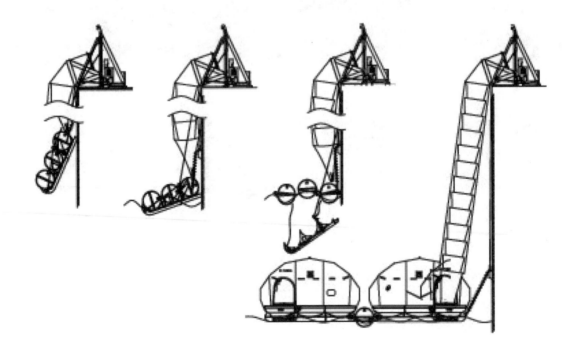

# VIKING Evacuation Chute System in action

The VEC system provides safe and rapid evacuation directly into liferafts, and protects evacuees from environmental hazards, such as severe weather conditions.

# Controlled descent

Access through the chute stowage box.

Controlled and protected descent to the liferafts. The passive descent technique does not require special training of crew or passengers.

# Passenger instructions

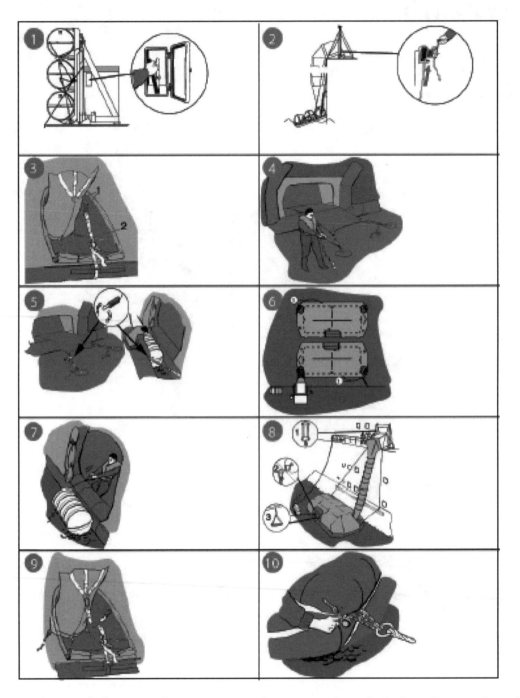

Step by step guides for preparing the VIKING Evacuation Chute system are designed to be clear and easy to understand.

## Safety of Life At Sea (SOLAS) Instructions
### ANNEX 1
### LIFERAFT SURVIVAL INSTRUCTIONS
### Part A
### INSTRUCTIONS FOR IMMEDIATE ACTION IN A LIFERAFT

The instructions concerning immediate action upon entering the liferaft should be written in easily legible type on waterproof material, and displayed so as to be easily seen by a person entering the liferaft. The instructions should be written in one of the official languages of the Organization in addition to the official language of the country.

1. Cut painter and get clear of ship.
2. Look for and pick up other survivors.
3. Ensure sea-anchor streamed when clear of ship.
4. Close up entrances.
5. Read survival instructions.

### LIFERAFT SURVIVAL INSTRUCTIONS
### Part B
### INSTRUCTIONS ON HOW TO SURVIVE IN A LIFERAFT

1. Identify person in charge of liferaft.
2. Post a look-out.
3. Open equipment pack.
4. Issue anti-seasickness medicine and seasickness bags.
5. Dry liferaft floor and inflate. if appropriate.
6. Administer first aid. if appropriate.
7. Maneuver towards other liferafts. Secure liferafts together and distribute survivors and equipment between survival craft.
8. Arrange watches and duties.
9. Check liferaft for correct operation and any damage and repair as appropriate (ventilate if $CO_2$ leaking into liferaft).
10. Check functioning of canopy light and if possible conserve power during daylight. Prepare and use detection equipment including radio equipment.
11. Gather up any useful floating objects.
12. Protect against heat, cold and wet conditions.
13. Decide on food and water rations.
14. Take measures to maintain morale.
15. Make sanitary arrangements to keep liferaft habitable.
16. Maintain liferaft including topping up of buoyancy tubes and canopy supports.
17. Make proper use of available survival equipment.
18. Prepare action for:
    1. arrival of rescue units;
    2. being taken in tow;
    3. rescue by helicopter; and
    4. landing and beaching.

Notes:
1. The order in which the above instructions are followed will depend on the particular circumstances.
2. The above instructions can stand alone or can be amplified as appropriate to the satisfaction of the Administration.

## Dedicated Fast Rescue Boat

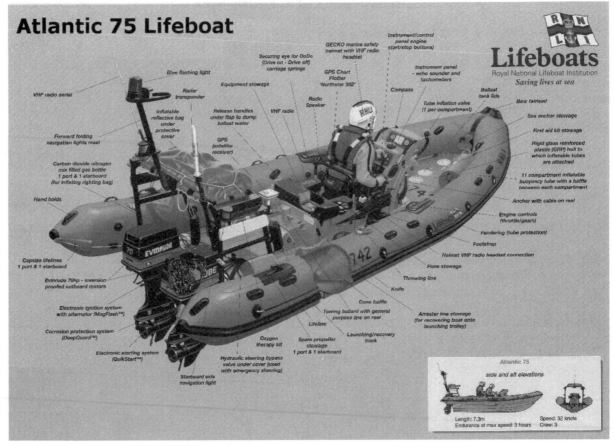